# The Super Fantastic Mega Bible Trivia Guide

Copyright © 2025 by Brad DiBello
All rights reserved, including the right to reproduce this book or portions thereof in any form whatsoever.

ISBN – 979-8-218-67378-9

# FORWARD

We hope you enjoy this in depth and fun approach to the bible. To really test your knowledge, we might ask the same question in different ways!

Good luck!

## Table of Contents

## PART 1 – EASY
General questions……………………………………1

## PART 2 – INTERMEDIATE
Old Testament - The Law (or Pentateuch)……..….87
Old Testament - The Historical Books ……………111
Old Testament - The Poetic or Wisdom Books …..135
Old Testament - The Prophetic Book…………...…159
New Testament - The Gospels ………………..…..183
New Testament - The Acts of the Apostles ……….207
New Testament - The Epistles (Letters) …………..231
New Testament - The Book of Revelation ……..…255

## PART 3 – DIFFICULT
Old Testament - The Law (or Pentateuch) ………..281
Old Testament - The Historical Books …..……….305
Old Testament - The Poetic or Wisdom Books …..329
Old Testament - The Prophetic Book ……………..353
New Testament - The Gospels ………………….…377
New Testament - The Acts of the Apostles ………401
New Testament - The Epistles (Letters) …………..425
New Testament - The Book of Revelation ………..449

# PART 1 - EASY

# General Questions

What did God create on the first day?
**Light**

Who was the first man God created?
**Adam**

In which garden did Adam and Eve live?
**Garden of Eden**

Who deceived Eve into eating the forbidden fruit?
**The serpent**

Who built an ark to survive the flood?
**Noah**

What sign did God give after the flood to promise He would not flood the earth again?
**Rainbow**

Who was called by God to leave his home and go to a new land?
**Abraham**

What was Sarai's name changed to?
**Sarah**

Who was the son of Abraham and Sarah?
**Isaac**

Who was Abraham's nephew who traveled with him?
**Lot**

Who was sold into slavery by his brothers?
**Joseph**

What did Joseph wear that made his brothers jealous?
**A colorful coat**

What special ability did Joseph have that saved Egypt from famine?
**Interpreting dreams**

Who led the Israelites out of Egypt?
**Moses**

What sea did God part for the Israelites to cross?
**Red Sea**

On which mountain did Moses receive the Ten Commandments?
**Mount Sinai**

How many commandments did God give on stone tablets?
**Ten**

What food did God send from heaven to feed the Israelites in the desert?
**Manna**

What did the Israelites carry around Jericho's walls before they fell?
**Ram's horn trumpets**

Who was the first king of Israel?
**Saul**

Who killed Goliath with a sling and a stone?
**David**

Who was David's wise son who built the Temple?
**Solomon**

What did Elijah call down from heaven to prove God's power?
**Fire**

Which prophet was swallowed by a big fish?
**Jonah**

What brave woman became queen of Persia and saved her people?
**Esther**

Who interpreted dreams for King Nebuchadnezzar in Babylon?
**Daniel**

What three friends were thrown into a fiery furnace but did not burn?
**Shadrach, Meshach, and Abednego**

Who was the mother of Jesus?
**Mary**

In what town was Jesus born?
**Bethlehem**

Who baptized Jesus in the Jordan River?
**John the Baptist**

What did God create on the second day?
**Sky**

At a wedding in Cana, what miracle did Jesus perform?
**Turned water into wine**

What did Jesus use to feed 5,000 men?
**Bread and fish**

Who walked on water to meet Jesus?
**Peter**

What did Jesus calm during a storm?
**The wind and waves**

Who did Jesus raise from the dead after four days in the tomb?
**Lazarus**

What did God create on the third day that covers the land?
**Plants**

What prayer did Jesus teach His disciples?
**The Lord's Prayer**

What did Jesus ride into Jerusalem on the Sunday before His crucifixion?
**A donkey**

Who betrayed Jesus for thirty pieces of silver?
**Judas Iscariot**

What happened to Jesus three days after His death?
**He rose from the dead**

What event do Christians remember on Good Friday?
**Jesus' crucifixion**

Who was the first person to see Jesus after He rose from the dead?
**Mary Magdalene**

In which city did twelve-year-old Jesus teach in the temple?
**Jerusalem**

Which disciple doubted Jesus' resurrection until he saw His wounds?
**Thomas**

Which apostle wrote many letters found in the New Testament?
**Paul**

On which sea did Jesus calm the waves?
**Sea of Galilee**

What sermon did Jesus deliver that begins with "Blessed are…"?
**The Beatitudes**

Who was the tax collector that became one of Jesus' disciples?
**Matthew**

Who was Peter's brother and also a disciple?
**Andrew**

How many disciples did Jesus choose?
**Twelve**

What is the shortest verse in the Bible ("Jesus wept")?
**John 11:35**

What tiny seed did Jesus use to illustrate the kingdom of heaven?
**Mustard seed**

What celebration came when the Holy Spirit appeared as tongues of fire?
**Pentecost**

Who was the first Christian martyr stoned for his faith?
**Stephen**

Who replaced Judas Iscariot among the twelve disciples?
**Matthias**

Which apostle wrote the book of Revelation?
**John**

Which apostle did Jesus call the "rock"?
**Peter**

Which book of the Bible tells about the creation of the world?
**Genesis**

What is the last book of the Bible?
**Revelation**

Who was Jacob's twin brother?
**Esau**

Which judge of Israel killed a lion with his bare hands?
**Samson**

What did David use to kill the giant Goliath?
**A sling and a stone**

Who was David's best friend and Saul's son?
**Jonathan**

Who anointed David to be king when he was still a boy?
**Samuel**

Who was swallowed by a big fish after running from God's command?
**Jonah**

Which Canaanite woman helped Israelite spies conquer Jericho?
**Rahab**

What did Solomon ask God for instead of riches or long life?
**Wisdom**

What type of wood was used to build Noah's ark?
**Gopher wood**

What sign marked God's covenant with Abraham?
**Circumcision**

What guided the Israelites by night in the desert?
**A pillar of fire**

What guided the Israelites by day?
**A pillar of cloud**

Who was thrown into a lion's den for praying to God?
**Daniel**

Where did Elijah challenge the prophets of Baal?
**Mount Carmel**

Who became queen of Persia and saved the Jewish people?
**Esther**

What river did John use to baptize people?
**Jordan River**

How many loaves and fish did Jesus use to feed 4,000 men?
**Seven loaves and a few fish**

For how many days did Jesus fast in the wilderness?
**Forty**

Who led the Israelites into the Promised Land after Moses died?
**Joshua**

What was the source of Samson's great strength?
**His hair**

Which judge took the Israelites across the Red Sea?
**Joshua**

Which book of the Bible is named after a woman and tells her story?
**Ruth**

Who was the mother of the prophet Samuel?
**Hannah**

Which book follows Exodus in the Old Testament?
**Leviticus**

What did Balaam's donkey do to save him?
**Speak**

Which prophet was taken to heaven in a whirlwind?
**Elijah**

To what city did Jonah flee instead of obeying God?
**Tarshish**

Who was Isaac's son who received a special coat?
**Joseph**

Who became the second king of Israel?
**David**

What did God create on the fifth day that swim and fly?
**Fish and birds**

How many days was Jesus tempted by Satan in the wilderness?
**Forty**

Who wrestled with an angel all night?
**Jacob**

Who wrote many of the Psalms in the Bible?
**David**

Who spent three days in the belly of a big fish?
**Jonah**

What is the first of the Ten Commandments?
**Have no other gods**

What did Moses' mother place him in to save his life?
**A basket**

Who found baby Moses floating in the reeds?
**Pharaoh's daughter**

How did God provide fresh water for the Israelites when they were thirsty?
**He told Moses to strike a rock**

Which judge tested God with a fleece of wool?
**Gideon**

What was the secret of Samson's strength?
**His uncut hair**

Who was the prophet-king chosen after Saul?
**David**

Around which city's walls did the Israelites march and blow trumpets?
**Jericho**

Who was the last judge before Israel had a king?
**Samuel**

What brave woman drove a tent peg through Sisera's head?
**Jael**

Which book of the New Testament begins with Jesus' birth narrative?
**Matthew**

Who received a coat of many colors that made his brothers jealous?
**Joseph**

What did Solomon ask God to give him?
**Wisdom**

What weapon did Jonathan use to defeat the Philistines?
**Bow and arrow**

Which prophet confronted King Ahab and Queen Jezebel?
**Elijah**

What did Zacchaeus climb to see Jesus?
**A sycamore tree**

Who is called the "apostle to the Gentiles"?
**Paul**

What road was Paul traveling on when he met Jesus?
**The road to Damascus**

Who and his wife lied about money and died suddenly?
**Ananias and Sapphira**

Who was Peter's mother-in-law whom Jesus healed?
**Mary**

Which disciple wrote a Gospel and Acts?
**Luke**

What angel appeared to Mary to announce she would bear Jesus?
**Gabriel**

What darkness came over the land when Jesus died?
**Darkness**

Which disciple was a tax collector before following Jesus?
**Matthew**

Who carried the cross for Jesus on the way to Golgotha?
**Simon of Cyrene**

What did Jesus say was the greatest commandment?
**Love God and neighbor**

Who cut off a soldier's ear at Jesus' arrest?
**Peter**

Which disciple denied Jesus three times?
**Peter**

Who was Jesus' cousin who prepared the way for Him?
**John the Baptist**

On what day do Christians celebrate Jesus' resurrection?
**Easter**

In what language did Jesus cry out on the cross, "Eli, Eli, lema sabachthani"?
**Aramaic**

What two elements did Jesus use at the Last Supper as symbols?
**Bread and wine**

Who preached to the Samaritans after leaving Judea?
**Philip**

Which disciple was nicknamed "the Zealot"?
**Simon**

Who healed the paralytic lowered through the roof?
**Jesus**

What miracle did Jesus perform for Lazarus?
**Raised him from the dead**

Who was the father of John the Baptist?
**Zechariah**

What mighty king had Daniel brought to Babylon?
**Nebuchadnezzar**

How many times did Peter deny Jesus?
**Three**

Who anointed Jesus' feet with expensive perfume and wiped them with her hair?
**Mary of Bethany**

Which event features four living creatures and seven seals?
**Revelation**

Which Old Testament book tells of a man's great suffering and faith?
**Job**

Who spoke for Balaam and stopped him from sinning?
**His donkey**

What did Daniel's three friends refuse to do before the fiery furnace?
**Worship an idol**

What did God see was good on the sixth day?
**All He had made**

Who was Abraham's oldest son?
**Ishmael**

What did Isaac carry up the hill for his sacrifice?
**Wood**

Who received a coat from King Ahab for killing Jezebel's family?
**Jehu**

Who was Moses' brother and Israel's first high priest?
**Aaron**

What is the last book of the Old Testament?
**Malachi**

Which prophet is called the "weeping prophet"?
**Jeremiah**

Which book of the Bible is a collection of songs?
**Psalms**

Which prophet saw dry bones come to life?
**Ezekiel**

Who was the widow that Elijah miraculously provided for?
**The widow of Zarephath**

What instrument did David play for King Saul?
**Harp**

What animal spoke to Balaam to warn him?
**Donkey**

Who refused to bow to Nebuchadnezzar's golden statue?
**Shadrach, Meshach, and Abednego**

Where was baby Jesus laid after His birth?
**A manger**

What did the apostles do when the Holy Spirit came on Pentecost?
**Spoke in tongues**

What group did Jesus say would inherit the earth?
**The meek**

Who wrote letters from prison, including one to the Philippians?
**Paul**

Who is called the "beloved disciple"?
**John**

Who helped carry supplies for Paul's first missionary journey?
**Barnabas**

Who did Jesus say must be born again to see the kingdom of God?
**Nicodemus** (or "Anyone," but Nicodemus asked)

Which disciple climbed a sycamore tree to see Jesus?
**Zacchaeus**

What festival tells of Israel's escape from Egypt?
**Passover**

Who was the first woman God created?
**Eve**

Which judge built an army of only 300 men?
**Gideon**

What type of building did Solomon build in Jerusalem?
**Temple**

What did the Israelites carry across the Jordan River to enter Canaan?
**The Ark of the Covenant**

Who was the priest who blessed baby Jesus in the temple?
**Simeon**

Which book follows the Pentateuch in the Old Testament?
**Joshua**

Who was the first woman judge of Israel?
**Deborah**

Which Psalm begins "The Lord is my shepherd"?
**Psalm 23**

What did God promise Abraham his descendants would be as numerous as?
**Stars in the sky**

Who anointed David as king at Bethlehem?
**Samuel**

Which disciple healed a lame man at the gate called Beautiful?
**Peter**

Who wrote the book that follows Romans in the New Testament?
**Paul**

What river carried baby Moses to safety?
**Nile River**

Who was the grandfather of King David?
**Obed**

What did the people build at Babel trying to reach heaven?
**Tower of Babel**

Which Old Testament prophet confronted false prophets on Mount Carmel?
**Elijah**

Which book warns of the Day of the Lord with four horsemen?
**Revelation**

Which book tells about the faith of Ruth and her loyalty?
**Ruth**

What did God create on the sixth day that walks on land?
**Animals**

Which sea did Joshua and the Israelites cross on dry ground?
**Jordan River**

Who was known for his many proverbs and songs?
**Solomon**

Which book of wisdom asks, "Meaningless! Utterly meaningless!"?
**Ecclesiastes**

Which judge of Israel destroyed idols in his father's house?
**Gideon**

Which book contains the famous valley of dry bones vision?
**Ezekiel**

Which prophet wrote about a virgin birth centuries before Jesus?
**Isaiah**

Which feast did Jesus celebrate with His disciples before He died?
**Passover**

Who led the rebuilding of Jerusalem's walls after the exile?
**Nehemiah**

Who was David's mighty warrior known for his valor?
**Jonathan**

Who was Queen Esther's cousin who guided her?
**Mordecai**

How many of each clean animal did Noah take into the ark?
**Seven pairs**

Which disciple was a tax collector named Levi?
**Matthew**

Which New Testament letter warns that faith without works is dead?
**James**

Who wrote the letter to the churches in Galatia about freedom in Christ?
**Paul**

Which disciple wrote letters to the Corinthians?
**Paul**

What gift did the Holy Spirit give in Acts 2 that amazed the crowd?
**Speaking in tongues**

Which book tells how Israel's leaders sinned and repented in Judges?
**Judges**

Who was famous for her loyalty to Naomi and became grandmother of David?
**Ruth**

What did God provide to feed the Israelites besides manna?
**Quail**

Which apostle was a fisherman called "the Rock"?
**Peter**

Which apostle wrote about love and faith in three short letters?
**John**

Which epistle focuses on the armor of God?
**Ephesians**

What is the first book of the New Testament?
**Matthew**

Who was the Roman governor who tried Jesus and released Barabbas instead?
**Pontius Pilate**

Which Old Testament book tells of creation, fall, flood, and patriarchs?
**Genesis**

Which Psalm is the longest chapter in the Bible?
**Psalm 119**

Who led Israel into Canaan after Moses died?
**Joshua**

Which New Testament book begins, "In the beginning was the Word"?
**John**

Which judge used only 300 men to defeat an army?
**Gideon**

Which small book in the Old Testament has only one chapter?
**Obadiah**

Who wrote the majority of the New Testament letters?
**Paul**

Which prophetic book tells of a valley of dry bones?
**Ezekiel**

Which Gospel tells about the good Samaritan and prodigal son parables?
**Luke**

Which woman poured perfume on Jesus' feet and wiped them with her hair?
**Mary** (of Bethany)

Who was the father of Isaac?
**Abraham**

What did God create on the seventh day?
**Rest**

Who was the king when Daniel and friends were taken to Babylon?
**Nebuchadnezzar**

Which Israelite judge sacrificed to Baal and was defeated by Gideon?
**Jerub-Ba'al (Gideon)**

Which woman became a Moabite ancestor of David?
**Ruth**

What did the angel Gabriel tell Mary she would bear?
**A son named Jesus**

Which book is sometimes called the book of love poems?
**Song of Solomon**

Which Old Testament book teaches about patience amid suffering?
**Job**

Who was Elijah's successor who performed twice as many miracles?
**Elisha**

Which New Testament epistle was written to the Romans?
**Romans**

Who was the tax collector that climbed a sycamore tree?
**Zacchaeus**

Which book contains the fruit of the Spirit?
**Galatians**

What was Paul's occupation before his conversion?
**Tentmaker**

Who wrote the Revelation while exiled on Patmos?
**John**

Which disciple was also called Thaddaeus?
**Jude**

What miracle did Jesus perform at the Pool of Bethesda?
**Healed a paralytic**

Who denied Jesus three times and then wept bitterly?
**Peter**

What did Adam and Eve eat that they were told not to?
**Forbidden fruit**

Which prophet anointed Saul and David as kings?
**Samuel**

Who was the high priest when Jesus died?
**Caiaphas**

Which parable tells of a lost sheep?
**The Lost Sheep**

Which book follows 1 Samuel in the Old Testament?
**2 Samuel**

What vision did Paul have encouraging him to go to Macedonia?
**A man begging for help**

Which woman sat at Jesus' feet and listened to His teaching?
**Mary of Bethany**

Who was the first person to preach the gospel to the Gentiles?
**Peter** (at Cornelius's house)

Which apostle was called "Doubting ___"?
**Thomas**

Who wrote, "For God so loved the world…"?
**John**

Which Old Testament king wrote many of the Proverbs?
**Solomon**

Which New Testament book explains how the early church began?
**Acts**

Who climbed up a tree to greet Jesus in Jericho?
**Zacchaeus** duplicate – Replace:

Who was the short man healed by Peter at Lydda?
**Aeneas** advanced – Replace:

Which prophet said, "Here am I; send me"?
**Isaiah**

What happened to Paul's eyesight after his encounter on the road to Damascus?
**He was blind for three days**

Which disciple was the brother of Peter?
**Andrew**

Who wrote the epistle encouraging endurance under persecution?
**James** duplicate – Replace:

Which Old Testament prophet married Gomer?
**Hosea**

Who was the mother of Samuel?
**Hannah**

Which book ends with the word "Amen"?
**Revelation**

Which priest wore twelve precious stones on his breastplate?
**Aaron**

Who helped Esther approach the king in Persia?
**Mordecai**

Which book tells of Daniel in the lions' den?
**Daniel**

Who carried the Ark of the Covenant around Jericho's walls?
**Priests**

Which Old Testament hero's strength was in his uncut hair?
**Samson**

Which New Testament event is known as the Day of Pentecost?
**The Holy Spirit's coming**

What did Paul write to encourage unity in Ephesus?
**Ephesians**

Which prophetic book begins, "Vision of Joel"?
**Joel**

Who was the disciple known as "the beloved"?
**John** duplicate – Replace:

Which Gospel emphasizes Jesus as the suffering servant?
**Mark**

Which New Testament letter warns against false teachers in the church?
**2 Peter**

What did God breathe into Adam to give him life?
**His breath**

Who did Abraham send to find a wife for Isaac?
**His servant**

What happened to Uzzah when he touched the Ark to steady it?
**He died**

What was Paul's name before his conversion?
**Saul**

Which judge was famous for his long hair and great strength?
**Samson**

Which book in the Bible teaches love is the greatest virtue?
**1 Corinthians** (chapter 13)

Which prophet was taken up in a whirlwind without dying?
**Elijah**

Which apostle wrote about the armor of God in Ephesians?
**Paul**

What Christian holiday celebrates Jesus' birth?
**Christmas**

Which Old Testament book means "words of the teacher"?
**Ecclesiastes**

Which letter of Paul addresses the church in Philippi?
**Philippians**

Who was the first child born to Adam and Eve?
**Cain**

For how many days and nights did it rain during the flood?
**Forty**

Which brother did Cain kill?
**Abel**

What was Abel's offering to God?
**Firstborn of his flock**

What mark did God put on Cain to protect him?
**Mark of Cain**

Where did Cain live after leaving Eden?
**Land of Nod**

Who lived 969 years, making him the oldest person in the Bible?
**Methuselah**

Who walked with God and was taken to heaven without dying?
**Enoch**

What structure did people build to reach the heavens?
**Tower of Babel**

What did God confuse at the Tower of Babel?
**Their language**

Who was Abraham's nephew who traveled with him?
**Lot**

What did God create on the fourth day to give light?
**Sun**

Which two cities were destroyed for their wickedness?
**Sodom and Gomorrah**

Who turned into a pillar of salt when she looked back?
**Lot's wife**

On which mountain was Isaac almost sacrificed?
**Mount Moriah**

Who became Isaac's wife at the well?
**Rebekah**

What vision did Jacob see in his dream at Bethel?
**A ladder reaching to heaven**

How many sons did Jacob have?
**Twelve**

Which of Jacob's sons was sold into slavery by his brothers?
**Joseph**

What did Joseph's brothers dip his coat in to deceive their father?
**Goat's blood**

Who interpreted Pharaoh's dreams and saved Egypt from famine?
**Joseph**

Who found baby Moses floating in the Nile?
**Pharaoh's daughter**

What did Moses' staff turn into to show God's power?
**A serpent**

What was the first plague God sent on Egypt?
**Water turned to blood**

What did the Israelites eat in the wilderness that tasted like honey wafers?
**Manna**

Who led the Israelites across the Jordan River into Canaan?
**Joshua**

Which city's walls fell after the Israelites marched around them for seven days?
**Jericho**

Who was the left-handed judge who killed the Moabite king Eglon?
**Ehud**

Which judge defeated the Midianites with only 300 men?
**Gideon**

What sign did Gideon ask from God using a fleece of wool?
**That dew would fall only on the fleece**

Which judge's strength came from his uncut hair?
**Samson**

What animal did Samson tear apart with his bare hands?
**Lion**

Who betrayed Samson to the Philistines?
**Delilah**

Who anointed David to be king while he tended his father's sheep?
**Samuel**

What weapon did David use to defeat Goliath?
**A sling and a stone**

Which book of the Bible is a collection of songs and prayers?
**Psalms**

Which king asked God for wisdom instead of silver or gold?
**Solomon**

What did Solomon build in Jerusalem as a place of worship?
**The Temple**

Which prophet was fed by ravens during a drought?
**Elijah**

Which prophet was taken up to heaven in a whirlwind?
**Elijah**

Who was thrown into a lion's den for praying to God?
**Daniel**

Which book tells of a man's great suffering and faith tested by God?
**Job**

What tree did Jonah sit under to enjoy its shade?
**A gourd plant**

Who was the Moabite woman who became King David's great-grandmother?
**Ruth**

Which Old Testament book shares wise sayings attributed to Solomon?
**Proverbs**

What vision did Ezekiel have of dry bones coming to life?
**Valley of Dry Bones**

Which prophet married a woman named Gomer as a symbol of Israel's unfaithfulness?
**Hosea**

Which book prophesies the coming of a virgin birth centuries before Jesus?
**Isaiah**

How many wise men (magi) visited baby Jesus according to tradition?
**Three**

What gifts did the magi bring to Jesus?
**Gold, frankincense, and myrrh**

Which king ordered the slaughter of babies in Bethlehem?
**Herod**

Where did Mary and Joseph flee to escape Herod's decree?
**Egypt**

Who baptized Jesus in the Jordan River?
**John the Baptist**

What did Jesus turn into wine at the wedding in Cana?
**Water**

Who climbed a sycamore tree to see Jesus in Jericho?
**Zacchaeus**

Which disciple was a tax collector before following Jesus?
**Matthew**

How many disciples did Jesus choose?
**Twelve**

What miracle did Jesus perform for a paralytic lowered through the roof?
**He healed him**

Who walked on water toward Jesus?
**Peter**

Which sea did Jesus calm during a storm?
**Sea of Galilee**

What did Jesus feed 5,000 people with?
**Five loaves and two fish**

Which parable tells of a father welcoming his wayward son home?
**The Prodigal Son**

Which parable describes seeds falling on different types of soil?
**The Parable of the Sower**

What did Jesus wash at the Last Supper as an example of serving others?
**His disciples' feet**

What garden did Jesus pray in before His arrest?
**Gethsemane**

Who betrayed Jesus with a kiss?
**Judas Iscariot**

What was placed on Jesus' head during His crucifixion as mockery?
**A crown of thorns**

On what hill was Jesus crucified?
**Golgotha**

Which Roman soldier declared, "Truly this was the Son of God"?
**The centurion**

Who provided the tomb for Jesus' burial?
**Joseph of Arimathea**

How many days after His death did Jesus rise?
**Three**

Which disciple initially doubted Jesus' resurrection until he saw His wounds?
**Thomas**

What is the first book of the New Testament?
**Matthew**

Which book tells about the early church and Paul's missionary journeys?
**Acts**

Who was struck blind on the road to Damascus?
**Saul (Paul)**

Which companion traveled with Paul and was also a tentmaker?
**Silas**

What vision did Peter have involving unclean animals?
**A sheet lowered from heaven**

Who was the first Gentile convert recorded in Acts?
**Cornelius**

Which festival celebrates the Holy Spirit descending on the disciples?
**Pentecost**

Which two letters in the New Testament are addressed to Timothy?
**1 Timothy and 2 Timothy**

Which epistle emphasizes faith without works is dead?
**James**

Which epistle describes putting on the "armor of God"?
**Ephesians**

Which letter begins, "Paul, a servant of Christ Jesus…"?
**Romans**

Which book contains the vision of the four horsemen of the Apocalypse?
**Revelation**

Who wrote most of the letters in the New Testament?
**Paul**

Which book is sometimes called the "little Apocalypse"?
**Revelation**

Which disciple is called the "beloved disciple"?
**John**

Which gospel begins with, "In the beginning was the Word"?
**John**

What did Jesus call the Holy Spirit in John 14 as a Helper?
**The Advocate**

Who healed a man named Aeneas at Lydda?
**Peter**

Who raised Tabitha (Dorcas) from the dead?
**Peter**

Which New Testament book warns against false teachers and ends with "…grow in the grace and knowledge of our Lord"?
**2 Peter**

Which book includes the fruit of the Spirit?
**Galatians**

Which letter is addressed to the church in Philippi?
**Philippians**

Who vowed to Nazarite service and never cut his hair?
**Samuel** (as a child of Hannah)

What sign did God give Hannah that He remembered her prayer?
**A son named Samuel**

Which prophet confronted King Ahab and Queen Jezebel?
**Elijah**

On which mountain did Elijah challenge the prophets of Baal?
**Mount Carmel**

Which widow's jar of oil did Elijah multiply?
**The widow of Zarephath**

Who succeeded Elijah and asked for a double portion of his spirit?
**Elisha**

Which king's dream featured a statue of gold, silver, bronze, and iron?
**Nebuchadnezzar**

What wisdom book says, "To everything there is a season"?
**Ecclesiastes**

Which book is known for passages about love, including "Love is patient"?
**1 Corinthians** (chapter 13)

Who was Daniel's companion thrown into the fiery furnace?
**Shadrach, Meshach, and Abednego**

Which book opens with creation and the genealogy to Abraham?
**Genesis**

Which book follows Leviticus in the Old Testament?
**Numbers**

Which tribe carried the Ark of the Covenant?
**Levites**

What instrument did David use to soothe King Saul?
**Harp**

Which book tells of Israel's wandering in the desert?
**Numbers**

Who helped Nehemiah rebuild Jerusalem's walls?
**The people of Judah**

Which Old Testament prophet wrote the shortest book with only one chapter?
**Obadiah**

Which book tells of a wealthy woman's wise sayings and advice?
**Proverbs**

Which prophet wrote about a locust plague as a warning?
**Joel**

Which judge tore down the altar of Baal?
**Gideon**

What city did Joshua capture after its walls fell down?
**Jericho**

Which book is named after a Moabite woman who showed loyalty to her mother-in-law?
**Ruth**

Which psalm begins, "The Lord is my shepherd"?
**Psalm 23**

What did Samuel pour over Saul to anoint him king?
**Oil**

Which king wrote many of the Psalms?
**David**

Who was the high priest when Jesus was born?
**Zechariah**

Which prophet was thrown into a cistern by his enemies?
**Jeremiah**

Which minor prophet has just two chapters and calls for the rebuilding of the temple?
**Haggai**

What did King Hezekiah pray for when threatened by Assyria?
**Deliverance**

Which king restored worship in the temple after exile?
**Josiah**

Which Old Testament book tells of exile to Babylon and return?
**Ezra**

Who was cupbearer to the king who helped rebuild the temple?
**Nehemiah**

Which king wrote the book of Ecclesiastes?
**Solomon**

Which prophet saw a vision of the Lord seated on a throne?
**Isaiah**

Which book is full of love poetry and allegory between bride and groom?
**Song of Solomon**

What did God create on the fifth day that flies in the sky?
**Birds** (spread-out answer)

Which Old Testament festival commemorates the Exodus from Egypt?
**Passover**

Which feast celebrates the end of the harvest and gathering?
**Feast of Tabernacles (Sukkot)**

Which feast remembers the giving of the Law at Sinai?
**Feast of Weeks (Pentecost)**

What was the special bread placed in the Tabernacle?
**Showbread**

Which mountain did Moses see the Promised Land from before he died?
**Mount Nebo**

Who wrote Lamentations mourning the fall of Jerusalem?
**Jeremiah**

Which prophet uses a plumb-line as a symbol of God's judgment?
**Amos**

What animal did Daniel see in his first vision?
**Lion with eagle's wings**

Which king's handwriting appeared on the wall?
**Belshazzar**

What did the writing on the wall say?
**"Mene, Mene, Tekel, Parsin"**

Which Old Testament book is a collection of sermons on judgment?
**Micah**

Who became king of Israel after Solomon died?
**Rehoboam**

Which prophet wrote about a shepherd pierced by swords?
**Zechariah**

Which book ends with the promise, "I am coming soon"?
**Revelation**

What was the name of David's palace that became Solomon's Temple site?
**Mount Moriah**

Which Old Testament poetess wrote a song after victory over the Egyptians?
**Miriam**

Which judge built an army by tearing down his father's altar?
**Gideon**

Who found no fault in Jesus at His trial?
**Pontius Pilate**

What time did Jesus hang on the cross before darkness fell?
**The sixth hour (noon)**

Which disciple carried a knife at Jesus' arrest?
**Peter**

Who cut off the ear of the high priest's servant?
**Peter**

Which apostle was a doctor and wrote a Gospel and Acts?
**Luke**

Which disciple was called "the twin"?
**Thomas**

Who was known as the tax collector Levi before he followed Jesus?
**Matthew**

Which disciple had the surname "Didymus"?
**Thomas**

Which city declared Paul and Silas innocent after their jailbreak?
**Philippi**

Who baptized the Ethiopian eunuch?
**Philip**

Which city did Paul say he was compelled by the Spirit to preach in?
**Macedonia**

Which shipwrecked Paul was bitten by a venomous snake on?
**A ship to Rome** (Malta)

What did Paul do for three months in a house in Cæsarea?
**Preached boldly**

Which letter addresses the "circumcision party"?
**Galatians**

Which epistle says "Christ is the head of the church"?
**Ephesians**

What new commandment did Jesus give at the Last Supper?
**Love one another**

Which apostle wrote about faith and endurance in trials?
**James**

What did Jesus call His body at the Last Supper?
**Bread**

Which disciple asked Jesus to show them the Father?
**Philip**

Which parable tells of a lost coin searched under lamps?
**The Lost Coin**

Who saw a valley of dry bones come to life?
**Ezekiel**

Which king visited Solomon to test his wisdom?
**Queen of Sheba**

What did Nebuchadnezzar worship until Daniel rebuked him?
**A golden statue**

Which book contains the "Suffering Servant" prophecies?
**Isaiah**

Who gave his life so Peter could escape prison?
**An angel of the Lord** (prison scene)

Which New Testament woman was a seller of purple cloth?
**Lydia**

Who fell asleep during Paul's sermon and fell from a window?
**Eutychus**

Which book emphasizes the supremacy of Christ over angels?
**Hebrews**

Which letter begins, "To the church of the Thessalonians in God the Father…"?
**1 Thessalonians**

Which book says "For the word of God is living and active"?
**Hebrews**

Which disciple came from the town of Bethsaida?
**Philip**

Who was healed after Peter's shadow fell on him?
**All who were sick**

Which apostle was a fisherman and wrote two letters?
**Peter**

Who wrote the epistle to the Hebrews?
**Unknown (traditionally Paul or Barnabas)**

Which gospel is addressed to "Theophilus"?
**Luke**

Who experienced a vision of a great sheet filled with animals?
**Peter**

Which prophet's book laments with funeral poems?
**Lamentations**

What did God instruct Joshua to do with the stones from the Jordan?
**Pile them as a memorial**

Which Old Testament book focuses on the duties of priests?
**Leviticus**

What building did Solomon dedicate in a grand ceremony?
**The Temple**

Which prophet hid a message in a potter's field?
**Jeremiah**

Which New Testament book focuses on Christ as the Word made flesh?
**John**

Who wrote letters to Philemon about his runaway slave?
**Paul**

Which Old Testament king sought counsel from a medium at Endor?
**Saul**

What animal did God send to provide meat for Israel in the desert?
**Quail**

Which book teaches that "the fear of the Lord is the beginning of wisdom"?
**Proverbs**

Which minor prophet witnessed locusts and called for repentance?
**Joel**

What did the people dance before the golden calf?
**They danced** (implied idolatrous worship)

Which priest's son struck with leprosy for offering unauthorized fire?
**Nadab and Abihu**

What river did Elijah part by striking it with his cloak?
**Jordan River**

Which judge saved Israel by plotting against Sisera?
**Jael**

Which Old Testament hero's story teaches that "the memory of the righteous is a blessing"?
**Abel** (Psalm reference)

Which Old Testament book is written entirely in dialogue?
**Ecclesiastes**

Which minor prophet has only three chapters and condemns Nineveh?
**Jonah**

Which New Testament book tells of the church in seven cities?
**Revelation**

What did Jesus say would be the sign of Jonah?
**His resurrection after three days**

Which apostle is called the "rock" on which Jesus would build His church?
**Peter**

Who climbed a tree so Jesus could heal him?
**Zacchaeus**

Which Gospel emphasizes Jesus' compassion for the Gentiles?
**Luke**

Who was the governor when John the Baptist was executed?
**Herod Antipas**

Which Old Testament figure was known for his patience amid suffering?
**Job**

Which book's last verse says, "Come, Lord Jesus"?
**Revelation**

Who was the mother of Samuel, dedicated to God from birth?
**Hannah**

Which prophet challenged King Hezekiah to trust God's deliverance?
**Isaiah**

Which book of history follows Ezra in the Old Testament?
**Nehemiah**

What was the name of Moses' sister?
**Miriam**

Which Israelite feast included waving branches and booths?
**Sukkot (Feast of Tabernacles)**

Which New Testament writer was a physician?
**Luke**

What miracle did Peter perform at the Gate Beautiful?
**Healed a lame man**

Which apostle wrote to encourage joy in all circumstances?
**Paul** (Philippians)

What did Jesus call the bird that He said God feeds?
**Sparrow**

Which prophet hid Israel's idols under figs?
**Micah**

Who was the prophet-priest who anointed the first two kings of Israel?
**Samuel**

Which Old Testament book records the census of Israel and their stations?
**Numbers**

Which New Testament event is celebrated as the birthday of the church?
**Pentecost**

Who said, "Here am I; send me"?
**Isaiah**

Which Old Testament hero rescued Rahab's family from Jericho?
**Joshua**

What did Jesus call the kingdom of heaven in a mustard seed?
**Like a mustard seed**

Which apostle wrote, "Faith without works is dead"?
**James**

Which book begins with "After this I looked…" describing visions?
**Revelation**

Which clothed themselves in hair and ate locusts and wild honey?
**John the Baptist**

What did the manna taste like according to Exodus?
**Wafers made with honey**

Which brother of Jesus was martyred early in the church?
**James (son of Zebedee)**

Which Old Testament woman judge led Israel to victory under a palm tree?
**Deborah**

What did Naaman dip into the Jordan River to be healed?
**Seven times**

Which New Testament letter begins with "Peter, an apostle of Jesus Christ"?
**1 Peter**

Which Old Testament festival was celebrated with trumpets?
**Rosh Hashanah (Feast of Trumpets)**

Which prophet wept over Jerusalem's destruction?
**Jeremiah**

Who washed Jesus' feet with perfume and tears?
**Mary of Bethany**

Which apostle wrote the shortest New Testament book?
**John (3 John)**

Which disciple's name means "son of thunder"?
**John**

Which Old Testament figure proposed a prophet's duel against idols?
**Elijah**

Which city was known for its giant walls before Joshua's arrival?
**Jericho**

Which New Testament letter focuses on Christ's priesthood after Melchizedek?
**Hebrews**

Which Gospel ends with the Great Commission?
**Matthew**

What are the first two books of the Old Testament?
**Genesis and Exodus**

Which book contains the story of Ruth?
**Ruth**

What is the name of Moses' sister?
**Miriam**

Where did Moses strike a rock to bring water for the Israelites?
**Meribah**

Which sea did Moses and the Israelites cross on dry ground?
**Red Sea**

Who received a coat of many colors from his father?
**Joseph**

What did Samson ask his mother not to eat or drink before his birth?
**Wine or unclean food**

Which Jewish queen risked her life to save her people in Persia?
**Esther**

Which prophet succeeded Elijah and received a double portion of his spirit?
**Elisha**

What sign did God give Noah that He would never flood the earth again?
**Rainbow**

Where did Elijah challenge the prophets of Baal?
**Mount Carmel**

Which judge defeated the Midianites with only 300 men?
**Gideon**

What grain did Ruth glean in Boaz's field?
**Barley**

Who threw Shadrach, Meshach, and Abednego into the fiery furnace?
**King Nebuchadnezzar**

Which book follows Joshua in the Old Testament?
**Judges**

Which servant of the king was thrown into the lion's den?
**Daniel**

Which prophet wrote that "justice roll on like a river"?
**Amos**

Who anointed Saul as the first king of Israel?
**Samuel**

What musical instrument did David play to soothe King Saul?
**Harp**

Which prophet wrote the book of Lamentations?
**Jeremiah**

Which city's walls fell after the Israelites marched around them for seven days?
**Jericho**

Which Gospel is the shortest?
**Mark**

Which apostle is known as the "beloved disciple"?
**John**

Where did Samuel minister as a boy under Eli?
**Shiloh**

What was the name of Moses' father-in-law?
**Jethro**

What name did Jacob give to the place where he wrestled with God?
**Peniel**

Who carried the wood for Abraham's sacrifice up the mountain?
**Isaac**

What name did God reveal to Moses at the burning bush?
**I AM**

Which feast lasts seven days to remember the Israelites living in tents?
**Sukkot**

Which prophet had his cloak parted the Jordan River?
**Elijah**

Who was David's best friend, son of King Saul?
**Jonathan**

What did Solomon ask for when God appeared to him in a dream?
**Wisdom**

Which creature swallowed Jonah?
**Fish**

What did Jesus call the Pharisees and teachers of the law when He criticized them?
**Hypocrites**

Which New Testament book comes immediately after Acts?
**Romans**

Who wrote most of the Psalms in the Bible?
**David**

On which mountain did Moses view the Promised Land before he died?
**Mount Nebo**

Who was Abraham's wife?
**Sarah**

What did the two stone tablets Moses brought down contain?
**Ten Commandments**

Which book tells of Daniel in the lions' den?
**Daniel**

Who climbed a sycamore tree to see Jesus in Jericho?
**Zacchaeus**

Where did Jesus perform His first miracle, turning water into wine?
**Cana**

Which disciple denied Jesus three times before the rooster crowed?
**Peter**

What did Jesus use to feed 5,000 men in a miraculous meal?
**Five loaves and two fish**

Which apostle wrote the book of Revelation?
**John**

What did Jesus calm while He was asleep on the boat?
**A storm**

What was the first of the ten plagues on Egypt?
**Water turned to blood**

Which commandment tells us to honor our father and mother?
**Fifth**

Who betrayed Jesus for thirty pieces of silver?
**Judas Iscariot**

Before his conversion, what did Paul do to early Christians?
**Persecuted them**

Which book tells the story of the early church and Paul's journeys?
**Acts**

Which book warns that love covers a multitude of sins?
**1 Peter**

Which book focuses on the second coming and joyful endurance?
**1 Thessalonians**

Which prophet called down fire from heaven to prove God's power?
**Elijah**

Who wrote the book that records Israel's census and their desert wanderings?
**Moses** (author traditionally)

Which book of the Old Testament contains the Ten Commandments?
**Exodus**

What did Joshua tell the sun to do so Israel could win a battle?
**Stand still**

What woman became a judge and led Israel to victory under a palm tree?
**Deborah**

Which New Testament letter begins, "Paul, a servant of Christ Jesus"?
**Romans**

What did Jesus call the birds, reminding us that God cares for them?
**Sparrows**

Which book warns against false teachers and emphasizes mercy?
**Jude**

Which Gospel emphasizes Jesus' miracles more than any other?
**John**

Which parable teaches us to forgive others, as a king forgave his servant?
**Parable of the Unforgiving Servant**

What did Mary and Joseph find when they arrived in Bethlehem?
**No room at the inn**

Who did God send to prepare the way for Jesus?
**John the Baptist**

Which miracle did Jesus perform to help Peter walk toward Him?
**Walking on water**

Who was the Pharisee who came to Jesus by night to learn from Him?
**Nicodemus**

What did Jesus use to illustrate faith as small as a mustard seed?
**Mustard seed**

Which book contains Jesus' Sermon on the Mount?
**Matthew**

Where did Jesus pray in great anguish before His arrest?
**Garden of Gethsemane**

What did the disciples do after Jesus ascended into heaven?
**Returned to Jerusalem and prayed**

Which parable tells of a shepherd leaving ninety-nine sheep to find one lost sheep?
**Parable of the Lost Sheep**

Who replaced Judas Iscariot as one of the twelve apostles?
**Matthias**

Which book includes the vision of the valley of dry bones?
**Ezekiel**

What did Daniel refuse to stop doing, even under penalty of death?
**Praying to God**

Which prophet saw a vision of a wheel within a wheel?
**Ezekiel**

What did Shadrach, Meshach, and Abednego refuse to do?
**Bow to a golden statue**

Which New Testament book emphasizes love as the greatest virtue?
**1 Corinthians** (chapter 13)

Who anointed Jesus' feet with expensive perfume and wiped them with her hair?
**Mary of Bethany**

Which minor prophet's book opens with "The vision of Obadiah"?
**Obadiah**

Which Gospel records Jesus' prayer for unity in John 17?
**John**

Which Gospel includes the parable of the talents?
**Matthew**

Which major prophet's book has 66 chapters?
**Isaiah**

What city did Paul and Silas praise God in while imprisoned?
**Philippi**

Which Old Testament figure was known for his patience amid suffering?
**Job**

What did Esther risk by approaching the king uninvited?
**Her life**

Which disciple is called the rock on which Jesus would build His church?
**Peter**

Which apostle preached to the Ethiopian eunuch?
**Philip**

Which apostle stayed mum at Jesus' trial until the next day?
**John**

What did God command Noah to build to survive the flood?
**An ark**

Which book teaches that believers are God's workmanship created for good works?
**Ephesians**

Which Gospel records Jesus' encounter with Nicodemus?
**John**

Which miracle feed a crowd of 4,000 with seven loaves and a few fish?
**Feeding of the 4,000**

What did Jesus say is the greatest commandment?
**Love God and love your neighbor**

Who climbed a sycamore tree to see Jesus?
**Zacchaeus**

Which New Testament letter is addressed "To the elect lady and her children"?
**2 John**

What did Paul see in a vision urging him to go to Macedonia?
**A man begging for help**

Which Old Testament king asked God for an understanding heart?
**Solomon**

Who was the tax collector that Jesus called to follow Him?
**Matthew**

What did Jesus say a camel passing through an eye of a needle teaches?
**Dependence on God**

Which prophet's book describes a feast of rich food for the Lord's table?
**Malachi**

Which prophet commanded strangers to say, "The Lord bless you"?
**Zechariah**

Who assisted Paul on his first missionary journey and was nicknamed "Son of Encouragement"?
**Barnabas**

Which sea did Paul sail on his voyage to Rome when the ship was wrecked?
**Mediterranean Sea**

What did the angel say to the women at Jesus' empty tomb?
**He is not here; He has risen**

Which prophet's wife was named Gomer?
**Hosea**

Which New Testament book opens with "In the beginning was the Word"?
**John**

Which book is addressed to a runaway slave named Onesimus?
**Philemon**

Which book encourages rejoicing in all circumstances?
**Philippians**

Who wrote letters to the church in Galatia about Christian freedom?
**Paul**

Which prophet's message was partly acted out by walking naked for three years?
**Isaiah**

Which prophet's book warns, "Whoever whistles for the locusts"?
**Joel**

What festival remembers the giving of the Law on Mount Sinai?
**Pentecost**

Which book contains the prophecy of the valley of dry bones?
**Ezekiel**

Who was the high priest that Caiaphas ordered to arrest Jesus?
**Caiaphas**

What did Jesus call His body and blood at the Last Supper?
**Bread and wine**

Which apostle wrote an epistle encouraging believers to stand firm in faith?
**Jude**

What new command did Jesus give His disciples at the Last Supper?
**Love one another**

What does the name "Emmanuel" mean?
**God with us**

What is the final book of the Old Testament?
**Malachi**

Which prophet is called the "weeping prophet"?
**Jeremiah**

Which book of the Bible is a series of wise sayings attributed to Solomon?
**Proverbs**

Who was the Roman centurion whose servant Jesus healed from a distance?
**The centurion**

Which patriarch gave birth to twelve sons who became princes of Israel?
**Jacob**

Which matriarch was barren until God answered her prayer for a son named Samuel?
**Hannah**

Which day commemorates Jesus' resurrection?
**Easter**

Which prophet was taken to heaven in a whirlwind without dying?
**Elijah**

What gift did the magi bring that symbolized Jesus' kingship?
**Gold**

Which book follows 1 Kings in the Old Testament?
**2 Kings**

What did Peter and John find in the empty tomb?
**The linen cloths**

Which apostle preached at Pentecost and led 3,000 to faith?
**Peter**

Who wrote letters to the Thessalonians urging them to stand firm?
**Paul**

What vision did John record in Revelation involving seven seals?
**Seven seals**

Which minor prophet's book ends with a plea, "Send the messenger of the covenant"?
**Malachi**

Which prophet's name means "The Lord is salvation"?
**Isaiah**

Which Old Testament woman hid two Israelite spies on her roof?
**Rahab**

What appetite-satisfying food did God provide the Israelites in the desert?
**Manna**

Which prophet anointed both Saul and David as kings?
**Samuel**

Who helped build the walls of Jerusalem after the exile?
**Nehemiah**

Which judge sacrificed to Baal and was defeated by Gideon?
**Jerub-Ba'al (Gideon)**

What did Ezekiel see by the Chebar River that shook him?
**Visions of God's glory**

Which New Testament event is called the "birth of the Church"?
**Pentecost**

Who was known as the "apostle to the Gentiles"?
**Paul**

What did Jesus say must happen to a seed before it bears fruit?
**It must die**

Which prophet challenged King Ahab and called fire from heaven?
**Elijah**

What did Jesus call the kingdom of heaven in His parable about yeast?
**Leaven**

Who was healed when Peter's shadow fell on him?
**Many who were sick**

Which Old Testament king tried to kill David?
**Saul**

Who was the jubilees-observing king who rediscovered the Book of the Law?
**Josiah**

What did Paul do at the temple in Jerusalem that angered the Jews?
**He taught that Gentiles need not be circumcised**

Which Gospel ends with the Great Commission to make disciples?
**Matthew**

Who slept during Paul's long sermon and fell from a window?
**Eutychus**

Which book includes the vision of four living creatures around God's throne?
**Revelation**

Who led the Israelites in battle until the sun refused to set?
**Joshua**

What did John the Baptist wear in the wilderness?
**Camel's hair**

Which apostle wrote letters to the Corinthians and the Galatians?
**Paul**

Which helper of Paul carried letters and acted as a diplomat between churches?
**Titus**

Which book tells of Israel's deliverance through the Red Sea?
**Exodus**

What did Solomon build in Jerusalem that took seven years to complete?
**The Temple**

Which apostle wrote about the armor of God?
**Paul** (Ephesians)

Who was the son of Jesse, a harpist and future king?
**David**

Which prophet's wife was unnamed but had her hair shaved?
**Isaiah's wife** (called "the prophetess")

What did Zacchaeus promise to give back to anyone he had cheated?
**Four times** the amount

Which Old Testament feast commemorates the day of atonement?
**Yom Kippur**

What did Jesus call the wind and waves when He stilled them?
**Obedient**

Which New Testament letter addresses false teachers in the church?
**2 Peter**

What did David call the Lord in Psalm 23?
**Shepherd**

Which epistle emphasizes that Jesus is the great high priest?
**Hebrews**

Who saw a vision of a scroll that said, "Eat it and it will make your stomach bitter but your mouth sweet"?
**Ezekiel**

Which Old Testament woman ushered in Israel's victory by driving a tent peg through an enemy's head?
**Jael**

Which Gospel emphasizes Jesus' compassion and parables about the poor?
**Luke**

Who was the first Gentile convert recorded in the book of Acts?
**Cornelius**

What did Paul call the old sinful nature he struggled with?
**Flesh**

Who was the first murderer in the Bible?
**Cain**

Who was the second son of Adam and Eve?
**Abel**

What type of offering did Abel bring?
**Firstborn of his flock**

Who is noted for being taken by God without dying?
**Enoch**

Who lived 969 years, the longest recorded human life?
**Methuselah**

Which prophet's ministry took place during the reign of King Hezekiah?
**Isaiah**

Which book follows Ruth in the Old Testament?
**1 Samuel**

What structure did people build in Shinar?
**Tower of Babel**

What did God confuse at Babel?
**Their language**

Who was Abraham's firstborn son?
**Ishmael**

What was Jacob's name changed to?
**Israel**

Which son of Jacob was sold by his brothers?
**Joseph**

Who was Joseph's master in Egypt?
**Potiphar**

Which ruler's dreams did Joseph interpret?
**Pharaoh**

What position did Pharaoh give Joseph?
**Second in command**

Who led Israel into the Promised Land?
**Joshua**

Which judge defeated the Midianites with 300 men?
**Gideon**

Who made a rash vow leading to his daughter's sacrifice?
**Jephthah**

What foreign woman became David's great-grandmother?
**Ruth**

Who was the prophet in King Ahab's day?
**Elijah**

What did Elijah call down to prove God's power?
**Fire**

Who was taken up in a whirlwind?
**Elijah**

Who received a double portion of Elijah's spirit?
**Elisha**

Which captive interpreted the king's handwriting on the wall?
**Daniel**

Which patriarch's sons became the twelve tribes of Israel?
**Jacob**

Which matriarch served her mother-in-law Naomi and stayed in Bethlehem?
**Ruth**

What feast commemorates Israel's deliverance from Egypt?
**Passover**

Which sea did Jesus walk on?
**Sea of Galilee**

Who baptized Jesus?
**John the Baptist**

Which miracle at Cana involved water?
**Turning water into wine**

What meal did Jesus feed 5,000 with loaves and fish?
**The feeding of the 5,000**

Who denied Jesus three times?
**Peter**

Which apostle replaced Judas Iscariot?
**Matthias**

Which prophet wrote, "But they who wait for the Lord shall renew their strength"?
**Isaiah**

Which minor prophet declared, "For I am mighty to save"?
**Zephaniah**

What gift came at Pentecost?
**Holy Spirit**

Who wrote most of the New Testament letters?
**Paul**

Which book follows the Gospels and tells of the early church?
**Acts**

Who baptized an Ethiopian eunuch?
**Philip**

Which apostle wrote Revelation?
**John**

Who was known as the apostle to the Gentiles?
**Paul**

Where was Paul headed when he saw a light from heaven?
**Damascus**

Which Gospel says Jesus was "God with us," Immanuel?
**Matthew**

Which Gospel records Jesus' turning over the temple tables?
**John**

Which prison did Paul and Silas pray in before an earthquake?
**Philippi jail**

Who fell asleep and fell from a window during Paul's sermon?
**Eutychus**

Which prophet wrote, "But they who wait for the Lord shall renew their strength"?
**Isaiah**

Which minor prophet declared, "For I am mighty to save"?
**Zephaniah**

Which epistle begins, "Paul, a servant of Christ Jesus"?
**Romans**

Which Gospel begins, "The book of the genealogy of Jesus Christ"?
**Matthew**

Which Psalm is known as the shepherd's psalm?
**Psalm 23**

Which prophet wrote about a plumb line showing Jerusalem was crooked?
**Amos**

Which prophet told of the "valley of dry bones" coming to life?
**Ezekiel**

What did God create on the seventh day?
**Rest**

Which servant in the palace interpreted the king's dream of the four beasts?
**Daniel**

Which prophet's book is only one chapter long?
**Obadiah**

Who was Abraham's nephew who escaped Sodom?
**Lot**

What did Lot's wife become when she looked back?
**A pillar of salt**

Who was Isaac's wife?
**Rebekah**

Which brother did Jacob wrestle with?
**God (angel)**

What did Jacob dream at Bethel?
**A ladder to heaven**

Who was Jacob's favorite son?
**Joseph**

What color was Joseph's special coat?
**Multicolored**

Who tempted Eve in the garden?
**The serpent**

How many days did it rain during the flood?
**Forty**

What sign did God set after the flood?
**Rainbow**

Who was Moses' brother and first priest?
**Aaron**

Who was Moses' sister?
**Miriam**

What miracle did God perform at the Red Sea?
**Parting the waters**

Which mountain did Moses ascend to receive the Law?
**Mount Sinai**

What did God give Moses on tablets?
**Ten Commandments**

What food did God send from heaven?
**Manna**

Who led the Israelites around Jericho's walls?
**Priests blowing trumpets**

What judge slew a lion with his bare hands?
**Samson**

What gave Samson his strength?
**His hair**

Where did Samson collapse the temple?
**Philistine temple**

Which book names the offerings and feasts Israel was to keep?
**Leviticus**

Which book continues the story of Israel's wilderness journey with their census?
**Numbers**

Who anointed David as king?
**Samuel**

Which prophet warned Nineveh to repent or be destroyed?
**Jonah**

Which prophet used a vision of locusts to symbolize God's judgment?
**Joel**

What weapon did David use against Goliath?
**Sling and stone**

Who was David's son known for wisdom?
**Solomon**

What did Solomon build?
**The Temple**

Which book contains wise sayings of Solomon?
**Proverbs**

Who was the weeping prophet?
**Jeremiah**

Which book mourns Jerusalem's fall?
**Lamentations**

Which prophet saw dry bones come to life?
**Ezekiel**

Who led a successful revolt for Israel under a palm tree?
**Deborah**

Which book tells of Nehemiah rebuilding walls?
**Nehemiah**

Who was Queen Esther's cousin?
**Mordecai**

What Persian king married Esther?
**Ahasuerus**

Who took Jesus' body down from the cross?
**Joseph of Arimathea**

Which disciple is called "the rock"?
**Peter**

What did Jesus call the bread at the Last Supper?
**His body**

What did Jesus call the cup at the Last Supper?
**His blood**

Who asked Jesus, "How can these things be?" about being born again?
**Nicodemus**

Which book describes the armor of God that believers must put on?
**Ephesians**

Which Gospel emphasizes Jesus' compassion?
**Luke**

What prayer did Jesus teach His disciples?
**The Lord's Prayer**

Which Old Testament woman judge sang a victory song?
**Miriam**

Which prophet confronted King Ahab beside a brook?
**Elijah**

Who was the king when Daniel interpreted dreams?
**Nebuchadnezzar**

What happened to Shadrach, Meshach, and Abednego in the furnace?
**They were unharmed**

Which king's handwriting appeared on the wall?
**Belshazzar**

What did the writing on the wall mean?
**God has numbered your days**

Who led the Israelites into Canaan after Moses?
**Joshua**

What river did Joshua cross on dry ground?
**Jordan River**

Who hid Israelite spies on her roof?
**Rahab**

Which poetic book is the longest chapter in the Bible?
**Psalm 119**

Which poetic book teaches "A gentle answer turns away wrath"?
**Proverbs**

Which servant of the Lord struck the Syrian army with blindness?
**Elisha**

Which servant of Moses saw the burning bush on Mount Sinai?
**Moses**

Which book addresses the priesthood of Christ in the order of Melchizedek?
**Hebrews**

Which book calls Jesus the faithful and true witness?
**Revelation**

Which poetic book is the longest chapter in the Bible?
**Psalm 119**

Which poetic book teaches "A gentle answer turns away wrath"?
**Proverbs**

Which judge defeated the Midianites at night?
**Gideon**

Who tested God with a fleece?
**Gideon**

Which book follows Judges?
**Ruth**

Who was Naomi's daughter-in-law?
**Ruth**

Who was the first female judge?
**Deborah**

Which book tells of Samuel's birth?
**1 Samuel**

Who anointed Saul as king?
**Samuel**

Which giant did David face?
**Goliath**

What musical instrument did David play?
**Harp**

Who wrote most of the Psalms?
**David**

Who was the disciple known for doubt?
**Thomas**

Which book begins with Cyrus's decree to let exiles return?
**Ezra**

Which book ends with the words, "The Spirit and the Bride say, 'Come!'"?
**Revelation**

Which disciple wrote five letters?
**Peter**

Which book tells of the fruit of the Spirit?
**Galatians**

Which epistle encourages Christian unity in one body?
**Ephesians**

Which letter addresses idolatry and immorality?
**1 Corinthians**

Who was the runaway slave mentioned in Philemon?
**Onesimus**

Which city did Jesus clear the temple?
**Jerusalem**

Which prophetis called to "prepare the way" for the Lord?
**John the Baptist**

What symbol descended on Jesus at baptism?
**A dove**

Who was the Roman governor at Jesus' trial?
**Pontius Pilate**

Who asked for Jesus' body before Pilate?
**Joseph of Arimathea**

What crown did Roman soldiers place on Jesus?
**Crown of thorns**

Who was laid in a garden tomb?
**Jesus**

Which day is "Good Friday"?
**The day Jesus was crucified**

Which day is "Easter Sunday"?
**The day Jesus rose**

Which Gospel begins with a genealogy of Jesus?
**Matthew**

Which Gospel begins at creation?
**John**

Who is called the "beloved physician"?
**Luke**

Which book speaks of Christ as the good shepherd?
**John's Gospel**

Who wrote letters from prison to the Philippians?
**Paul**

Which letter says we take up "the shield of faith"?
**Ephesians**

Which prophet saw a chariot of horses with fire-breathing creatures?
**Zechariah**

Which prophet's wife was called the "prophetess"?
**Isaiah's wife**

What does "Emmanuel" mean?
**God with us**

Which Old Testament book contains songs of praise?
**Psalms**

Which prophet's book is the shortest in the Old Testament?
**Obadiah**

Which book tells of Israel's census in the wilderness?
**Numbers**

Which book details priestly duties and sacrifices?
**Leviticus**

Who led Israel after Eli died?
**Samuel**

Which judge killed Eglon, king of Moab?
**Ehud**

Which prophet was commanded to marry an unfaithful wife?
**Hosea**

Which prophet declared "Prepare the way of the Lord"?
**Isaiah**

Which book warns of a day of the Lord with four horsemen?
**Revelation**

Which book records Jesus' birth narrative with shepherds and angels?
**Luke**

Which Gospel details the journey of the Magi?
**Matthew**

Which church did Jesus say had lost its first love?
**Ephesus**

Which church did Jesus commend for keeping His word?
**Smyrna**

Which church did Jesus love but rebuke for tolerating false teaching?
**Thyatira**

Which minor prophet wrote about locusts?
**Joel**

Which feast celebrates the giving of the Law?
**Pentecost (Weeks)**

Which woman disciple hosted Jesus at her home?
**Mary of Bethany**

Which disciple witnessed Jesus' transfiguration?
**Peter**

Which prophet wept for his people?
**Jeremiah**

Which city's destruction did Ezekiel prophesy with a model?
**Jerusalem**

Which king tore his clothes upon hearing the law?
**Hezekiah**

Which prophet's lips were touched with a live coal?
**Isaiah**

Who was taken by chariots of fire into heaven?
**Elijah**

Who was the first to see the angel at the empty tomb?
**Mary Magdalene**

Which Old Testament book tells of a lion's den?
**Daniel**

Which Gospel records the ascension of Jesus?
**Luke**

Which apostle wrote the book of Hebrews?
**Unknown**

Which letter says "the Lord is near"?
**Philippians**

Who wrote, "Rejoice in the Lord always"?
**Paul** (Philippians)

What did Jesus call prayer in secret?
**Your private prayer**

Which prophet saw a vision of flying scrolls?
**Zechariah**

Which feast involved blowing trumpets?
**Feast of Trumpets**

Which book begins with the phrase, "In those days there was no king in Israel"?
**Judges**

Which book follows Judges and tells of Naomi and Ruth?
**Ruth**

Who anointed David before he became king?
**Samuel**

Which prophet hid his message in a clay jar?
**Jeremiah**

Which judge saved Israel from Canaanites under his uncle's roof?
**Ehud**

Who was the king known for listening to a poor man's plea?
**Solomon**

Who chased Elijah after Jezebel threatened him?
**Elijah himself** (he fled)

Which New Testament letter warns against loving the world?
**1 John**

Who tried to build a tower to heaven?
**People of Babel**

What did Jesus call the Pharisees' righteousness?
**Filthy rags**

Which ex-apostle was also a tax collector?
**Matthew**

Which book encourages young men to flee youthful passions?
**2 Timothy**

Which patriarch wrestled all night with a man who turned out to be God's messenger?
**Jacob**

Which patriarch was nearly sacrificed on Mount Moriah?
**Isaac**

Which disciple had his name changed from Saul?
**Paul**

What did Paul call the love chapter?
**1 Corinthians 13**

Which minor prophet speaks of a refiner's fire?
**Malachi**

What did the master bury in the Parable of the Talents that was unproductive?
**One talent**

What did the servant receive in the Parable of the Talents who had been most faithful?
**Five talents**

Which parable tells of a man who found treasure hidden in a field?
**Hidden Treasure**

Which parable describes a merchant searching for fine pearls?
**Pearl of Great Price**

Which parable compares the kingdom of heaven to a fishing net?
**Dragnet**

Which parable describes mercy shown to a man beaten and left half dead?
**Good Samaritan**

Which parable warns against sowing seeds among thorns?
**Parable of the Sower**

Which parable features a prodigal son's return?
**Prodigal Son**

Which parable tells of a lost coin hidden until found?
**Lost Coin**

Which parable is about a wedding feast with invited guests refusing to come?
**Wedding Feast**

Which parable tells of workers hired at different hours receiving the same pay?
**Laborers in the Vineyard**

Which master forgave a servant a huge debt and then that servant refused to forgive a friend?
**Unforgiving Servant**

How many wise virgins were ready when the bridegroom came?
**Five**

Which miracle involved Jesus healing ten men with skin disease?
**Ten Lepers**

How many of the healed lepers returned to thank Jesus?
**One**

Who was the blind man healed near Jericho who called out, "Jesus, Son of David, have mercy on me"?
**Bartimaeus**

Which miracle saw Jesus raise a widow's son from the dead at Nain?
**Widow's Son at Nain**

Who had a high fever that Jesus healed after touching her hand?
**Peter's mother-in-law**

Whose ear did Peter cut off in the garden, which Jesus then healed?
**Malchus**

Which Roman soldier's servant was healed from a distance by Jesus?
**Centurion's servant**

What illness did the woman have who touched Jesus' cloak to be healed?
**Hemorrhage**

Which parable compares the kingdom of heaven to yeast hidden in dough?
**Yeast**

Which parable warns against greed using a man who stored up grain and died that night?
**Rich Fool**

Who did Jesus raise from the dead after being told her spirit had left?
**Jairus's daughter**

Who baptized about 3,000 people on the Day of Pentecost?
**Peter**

Which brother of John was an apostle and son of Zebedee?
**James**

How many disciples followed Jesus?
**Twelve**

Which Psalm speaks of making a joyful noise to the Lord?
**Psalm 100**

How many days did Jesus appear to His disciples after His resurrection?
**Forty**

What event marks the coming of the Holy Spirit on Jesus' followers?
**Pentecost**

Which poetic book in the Old Testament is also called Song of Songs?
**Song of Solomon**

Who confronted King David about his sin with Bathsheba?
**Nathan**

Which sea is also known as the Salt Sea?
**Dead Sea**

Which king dreamed of a large tree being chopped down before Daniel interpreted it?
**Nebuchadnezzar**

What did Elijah ask God to send so the drought would end?
**Rain**

Which prophet warned Israel with a vision of locusts devouring the land?
**Amos**

Which minor prophet's book has only two chapters?
**Haggai**

Which Gospel is the only one to mention the visit of the Magi?
**Matthew**

What did the wise men follow to find Jesus?
**Star**

Who warned Joseph in a dream to flee to Egypt with Mary and Jesus?
**Angel**

Which apostle wrote that the greatest gift is love in 1 Corinthians 13?
**Paul**

Which Gospel begins with the preaching of John the Baptist in the wilderness?
**Mark**

Which New Testament book says, "God is love"?
**1 John**

Which Jewish festival did Jesus attend when He was twelve years old?
**Passover**

Which disciple confessed that Jesus was the Messiah at Caesarea Philippi?
**Peter**

How many days did Jonah warn Nineveh would be overturned?
**Forty**

Which prophet's book opens with the words, "Hear this word that the Lord has spoken"?
**Haggai**

Which book tells how Joshua led the Israelites into Canaan?
**Joshua**

Which book opens with "The Revelation of Jesus Christ"?
**Revelation**

Which book ends with a vision of a new heaven and new earth?
**Revelation**

Which New Testament letter begins with a greeting "To the seven churches in Asia"?
**Revelation**

Which Gospel opens with a genealogy of Jesus through Abraham?
**Matthew**

Which Gospel records the Magnificat of Mary after the angel's visit?
**Luke**

Which apostle wrote most of the letters in the New Testament?
**Paul**

Which leader in the early church was nicknamed "Son of Encouragement"?
**Barnabas**

Who was known as the "beloved disciple"?
**John**

Which apostle was a fisherman before Jesus called him?
**Peter**

Which apostle wrote the Book of Acts along with one of the Gospels?
**Luke**

Which woman hosted Paul and Silas and was a dealer in purple cloth?
**Lydia**

Which believer in Philippi was raised from the dead by Peter?
**Tabitha (Dorcas)**

Which Roman centurion became a Christian after hearing Peter's sermon?
**Cornelius**

Which companion of Paul was a silversmith by trade?
**Silas**

Who was jailed with Paul in Philippi until an earthquake freed them?
**Silas**

Which companion of Paul later became bishop of Ephesus?
**Timothy**

Which companion of Paul wrote two New Testament letters to encourage him?
**Timothy**

Which centurion protected Paul when Jews tried to kill him in Jerusalem?
**Claudius Lysias (the centurion)**

Which Old Testament festival commemorates Israel's deliverance from Egypt?
**Passover**

Which festival lasts seven days and involves living in temporary shelters?
**Sukkot**

Which festival celebrates the giving of the Law on Mount Sinai?
**Weeks (Pentecost)**

Which festival begins the Jewish New Year with trumpet blasts?
**Rosh Hashanah (Trumpets)**

Which fast day remembers the Day of Atonement?
**Yom Kippur**

What was placed inside the Holy of Holies in the Tabernacle?
**Ark of the Covenant**

What was kept burning continually outside the Tabernacle?
**Lampstand**

Which Levites carried the Ark during the crossing of the Jordan River?
**Priests**

Which food did God send that tasted like wafers with honey?
**Manna**

Which animals did Noah send out from the ark to test for dry land?
**Dove and raven**

Which prophet struck the rock twice to bring water instead of speaking to it?
**Moses**

Which prophet raised the widow's son and gave him back to his mother?
**Elijah**

Which judge tested God with a fleece of wool?
**Gideon**

Which judge slew Eglon, king of Moab, with a hidden dagger?
**Ehud**

Which judge led Israel with the help of a thousand men armed with pitchers and lamps?
**Gideon**

Which judge's strength came from not cutting his hair?
**Samson**

Which judge plotted against Sisera by inviting him into her tent?
**Jael**

Who anointed David to be king while he was tending sheep?
**Samuel**

Which king built the first Temple in Jerusalem?
**Solomon**

Which king prayed for wisdom and received it in a dream?
**Solomon**

Which king's heart was torn when he heard the Book of the Law read after the exile?
**Josiah**

Which king's high priest was Hilkiah when the Law was rediscovered?
**Josiah**

Which prophet's wife died and was not mourned by Judah?
**Ezekiel's wife**

Which prophet lay on his side for 390 days as a sign to Israel?
**Ezekiel**

Which prophet watched dry bones come together and live?
**Ezekiel**

Which disciple wrote the book that begins, "I, Paul, a prisoner of Christ Jesus"?
**Paul**

Which companion of Paul was also a doctor?
**Luke**

Which companion of Paul was jailed with him in Philippi?
**Silas**

Which friend of Jesus provided the tomb for His burial?
**Joseph of Arimathea**

Which friend anointed Jesus' feet with costly perfume and wiped them with her hair?
**Mary of Bethany**

Which woman was the first to witness Jesus' empty tomb?
**Mary Magdalene**

Which woman was known for her hospitality to Paul and Peter?
**Lydia**

Which woman was raised from the dead by Peter in Joppa?
**Tabitha (Dorcas)**

Which Jewish carpenter was Jesus' earthly father?
**Joseph**

Which prophet lamented, "Even jackals offer the breast; they nurse their young"?
**Hosea**

Which prophet's writing warns that those who do not speak the word given will die?
**Ezekiel**

Which town was Jesus' childhood home?
**Nazareth**

Which town did Jesus choose to start His ministry after baptism?
**Capernaum**

Which town did Zacchaeus climb a sycamore tree in order to see Jesus?
**Jericho**

Which region did Jesus grow up in?
**Galilee**

Which wilderness did Jesus fast in for forty days?
**Judean Desert**

Which river did John baptize people in?
**Jordan River**

Which mountain did Jesus pray on before His transfiguration?
**Mount of Olives**

Which mountain did Moses climb to receive the Ten Commandments?
**Mount Sinai**

Which mountaintop did Jesus take Peter, James, and John to see Him transfigured?
**Mount Tabor** (tradition) but acceptable

Which garden did Jesus pray in the night before His arrest?
**Gethsemane**

Which historical book highlights Samuel's leadership and Israel's demand for a king?
**1 Samuel**

Which book describes Solomon's building of the temple in Jerusalem?
**1 Kings**

Which hill is called the place of the skull where Jesus was crucified?
**Golgotha**

Which gate did Jesus enter Jerusalem through on Palm Sunday?
**Golden Gate** (tradition; kids-level)

Which coat did Joseph wear that caused his brothers to envy him?
**Multicolored coat**

Which tower was being built that led God to confuse the people's language?
**Tower of Babel**

Which flood survivor built an altar to the Lord after leaving the ark?
**Noah**

Which animal did Noah send out to check if the waters had receded?
**Dove**

Which patriarch dreamed of a ladder reaching to heaven?
**Jacob**

Which matriarch was Abraham's sister as well as his wife?
**Sarah**

Which servant watered Abraham's camels when looking for Isaac's wife?
**Rebekah**

Which servant of Abraham found a wife for Isaac by prayer at a well?
**Eliezer**

Which servant of God asked to be remembered and called out, "Man of God, help me"?
**Elisha**

Which servant of Solomon became his secretary and helped him choose materials for the Temple?
**Ahijah** (advanced – acceptable)

Which prophet saw the end of exile and a restored Jerusalem in vision?
**Zechariah**

Which prophet told of a coming day when the sun would be darkened?
**Zephaniah**

Which prophet encouraged rebuilding the temple after the exile?
**Haggai**

Which prophet used a vision of the Lord high and lifted up in a temple?
**Isaiah**

Which prophet's book opens with "The word of the Lord that came to Joel"?
**Joel**

Which prophet announced the return from Babylon under Cyrus?
**Isaiah**

Which prophet was commanded to bury a loincloth as a sign against Judah?
**Jeremiah**

Which prophet wept over Jerusalem's coming destruction?
**Jeremiah**

Which minor prophet's name means "my messenger"?
**Malachi**

Which prophet declared, "Behold, I will send you Elijah before the great and awesome day of the Lord"?
**Malachi**

Which prophet wrote about a shepherd pierced by swords?
**Zechariah**

Which prophet confronted King Ahab with a drought?
**Elijah**

Which book prophesies about the Messiah being born of a virgin?
**Isaiah**

Which prophet's vision included four living creatures and wheels within wheels?
**Ezekiel**

Which prophet was taken up to heaven in a whirlwind?
**Elijah**

Which prophet asked God to "tear open the heavens" and come down?
**Isaiah**

Which minor prophet's book calls Israel "My vineyard"?
**Isaiah** (chapter 5)

Which prophet compared Israel to a stick that two sticks become one?
**Ezekiel**

Which prophet wrote about a future branch from Jesse?
**Isaiah**

Which prophet was active just before the exile to Babylon?
**Jeremiah**

Which prophet wrote, "My thoughts are not your thoughts"?
**Isaiah**

Which prophet's call began with "In the year that King Uzziah died"?
**Isaiah**

Which prophet's book emphasizes that "the righteous shall live by faith"?
**Habakkuk**

Which minor prophet's two-chapter book calls people to "Return to the Lord"?
**Haggai**

Which prophet's vision included a golden lampstand?
**Zechariah**

Which prophet was told to eat a scroll that tasted sweet and then bitter?
**Ezekiel**

Which prophet had to marry an unfaithful wife to illustrate Israel's sin?
**Hosea**

Which book records Israel's transition from judges to kings?
**1 Samuel**

Which book tells of David's reign and Solomon's rise?
**2 Samuel**

Which book continues Israel's history under Solomon and subsequent kings?
**1 Kings**

Which book tells of the fall of Jerusalem and exile to Babylon?
**2 Kings**

Which book records the return from exile and rebuilding of Jerusalem's walls?
**Nehemiah**

Which book tells of the returned exiles rebuilding the temple under Zerubbabel?
**Ezra**

Which poetic book asks, "Who can ascend the hill of the Lord?"
**Psalms**

Which poetic book explores life's meaning with "vanity of vanities"?
**Ecclesiastes**

Which poetic book contains love poems between bride and groom?
**Song of Solomon**

Which prophetic book follows Lamentations?
**Ezekiel**

Which book tells of Daniel interpreting dreams for three kings?
**Daniel**

Which book begins, "In the beginning God created the heavens and the earth"?
**Genesis**

Which book records Moses' laws and the tabernacle instructions?
**Exodus**

Which book ends with Israel poised to enter Canaan under Joshua's command?
**Deuteronomy**

Which book lists the Israelites' camps and tribal assignments?
**Numbers**

Which book records Elijah's ministry and miracles before Elisha's rise?
**1 Kings**

Which book records Elisha's ministry and twice-as-many miracles?
**2 Kings**

Which book tells how Esther became queen of Persia?
**Esther**

Which book recounts Job's trials and his faithful endurance?
**Job**

Which book tells about the rebuilding of Jerusalem's walls in 52 days?
**Nehemiah**

Which book's final verse is "Amen. Come, Lord Jesus"?
**Revelation**

Which book records Paul's journeys with Luke as his companion?
**Acts**

Which book gives an account of the Apostle Paul's letters to seven churches?
**Romans**

Which book opens with "Paul, a servant of Christ Jesus, called to be an apostle"?
**Romans**

Which book encourages generosity by giving like the Macedonians?
**2 Corinthians**

Which book addresses unity and spiritual gifts in the church?
**1 Corinthians**

Which Gospel tells of the parable of the rich young ruler?
**Luke**

Which Gospel opens with "The beginning of the gospel of Jesus Christ, the Son of God"?
**Mark**

Which disciple's name means "son of encouragement"?
**Barnabas**

Which disciple was the first martyr of the church?
**Stephen**

Which patriarch's name was changed to Israel?
**Jacob**

# PART 2 – INTERMEDIATE

# Old Testament - The Law (or Pentateuch)

What is the first book of the Bible?
**Genesis**

Who created the heavens and the earth?
**God**

What did God create on the first day?
**Light**

What did God create on the second day?
**Sky**

What did God create on the third day?
**Land and plants**

What did God create on the fourth day?
**Sun, moon, and stars**

What did God create on the fifth day?
**Fish and birds**

What did God create on the sixth day?
**Animals and humans**

On which day did God rest?
**Seventh**

Who was the first man?
**Adam**

Who was the first woman?
**Eve**

In which garden did they live?
**Eden**

Who tempted Eve to eat the forbidden fruit?
**The serpent**

What fruit did they eat that God told them not to?
**Fruit from the tree of knowledge**

Who was the first murderer?
**Cain**

Who was murdered by his brother?
**Abel**

What offering pleased God from Abel?
**Firstborn of his flock**

Who built the ark?
**Noah**

How many days and nights did it rain during the flood?
**Forty**

What sign did God give after the flood?
**Rainbow**

Who is called the father of many nations?
**Abraham**

Who was Abraham's wife?
**Sarah**

What was their son's name?
**Isaac**

Who was Isaac's wife?
**Rebekah**

Which twin was born first?
**Esau**

Which twin bought his brother's birthright?
**Esau**

Who deceived Isaac to receive the blessing?
**Jacob**

What new name did God give Jacob?
**Israel**

How many sons did Jacob have?
**Twelve**

Which son was sold by his brothers?
**Joseph**

What special coat did Joseph wear?
**Coat of many colors**

Who interpreted Pharaoh's dreams?
**Joseph**

What did Joseph become in Egypt?
**Governor**

Who was Moses' sister?
**Miriam**

In what did Moses float down the Nile?
**Basket**

Who found Moses as a baby?
**Pharaoh's daughter**

What did Moses' staff turn into before Pharaoh?
**A serpent**

Which river turned to blood as a plague?
**Nile**

What meal did the Israelites eat on the night of the tenth plague?
**Passover meal**

What food fell from heaven to feed the Israelites?
**Manna**

What sea did the Israelites cross on dry ground?
**Red Sea**

Where did Moses receive the Ten Commandments?
**Mount Sinai**

How many tablets were the Ten Commandments written on?
**Two**

What festival remembers the Exodus from Egypt?
**Passover**

Which tribe served as priests?
**Levi**

What was the portable dwelling place for God called?
**Tabernacle**

On which mountain did Moses view the Promised Land before he died?
**Mount Nebo**

Which book lists the census and desert wanderings?
**Numbers**

How many spies did Moses send into Canaan?
**Twelve**

Which two spies trusted God's promise?
**Joshua and Caleb**

What punishment did God give for the people's disbelief?
**Forty years of wandering**

Which river did the Israelites cross to enter Canaan?
**Jordan**

What miracle stopped the Jordan's flow?
**The waters stood up**

What did Moses strike to bring water at Meribah?
**A rock**

Which son of Aaron died for offering unauthorized fire?
**Nadab and Abihu**

What metal serpent did Moses raise for healing snake bites?
**Bronze serpent**

Which book means "second law"?
**Deuteronomy**

What prayer begins, "Hear, O Israel: The LORD our God, the LORD is one"?
**Shema**

Which day each week were Israelites commanded to rest?
**Sabbath**

Which feast celebrated the first fruits of the harvest?
**Weeks (Pentecost)**

Which feast commemorated living in tents in the desert?
**Tabernacles**

Which feast marked the blowing of trumpets?
**Trumpets**

Which feast was the Day of Atonement?
**Yom Kippur**

Which commandment forbids stealing?
**Eighth**

Which commandment forbids lying?
**Ninth**

Which commandment forbids coveting?
**Tenth**

Which plague brought frogs?
**Second**

Which plague brought gnats?
**Third**

Which plague brought darkness?
**Ninth**

Which plague killed the firstborn?
**Tenth**

What did the Israelites paint on their doorposts?
**Lamb's blood**

Which mountain did Moses ascend to receive the Law?
**Mount Sinai**

Who helped Moses hold up his arms during battle?
**Aaron and Hur**

Which animal's horns were used to make trumpets?
**Rams**

What did the Israelites carry around Jericho's walls?
**The Ark of the Covenant**

Which day of the month was the Day of Atonement?
**Tenth**

What type of wood was used for the tabernacle's poles?
**Acacia wood**

Which body of water did God turn into a pathway?
**Red Sea**

Who wrote the final book of the Pentateuch?
**Moses**

What command did Moses repeat five times in Deuteronomy?
**"Hear, O Israel"**

What did the people eat before manna that they later missed?
**Leeks and onions**

Which tribe's inheritance stayed east of the Jordan?
**Reuben, Gad, half of Manasseh**

Which book ends with Israel poised to enter Canaan?
**Deuteronomy**

What is the first commandment?
**No other gods**

Which commandment tells us not to misuse God's name?
**Third**

Which commandment tells us to remember the Sabbath?
**Fourth**

Which commandment tells us not to murder?
**Sixth**

Which commandment tells us not to commit adultery?
**Seventh**

Where did Moses break the first set of tablets?
**Mount Sinai**

Which patriarch's name means "father of many"?
**Abraham**

What city did Lot's wife look back at and turn into salt?
**Sodom**

Who closed the womb of Sarah until old age?
**God**

Which patriarch dreamed of a ladder reaching to heaven?
**Jacob**

On which mountain did Abraham almost sacrifice Isaac?
**Mount Moriah**

Which son of Jacob had a dream of the sun, moon, and stars bowing to him?
**Joseph**

What did Joseph's brothers dip his coat into to deceive their father?
**Goat's blood**

Which son of Levi led the Israelites out of Egypt as priest?
**Aaron**

What sign did God place in Abraham's flesh as a covenant?
**Circumcision**

Who was Pharaoh's chief baker in Joseph's prison?
**The baker**

Which plague killed livestock of the Egyptians?
**Fifth**

What did God tell the Israelites to put on their doorposts for protection from the plague of death?
**Blood of the lamb**

Which book begins with "These are the generations of…"?
**Genesis**

Which book contains the story of the burning bush?
**Exodus**

Which book outlines offerings and sacrifices?
**Leviticus**

Which book tells of Balaam's talking donkey?
**Numbers**

Which book repeats the law before Israel enters Canaan?
**Deuteronomy**

Which winged creatures overshadowed the Ark in the Most Holy Place?
**Cherubim**

What was the outer court of the tabernacle called?
**Court of the Israelites**

Which tribe carried the tabernacle and its furnishings?
**Levites**

What was worn by the high priest on his breastplate?
**Twelve stones**

What meal commemorates God passing over Hebrew homes?
**Passover**

Which festival celebrates the giving of the Law?
**Weeks (Pentecost)**

Which festival involves living in booths?
**Tabernacles**

Which book's name means "and these are the words"?
**Deuteronomy**

Who led the people in numbering them in the wilderness?
**Moses**

Which plague turned water into blood?
**First**

Which plague filled the land with flies?
**Fourth**

Which plague brought hail and fire?
**Seventh**

Which plague struck Egyptian livestock?
**Fifth**

Which plague brought darkness so thick it could be felt?
**Eighth**

What command did God give about making idols?
**Do not make idols**

What did the Israelites eat on the sixth day because none fell on the Sabbath?
**Double portion of manna**

Which book gives laws on clean and unclean animals?
**Leviticus**

What did Aaron's staff do to Bud?
**Budded**

What act showed Korah's rebellion against Moses?
**Earth opened and swallowed him**

Which son of Jacob married an Egyptian wife named Asenath?
**Joseph**

What was Joseph's final act before his brothers died?
**Forgave them**

Which command did Moses remind Israel to teach their children?
**God's commandments**

What does "Moses" mean?
**Drawn out**

In which book does God promise a prophet like Moses?
**Deuteronomy**

Which tribe encamped around the tabernacle?
**Levites**

What did Moses break in anger at the Israelites' idolatry?
**Stone tablets**

Which offerer brought grain as a gift to God?
**Grain offering**

Which sacrifice included an offering for sin?
**Sin offering**

Which sacrifice had a male without defect?
**Burnt offering**

What was the tenth plague on Egypt?
**Death of the firstborn**

Which pillar guided Israel by night?
**Pillar of fire**

Which river did Aaron's staff blossom near?
**Jordan**

Which two books tell of Israel's laws and festivals?
**Leviticus and Numbers**

Which mountain was named "the mountain of God"?
**Mount Sinai**

Which book ends with Moses' death?
**Deuteronomy**

Which book introduces the creation account?
**Genesis**

Where did Abraham almost sacrifice Isaac?
**Mount Moriah**

Which book recounts Israel's exodus from Egypt?
**Exodus**

Which book is also called "The Law of Moses"?
**Torah**

Which book lists the rules for the priesthood?
**Leviticus**

Which book contains the census in chapters 1 and 26?
**Numbers**

Which book restates the law before entering Canaan?
**Deuteronomy**

Which book recounts the story of Joseph and his brothers?
**Genesis**

Who married Zipporah, daughter of Jethro?
**Moses**

Which book tells of the construction of the tabernacle?
**Exodus**

Which river swallowed up Korah and his followers?
**Earth (opened)**

Which book lists the Ten Commandments twice?
**Exodus and Deuteronomy**

Which book records Moses' farewell speeches?
**Deuteronomy**

What did Israel carry as a testimony in the desert?
**Ark of the Covenant**

Which pillar guided Israel by day?
**Pillar of cloud**

Which book contains the story of the bronze serpent?
**Numbers**

Which book outlines the Jubilee year?
**Leviticus**

Which book describes the burning of Nadab and Abihu?
**Leviticus**

Which book begins with the words "These are the generations of"?
**Genesis**

Which book describes manna as "bread from heaven"?
**Exodus**

Which book recounts Miriam's complaint and punishment?
**Numbers**

Which book tells of Balaam's donkey speaking?
**Numbers**

Which book includes the command to "love your neighbor as yourself"?
**Leviticus**

Which book commands cities of refuge for accidental killers?
**Numbers**

Which book requires the Israelites to tithe every third year for the Levites?
**Deuteronomy**

Which book warns against false prophets in chapter 13?
**Deuteronomy**

Which book includes the blessing of the tribes in chapter 49?
**Genesis**

Which book describes human lifespans often over 900 years?
**Genesis**

Which book records the institution of the priesthood?
**Exodus**

Which book details the sin offering for unintentional sin?
**Leviticus**

Which book lists the laws for vows?
**Numbers**

Which book includes the command to remember Amalek?
**Exodus**

Which book instructs to teach the law to children in Deuteronomy 6?
**Deuteronomy**

Which book opens with the words "And Noah was six hundred years old"?
**Genesis**

Which book describes the rainbow as the sign of the covenant?
**Genesis**

Which book forbids boiling a young goat in its mother's milk?
**Exodus**

Which book contains the law about not muzzling an ox while it treads out the grain?
**Deuteronomy**

Which book tells of Aaron's rod that budded to prove his priesthood?
**Numbers**

Which book describes the dedication of the tabernacle in detail?
**Leviticus**

Which book includes Joshua's request to Moses in Deuteronomy 31?
**Deuteronomy**

Which book commands not to oppress strangers because you were strangers in Egypt?
**Exodus**

Which book warns against idolatry with Molech in Leviticus 18?
**Leviticus**

Which book describes the Amalekites' defeat after Moses held up his hands?
**Exodus**

Which book commands the Israelites to appoint judges and officers in all their towns?
**Deuteronomy**

Which book ends with the words "And there arose not a prophet since in Israel like Moses"?
**Deuteronomy**

Which book includes the law about gleaning fields for the poor and the foreigner?
**Leviticus**

Which book describes the census in the plains of Moab?
**Numbers**

Which book tells of the dedication of the golden altar?
**Exodus**

Which book lists the cities to be set aside for Levites?
**Numbers**

Which book records the incident of the talking donkey?
**Numbers**

Which book commands the Israelites to rejoice in the festivals?
**Leviticus**

Which book provides the law about the scapegoat on the Day of Atonement?
**Leviticus**

Which book commands the writing of the law on doorframes?
**Deuteronomy**

Which book ends with "Blessed is the man who does this and blessed are the people of Israel" (last verse)?
**Deuteronomy**

Which book begins with a genealogy from Adam to Noah?
**Genesis**

Which book titles mean "words" and "account"?
**Exodus**

Which book's name means "holy things"?
**Leviticus**

Which book's name means "in the wilderness"?
**Numbers**

Which book's name means "these words"?
**Deuteronomy**

Which book records the laws of the covenant in Exodus 20?
**Exodus**

Which book warns against consulting mediums and spiritists?
**Leviticus**

Which book instructs the Israelites to tithe on everything they produce?
**Leviticus**

Which book describes Moses' birth and early life?
**Exodus**

Which book records Israel's complaints about water at Massah?
**Exodus**

Which book includes statutes on sexual morality?
**Leviticus**

Which book recounts the rebellion of Korah, Dathan, and Abiram?
**Numbers**

Which book commands blessing and cursing Mount Gerizim and Mount Ebal?
**Deuteronomy**

Which book tells how Jacob's family moved to Egypt?
**Genesis**

Which book introduces the name Yahweh for God?
**Exodus**

Which book records the cost of the tabernacle items in detail?
**Exodus**

Which book includes the law about the Sabbath year?
**Leviticus**

Which book tells of the birth of Moses in the house of Levi?
**Exodus**

Which book names the place of God's testing as Massah and Meribah?
**Exodus**

Which book describes the consecration of the Levites on the Day of Atonement?
**Numbers**

Which book commands the Israelites to remember being slaves in Egypt in Deuteronomy 5?
**Deuteronomy**

Which book includes Aaron's garments for the high priest?
**Exodus**

Which book defines uncleanness for women after childbirth?
**Leviticus**

Which book contains the command, "Honor your father and your mother"?
**Exodus**

Which book describes the offering of first fruits in Exodus 23?
**Exodus**

Which book includes Moses' blessing to Israel in chapter 33?
**Deuteronomy**

Which book warns against carrying gods made of wood or stone?
**Deuteronomy**

Which book describes the bronze laver for priests to wash at the tabernacle?
**Exodus**

Which book recounts the command to build an altar of earth on entering the Promised Land?
**Deuteronomy**

Which book mentions the role of the daughters of Zelophehad in inheritance laws?
**Numbers**

Which book includes the law about the redemption of land in the Jubilee year?
**Leviticus**

Which book records Moses' final song in chapter 32?
**Deuteronomy**

Which book instructs the Israelites to choose life by loving and obeying God?
**Deuteronomy**

Which book commands not to boil a young goat in its mother's milk?
**Exodus**

Which book describes the garments of the high priest?
**Exodus**

Which book contains laws about birds, fish, and creeping things?
**Leviticus**

Which book instructs not to muzzle an ox during threshing?
**Deuteronomy**

Which book tells how God provided quail for meat in the wilderness?
**Numbers**

Which book details the census of the Levites by family heads?
**Numbers**

Which book includes the law of fair weights and measures?
**Leviticus**

Which book tells of Moses' bitter complaint at Meribah?
**Numbers**

Which book describes the covenant renewal ceremony at Shechem?
**Deuteronomy**

Which book begins with "The LORD spoke to Moses…"?
**Leviticus**

Which book contains the blessing Aaron gave in chapter 6?
**Numbers**

Which book instructs the Israelites to tithe every year?
**Deuteronomy**

Which book records the laws about rebellious children?
**Deuteronomy**

Which book describes the institution of the Sabbath as a covenant?
**Exodus**

Which book commands not to charge interest to a fellow Israelite?
**Deuteronomy**

Which book tells how Israel defeated the Amalekites at Rephidim?
**Exodus**

Which book includes the law about the red heifer and purification?
**Numbers**

Which book commands the use of salt in all offerings?
**Leviticus**

Which book lists the blessings and curses on Mount Gerizim and Ebal?
**Deuteronomy**

Which book explains the sanctity of firstborn animals?
**Exodus**

Which book instructs the Israelites to keep the Feast of Unleavened Bread seven days?
**Numbers**

Which book warns against joining with the pagan nations in worship?
**Deuteronomy**

Which book describes the census of those able to fight by tribe?
**Numbers**

Which book ends with the words, "There has not risen a prophet since in Israel like Moses"?
**Deuteronomy**

Where did Abraham live when God called him?
**Ur of the Chaldeans**

What was Abraham's original name?
**Abram**

What was Sarai's new name?
**Sarah**

How old was Abraham when Isaac was born?
**One hundred**

Who did Isaac marry?
**Rebekah**

At which well did Abraham's servant meet Rebekah?
**Well of Nahor**

Who wrestled with a man at the ford of Jabbok?
**Jacob**

What name did God give Jacob?
**Israel**

Which of Jacob's sons was sold into slavery by his brothers?
**Joseph**

How many years of plenty were in Pharaoh's dream?
**Seven**

What miracle sweetened the bitter water at Marah?
**Bitter water made sweet**

On which day did God create land animals and humans?
**Sixth**

Which day is set apart as a holy rest day?
**Seventh day**

Which tribe did not receive a land inheritance?
**Levites**

Who was Moses' father-in-law?
**Jethro**

How many plagues struck Egypt?
**Ten**

Which sea parted for Israel to cross?
**Red Sea**

What food fell from heaven each day?
**Manna**

What did the Israelites gather twice as much of on the sixth day?
**Manna**

Where did Moses receive the Ten Commandments?
**Mount Sinai**

How many tablets held the Ten Commandments?
**Two**

Which book details laws for sacrifices and the priesthood?
**Leviticus**

How many spies were sent into Canaan?
**Twelve**

Which two spies trusted God about Canaan?
**Joshua and Caleb**

How many years did Israel wander in the wilderness?
**Forty years**

Which river did Israel cross into the Promised Land?
**Jordan**

Which book restates Moses' farewell speeches?
**Deuteronomy**

Which prayer begins "Hear, O Israel"?
**Shema**

Which festival celebrates the Exodus from Egypt?
**Passover**

Which festival celebrates the giving of the Law?
**Pentecost**

Which festival involves dwelling in temporary shelters?
**Tabernacles**

Which celebration begins with trumpet blasts?
**Feast of Trumpets**

What is the holy day on the tenth of Tishri called?
**Day of Atonement**

Which commandment forbids murder?
**Sixth**

Which commandment forbids adultery?
**Seventh**

What did the first plague on Egypt do?
**Turned water to blood**

Which plague brought frogs onto the land?
**Second**

Which plague brought gnats on man and beast?
**Third**

Which plague brought swarms of flies?
**Fourth**

Which plague struck Egyptian livestock?
**Fifth**

What was kept inside the Ark of the Covenant?
**Tablets of the Law**

Which wood was used for the ark's poles?
**Acacia**

What metal overlaid the altar of incense?
**Gold**

How many cities of refuge were set apart?
**Six**

Who composed the song in Deuteronomy chapter 32?
**Moses**

Which book recounts laws about firstborn consecration?
**Exodus**

Which book details the census of Israel in the wilderness?
**Numbers**

# INTERMEDIATE

# Old Testament - The Historical Books

Who succeeded Moses as leader of Israel?
**Joshua**

Which city's walls fell after Israelites marched around them for seven days?
**Jericho**

Who hid two Israelite spies on her roof?
**Rahab**

Which river did the Israelites cross on dry ground under Joshua?
**Jordan River**

Where did the Israelites camp after crossing the Jordan?
**Gilgal**

What memorial did Joshua set up after crossing the Jordan?
**Twelve stones**

Who commanded the sun and moon to stand still?
**Joshua**

Which city made peace treaty with Israel through deception?
**Gibeon**

Who was the first judge of Israel?
**Othniel**

Who killed the Moabite king Eglon with a hidden sword?
**Ehud**

Which judge made a vow that led to his daughter's sacrifice?
**Jephthah**

Which judge tore a lion apart with his bare hands?
**Samson**

Who betrayed Samson for silver?
**Delilah**

Which judge defeated the Midianites with only 300 men?
**Gideon**

What sign did Gideon request with a fleece of wool?
**Dew on the fleece only**

Who was the only female judge of Israel?
**Deborah**

Which general under Deborah was Barak's commander?
**Sisera**

Who drove a tent peg through Sisera's head?
**Jael**

Which judge struck down 600 Philistines with an ox goad?
**Shamgar**

What pattern described Israel's cycle in the Book of Judges?
**Sin, oppression, repentance, deliverance**

Who stayed with her mother-in-law Naomi after her husband died?
**Ruth**

Who was Ruth's mother-in-law?
**Naomi**

In which country did Naomi and her family live before returning to Israel?
**Moab**

Who became Ruth's kinsman-redeemer?
**Boaz**

In whose field did Ruth glean grain?
**Boaz's field**

What crop did Ruth harvest?
**Barley**

Who blessed Ruth for her loyalty to Naomi?
**Boaz**

Which judge served Israel for 23 years?
**Tola**

Which judge served Israel for 22 years?
**Jair**

Which judge served for eight years and delivered Israel from Moabites?
**Ehud**

Which judge served for six years and delivered Israel from Ammonites?
**Jephthah**

Which judge served Israel for 40 years after Gideon?
**Abimelech** (as self-proclaimed king)

What was the era before Israel had kings called?
**The period of the Judges**

Which book immediately follows Joshua?
**Judges**

Which book tells the story of a Moabite woman's loyalty?
**Ruth**

Which judge's name means "he who redeems"?
**Ehud**

Which judge's story ends with a collection of songs and poems?
**Deborah**

Which tribe did Shamgar belong to?
**Naphtali**

Which judge's story shows God using a weak vessel to defeat enemies?
**Gideon**

What did God use to soften the hearts of Israel's enemies in Judges?
**Sin and deliverance**

Which city's defeat involved the sun standing still?
**Gibeon** (battle there)

What symbol of God's presence camped at Shiloh in Judges?
**Ark of the Covenant**

Which judge began his story with Israel doing evil in the eyes of the Lord?
**Othniel**

What was the name of Naomi's husband?
**Elimelech**

Which book ends with the words "So the land had rest for eighty years"?
**Judges**

Which judge's birth involved an angel's announcement to his mother?
**Samson**

What was the original name of the city of Boaz's family?
**Bethlehem**

What piece of clothing did Ruth pick up at the threshing floor?
**Boaz's sandal**

Who was the chief city of Moab that oppressed Israel in Judges?
**Gilead**

Which judge's story involves an annual Philistine oppression?
**Shamgar**

Which book begins with "Now after the death of Joshua"?
**Judges**

Which judge's story shows God's power working through a weak person?
**Gideon**

Which judge's name is associated with "rest"?
**Othniel**

Which book's central theme is "everyone did what was right in their own eyes"?
**Judges**

Who was the prophet that succeeded Moses as Israel's leader?
**Joshua**

Which city's walls collapsed after the Israelites marched around them?
**Jericho**

Who hid two Israelite spies on her roof?
**Rahab**

Which river did the Israelites cross on dry ground under Joshua's command?
**Jordan River**

Where did the Israelites camp immediately after crossing the Jordan?
**Gilgal**

What memorial did Joshua set up at Gilgal?
**Twelve stones**

Which judge of Israel was also a prophetess?
**Deborah**

Who was Deborah's military commander in defeat of Jabin's army?
**Barak**

Who drove a tent peg through the head of Sisera?
**Jael**

Which judge tore apart a lion with his bare hands?
**Samson**

Who betrayed Samson for thirty pieces of silver?
**Delilah**

Which judge defeated the Midianites with 300 men?
**Gideon**

What sign did Gideon ask God to confirm His promise?
**Fleece of wool**

Which tribe had no inheritance of land but were assigned cities?
**Levites**

Who became king of Israel after Saul's death?
**David**

Who was David's loyal friend and Saul's son?
**Jonathan**

Which prophet anointed David as king?
**Samuel**

Who succeeded David as king of Israel?
**Solomon**

Which queen visited Solomon to test his wisdom?
**Queen of Sheba**

What did Solomon build in Jerusalem?
**The Temple**

Which judge's story involves a great deliverance with only 300 men?
**Gideon**

Which prophet confronted King Ahab with a drought?
**Elijah**

Who raised the widow of Zarephath's son from the dead?
**Elijah**

Who succeeded Elijah and performed twice as many miracles?
**Elisha**

Which Syrian general was healed by Elisha after his servants prayed?
**Naaman**

Which king of Judah was known for his trust in God during Sennacherib's siege?
**Hezekiah**

Which Assyrian king's army was destroyed by an angel in one night?
**Sennacherib**

Who was the last king of Judah before the Babylonian exile?
**Zedekiah**

Which ruler in Persia allowed the Jews to return and rebuild the temple?
**Cyrus**

Who led the first group of exiles back to Jerusalem?
**Zerubbabel**

Which prophet encouraged Zerubbabel to complete the rebuilding of the temple?
**Haggai**

Who served as high priest during the foundation laying of the second temple?
**Joshua**

Which cupbearer to King Artaxerxes rebuilt the walls of Jerusalem?
**Nehemiah**

How many days did it take Nehemiah to rebuild Jerusalem's walls?
**Fifty-two**

Which official mocked Nehemiah and plotted against him?
**Sanballat**

Who was appointed governor of Judea after the exile?
**Nehemiah**

Which scribe read the Law to the people in Nehemiah's time?
**Ezra**

In which Persian city did Esther become queen?
**Susa**

Who was Esther's cousin and guardian?
**Mordecai**

Which king decreed Esther's people could defend themselves on one day?
**Artaxerxes**

What festival commemorates the Jews' deliverance in Esther's time?
**Purim**

Which book retells Israel's history from Adam to the exile?
**1 Chronicles**

Which book covers Israel's history from Solomon to the Babylonian exile?
**2 Chronicles**

Which prophet read the Law to King Josiah, prompting a revival?
**Shaphan** (scribe)

Which king discovered the Book of the Law during temple repairs?
**Josiah**

Which book tells of the return from exile and temple completion under Zerubbabel?
**Ezra**

Which book recounts Nehemiah's efforts to restore Jerusalem's walls?
**Nehemiah**

Who was king when Ezra led a second group of exiles to Jerusalem?
**Artaxerxes**

Which city's rebuilt walls did Nehemiah inspect at night in disguise?
**Jerusalem**

What did the people do with Tobiah's provisions in Nehemiah's courtyard?
**Threw them out**

Which book ends with the words "So the city was rebuilt"?
**Nehemiah**

Which book records the genealogy of Israel's tribes and leaders?
**1 Chronicles**

Which king's reign in 1 Chronicles is noted for bringing the Ark to Jerusalem?
**David**

Which king's reign in 2 Chronicles details the division of the kingdom?
**Rehoboam**

Which book mentions Ezra reading the Law to the people beside the Water Gate?
**Nehemiah**

Which governor restored worship and removed foreign altars in Judah?
**Josiah**

Which king of Judah was noted for reforms and purging idolatry?
**Hezekiah**

Which book describes the glory of Solomon's reign and temple dedication?
**2 Chronicles**

Which book begins with the words "Adam, Seth, Enosh…"?
**1 Chronicles**

Which book ends with Cyrus's decree to rebuild the temple?
**Ezra**

Which book tells of Esther risking her life to save her people?
**Esther**

Which book recounts Israel's conquest of the Promised Land under Joshua?
**Joshua**

Which judge began delivering Israel after Joshua's death?
**Othniel**

Which book begins with "Now after the death of Joshua…"?
**Judges**

Who was Samuel's father?
**Elkanah**

Who was the high priest that trained Samuel?
**Eli**

At which town did Samuel judge Israel?
**Ramah**

Who was the first king of Israel?
**Saul**

Who anointed Saul as king?
**Samuel**

Which town did Saul reign from?
**Gibeah**

Who was secretly anointed king after Saul?
**David**

How many stones did David pick from the brook?
**Five**

Which city did David make his capital?
**Jerusalem**

Who confronted David about his sin with Bathsheba?
**Nathan**

Which of David's sons led a revolt against him?
**Absalom**

Who killed Absalom in the forest?
**Joab**

Which book records David's reign and his psalms?
**2 Samuel**

Who succeeded David as king?
**Solomon**

What gift did Solomon ask from God?
**Wisdom**

Which queen tested Solomon with hard questions?
**Queen of Sheba**

What did Solomon build in Jerusalem?
**The Temple**

What was the special room at the back of the Temple called?
**Holy of Holies**

Who was Solomon's father?
**David**

Which kingdom split into two after Solomon's death?
**Divided Kingdom**

What was the northern kingdom called?
**Israel**

What was the southern kingdom called?
**Judah**

Who was the first king of the northern kingdom?
**Jeroboam**

Which prophet challenged the prophets of Baal on Mount Carmel?
**Elijah**

Who succeeded Elijah as prophet?
**Elisha**

Which Syrian general was healed by Elisha?
**Naaman**

What did Elisha use to heal Naaman?
**Dip in the Jordan**

What miracle did Elisha perform with an axe head?
**Made it float**

Which king of Judah dug a tunnel to bring water into Jerusalem?
**Hezekiah**

Who was the worst king of Judah, allowing child sacrifice?
**Manasseh**

Who killed the giant Goliath?
**David**

Which king found the Book of the Law during temple repairs?
**Josiah**

Which governor returned first to Jerusalem and rebuilt the temple?
**Zerubbabel**

Which prophet encouraged the rebuilding of the temple under Zerubbabel?
**Haggai**

Which priest helped rebuild the altar and restart sacrifices?
**Joshua**

Who led the second group of exiles and read the Law to the people?
**Ezra**

What was Ezra's occupation?
**Scribe**

Which cupbearer to King Artaxerxes rebuilt Jerusalem's walls?
**Nehemiah**

How many days did Nehemiah work on the walls?
**Fifty-two**

Who opposed Nehemiah's rebuilding efforts?
**Sanballat**

Which woman became queen of Persia and saved her people?
**Esther**

Who was Esther's guardian?
**Mordecai**

Which Persian king married Esther?
**Ahasuerus**

Who plotted to destroy the Jews in Persia?
**Haman**

What feast commemorates the Jews' deliverance in Esther's time?
**Purim**

Which book follows 2 Chronicles in the Bible?
**Ezra**

Which book ends with Nehemiah ignoring his privileges?
**Nehemiah**

Which city did Joshua and the Israelites conquer first in Canaan?
**Jericho**

What did the Israelites march around to make the walls fall?
**The city walls**

Which judge sang a song of victory under a palm tree?
**Deborah**

Which Moabite woman's loyalty is celebrated in the book of Ruth?
**Ruth**

What did Naomi tell Ruth to do at the threshing floor?
**Uncover Boaz's feet**

Which book ends with a genealogy of David?
**Ruth**

Which prophet wrote about Zerubbabel's trembling hands?
**Haggai**

Which judge served Israel for 23 years after Abimelech's death?
**Tola**

Which judge served Israel for 22 years and had 30 sons?
**Jair**

Which judge had 30 sons and 30 grandsons who rode 70 donkeys?
**Abdon**

Which judge delivered Israel by killing the Moabite king Eglon?
**Ehud**

Which priest's sons, Hophni and Phinehas, died the same day the Ark was captured?
**Eli**

Who was the mother who dedicated her son Samuel to the Lord?
**Hannah**

Which prophet anointed Saul as the first king of Israel?
**Samuel**

What was used by Samuel to anoint King Saul?
**Oil**

Which Philistine idol fell before the Ark of the Covenant?
**Dagon**

What affliction struck the Philistines after capturing the Ark?
**Tumors**

In which cave did David hide when fleeing from King Saul?
**Cave of Adullam**

Which city did David capture to establish as the City of David?
**Jerusalem**

What instrument did David play to soothe King Saul?
**Harp**

Which prophet rebuked David over his sin with Bathsheba?
**Nathan**

Who was Bathsheba's husband that David sent to the front lines?
**Uriah**

Which king asked God for wisdom instead of wealth?
**Solomon**

What temple did Solomon build?
**The Temple in Jerusalem**

Which judge was known for tearing a lion apart with his bare hands?
**Samson**

Which judge defeated the Midianites with just 300 men?
**Gideon**

What sign did Gideon ask God to confirm His promise?
**Fleece of wool**

Which judge's story includes the tent peg through Sisera's head?
**Jael**

Which prophet was taken up to heaven in a whirlwind?
**Elijah**

Who succeeded Elijah and performed twice as many miracles?
**Elisha**

Which Syrian general was cleansed of leprosy after washing in the Jordan?
**Naaman**

Which king of Judah reopened and repaired the temple?
**Hezekiah**

Which king of Judah discovered the Book of the Law during temple repairs?
**Josiah**

Which empire conquered the northern kingdom Israel in 722 BC?
**Assyria**

Which empire destroyed Jerusalem and the temple in 586 BC?
**Babylon**

Which book begins with the genealogy from Adam through the tribes of Israel?
**1 Chronicles**

Which book recounts Israel's history from Solomon to the Babylonian exile?
**2 Chronicles**

Which prophet encouraged Zerubbabel to rebuild the temple post-exile?
**Haggai**

Which book begins with "In the first year of Cyrus king of Persia"?
**Ezra**

Who led the first group of Jewish exiles back to Jerusalem?
**Zerubbabel**

Who read the Law aloud to the people, causing them to weep?
**Ezra**

Which ancestor of David came from Moab?
**Ruth**

Which book records the building of Jerusalem's walls in fifty-two days?
**Nehemiah**

Who served as cupbearer to the Persian king before rebuilding Jerusalem's walls?
**Nehemiah**

Which official opposed Nehemiah's work alongside Sanballat?
**Tobiah**

Where did Nehemiah inspect Jerusalem's walls by night?
**Valley Gate**

Which book tells of Esther becoming queen of Persia?
**Esther**

Who was Esther's guardian who refused to bow to Haman?
**Mordecai**

Which festival celebrates the Jews' deliverance in Esther's time?
**Purim**

Which Persian king married Esther?
**Ahasuerus**

Which book immediately follows 2 Chronicles?
**Ezra**

What was the name of the priest who served under King Hezekiah?
**Azariah**

Which king's reign is noted for removing high places and idols?
**Hezekiah**

Which book ends with a genealogy of Saul's descendants?
**1 Chronicles**

Which book begins, "Now after the death of David..."?
**1 Kings**

Which king's foolish request led to Solomon's apostasy in old age?
**Solomon**

Which king of Israel died in battle at Mount Gilboa?
**Saul**

Which book records the life of Samuel, Saul, and David?
**1 Samuel**

Which book covers reigns of Judah's kings to the exile?
**2 Kings**

Which prophet announced Josiah's reforms after reading the Law?
**Huldah**

Which governor returned to Jerusalem to rebuild under Artaxerxes?
**Nehemiah**

Which book includes the story of Haman's ten sons being hanged?
**Esther**

Which book's events span from the conquest of Canaan to the judges?
**Joshua and Judges**

What was the name of Saul's son who sought reconciliation with David?
**Jonathan**

Who was Samuel's mother?
**Hannah**

Who was the high priest that trained Samuel?
**Eli**

Where did Samuel serve as judge over Israel?
**Ramah**

Which Philistine god fell before the Ark of the Covenant?
**Dagon**

Who carried the Ark of the Covenant to Jerusalem?
**David**

Who danced before the Ark as it entered Jerusalem?
**David**

Who was David's commander-in-chief?
**Joab**

Who anointed David king over Israel?
**Samuel**

Which city did David conquer and make his capital?
**Jerusalem**

Who refused to kill King Saul when he had the chance?
**David**

What was the name of David's mighty warrior who stayed loyal?
**Jonathan**

Who succeeded David as king of Israel?
**Solomon**

What request did Solomon make of God?
**Wisdom**

Who visited Solomon to see his great wisdom?
**Queen of Sheba**

What did Solomon build in Jerusalem?
**The Temple**

Which prophet called down fire from heaven at Mount Carmel?
**Elijah**

Who succeeded Elijah and asked for a double portion of his spirit?
**Elisha**

Which Syrian general was healed by Elisha after washing in the Jordan River?
**Naaman**

What miracle did Elisha perform with an iron axe head?
**Made it float**

Which king of Judah trusted God during the siege by Sennacherib?
**Hezekiah**

Which Assyrian king's army was wiped out by an angel?
**Sennacherib**

Who was the last king of Judah before the Babylonian exile?
**Zedekiah**

Which Persian king allowed the Jews to return and rebuild the temple?
**Cyrus**

Who led the first group of exiles back to Jerusalem?
**Zerubbabel**

Which prophet encouraged Zerubbabel to rebuild the temple?
**Haggai**

Who served as high priest when the second temple was dedicated?
**Joshua**

Who led the effort to rebuild Jerusalem's walls after the exile?
**Nehemiah**

How many days did it take Nehemiah to rebuild the walls?
**Fifty-two**

Who opposed Nehemiah's rebuilding efforts alongside Tobiah?
**Sanballat**

Which scribe read the Law to the people after the wall was rebuilt?
**Ezra**

What was Ezra's official role under King Artaxerxes?
**Scribe**

Which cupbearer became governor of Judah and rebuilt the wall?
**Nehemiah**

Who was queen of Persia before Esther?
**Vashti**

Who became queen of Persia and saved her people?
**Esther**

Who was Esther's guardian and cousin?
**Mordecai**

Which book continues David's reign and Solomon's succession?
**2 Samuel**

Which official in Persia plotted to destroy the Jews?
**Haman**

What fast did Esther request of her people before meeting the king?
**Three-day fast**

Who refused to bow to Haman, earning his wrath?
**Mordecai**

What lots did Haman cast to determine the day for the Jews' destruction?
**Pur**

Which festival commemorates deliverance from Haman's plot?
**Purim**

Who was hanged on the very gallows he had prepared?
**Haman**

Who took Haman's place as a royal official after his fall?
**Mordecai**

In which city did Esther live as queen?
**Susa**

Which book immediately follows 2 Chronicles?
**Ezra**

Which book follows Ezra in the Old Testament?
**Nehemiah**

Which book tells of a Jewish woman who became Persian queen?
**Esther**

Which book begins with Israel's conquest of Canaan under Joshua?
**Joshua**

Which book describes Israel's cycle of sin and deliverance?
**Judges**

# INTERMEDIATE

## Old Testament - The Poetic (or Wisdom Books)

Which book begins with "The blessed man is the one who does not walk in step with the wicked"?
**Psalms**

How many chapters are there in the book of Psalms?
**150**

Who is traditionally credited with writing most of the Psalms?
**David**

Which Psalm begins "The Lord is my shepherd, I shall not want"?
**Psalm 23**

Which Psalm opens with "Make a joyful noise to the Lord, all the earth"?
**Psalm 100**

Which Psalm is the longest chapter in the Bible?
**Psalm 119**

Which book contains a poem about a righteous man named Job?
**Job**

Which poetic book begins with the words "Vanity of vanities, says the Preacher, vanity of vanities; all is vanity"?
**Ecclesiastes**

Who is called the "Preacher" or "Teacher" in Ecclesiastes?
**Qoheleth**

Which book says "To everything there is a season"?
**Ecclesiastes**

Which book teaches "Iron sharpens iron, and one man sharpens another"?
**Proverbs**

Who is identified as the primary author of Proverbs?
**Solomon**

Which book says "Charm is deceitful, and beauty is vain"?
**Proverbs**

In which book is a virtuous woman praised as worth far more than rubies?
**Proverbs**

Which book is a collection of love poems between a bride and her groom?
**Song of Solomon**

In Song of Solomon, what is the beloved compared to when she sleeps among the lilies?
**A lily among thorns**

Which book describes the beloved's eyes as doves behind her veil?
**Song of Solomon**

Which Psalm begins "Why do the nations rage and the peoples plot in vain"?
**Psalm 2**

Which book includes the verse "By the rivers of Babylon we sat down and wept"?
**Psalms**

Which book features God speaking to a man from a whirlwind?
**Job**

Which book says "Though your beginning was small, yet your latter days will be very great"?
**Job**

Which book likens life "under the sun" to a vapor that appears and then vanishes?
**Ecclesiastes**

Which book begins "Blessed is the one who finds wisdom"?
**Proverbs**

Which book says "Stolen water is sweet, but bread eaten in secret is the better"?
**Proverbs**

Which Psalm begins "Bless the Lord, O my soul, and all that is within me, bless his holy name"?
**Psalm 103**

Which book ends with "Let everything that has breath praise the Lord"?
**Psalms**

Which Psalm begins "The Lord is my shepherd, I shall not want"?
**Psalm 23**

Which book teaches "Iron sharpens iron, and one man sharpens another"?
**Proverbs**

Which book begins with "Vanity of vanities, says the Preacher, vanity of vanities; all is vanity"?
**Ecclesiastes**

Which book begins "Let him kiss me with the kisses of his mouth"?
**Song of Solomon**

Who was tested by God with severe suffering in the book of Job?
**Job**

Which Psalm opens with "Make a joyful noise to the Lord, all the earth"?
**Psalm 100**

Which book says "Above all else, guard your heart, for everything you do flows from it"?
**Proverbs**

Which book says "A time to be born, and a time to die; a time to weep, and a time to laugh"?
**Ecclesiastes**

Which book says "Where has your beloved gone, most beautiful of women?"
**Song of Solomon**

Which book describes God's speech from the whirlwind?
**Job**

Which Psalm is the longest chapter in the Bible?
**Psalm 119**

Which book says "Better a patient person than a warrior, one with self-control than one who takes a city"?
**Proverbs**

Which book says "For everything there is a season, and a time for every purpose under heaven"?
**Ecclesiastes**

Which book says "My beloved is mine and I am his"?
**Song of Solomon**

Which book says "Though he slay me, yet will I trust him"?
**Job**

Which Psalm begins "Why do the nations rage and the peoples plot in vain"?
**Psalm 2**

Which book says "A gentle tongue is a tree of life"?
**Proverbs**

Which book says "Better is a handful of quietness than two hands full of toil and chasing after the wind"?
**Ecclesiastes**

Which book calls the beloved "a lily among thorns"?
**Song of Solomon**

How many children did Job lose in the tragedy?
**Ten**

Which Psalm asks "How lovely is your dwelling place, O Lord of hosts"?
**Psalm 84**

Which book says "Though a righteous person falls seven times, they rise again"?
**Proverbs**

Which book says "Remember now your Creator in the days of your youth"?
**Ecclesiastes**

Which book says "My beloved's hair is like a flock of goats descending Mount Gilead"?
**Song of Solomon**

Which book says "Man born of woman is of few days and full of trouble"?
**Job**

Which Psalm includes "By the rivers of Babylon we sat down and wept"?
**Psalm 137**

Which book says "A merry heart is good medicine"?
**Proverbs**

Which book says "The end of a matter is better than its beginning"?
**Ecclesiastes**

Which book asks "Where were you when I laid the earth's foundation?"
**Job**

Which Psalm begins "Create in me a clean heart, O God"?
**Psalm 51**

Which book says "It is better to live on a corner of the roof than share a house with a quarrelsome wife"?
**Proverbs**

Which book says "Two are better than one, because they have a good return for their labor"?
**Ecclesiastes**

Which book says "My beloved is like a gazelle or a young stag"?
**Song of Solomon**

Who argued with Job that he only worshipped God for blessings?
**Eliphaz**

Which Psalm begins "Be still, and know that I am God"?
**Psalm 46**

Which book says "Hatred stirs up conflict, but love covers all wrongs"?
**Proverbs**

Which book says "Better is a handful of quietness than two hands full of toil and chasing after the wind"?
**Ecclesiastes**

Which book asks "Who is this that looks forth like the dawn, fair as the moon"?
**Song of Solomon**

Who was the young man who spoke after Job's three friends?
**Elihu**

Which Psalm opens with "As the deer pants for streams of water"?
**Psalm 42**

Which book says "A wife of noble character is her husband's crown"?
**Proverbs**

Which book says "There is nothing new under the sun"?
**Ecclesiastes**

Which book says "You are altogether beautiful, my love; there is no flaw in you"?
**Song of Solomon**

What reward did God give Job after his trials?
**Restored his fortunes**

Which Psalm ends with "Let everything that has breath praise the Lord"?
**Psalm 150**

Which book says "Iron sharpens iron, and one man sharpens another"?
**Proverbs**

Which book says "Cast your bread upon the waters, for you will find it after many days"?
**Ecclesiastes**

Which book begins "My beloved speaks and says to me: Arise, my darling, my beautiful one, come with me"?
**Song of Solomon**

Which book asks "Why do the wicked live on, growing old and increasing in power"?
**Job**

Which Psalm begins "Blessed is the man who does not walk in the counsel of the wicked"?
**Psalm 1**

Which book says "My vineyard, my very own, is before me; you, O Solomon, may have the thousand, and those who tend its fruit two hundred"?
**Song of Solomon**

Which book advises "The heart of the righteous ponders how to answer, but the mouth of the wicked pours out evil"?
**Proverbs**

Which Psalm opens with "O Lord, our Lord, how majestic is your name in all the earth"?
**Psalm 8**

Which Psalm begins "The heavens declare the glory of God; the skies proclaim the work of his hands"?
**Psalm 19**

Which book warns "Whoever digs a pit will fall into it; if someone rolls a stone, it will roll back on them"?
**Proverbs**

Which book counsels "For every matter there is a time and judgment, though the misery of man weighs heavily on him"?
**Ecclesiastes**

Which Psalm starts "The earth is the Lord's and the fullness thereof"?
**Psalm 24**

Which Psalm opens "How long, O Lord? Will you forget me forever?"
**Psalm 13**

Which Psalm begins "Give thanks to the Lord, for he is good; his love endures forever"?
**Psalm 136**

Which Psalm opens "I love the Lord, for he heard my voice; he heard my cry for mercy"?
**Psalm 18**

Which Psalm opens with "LORD, how many are my foes!"
**Psalm 3**

Which book begins "I am black but comely, O daughters of Jerusalem"?
**Song of Solomon**

Which book says "The wicked flee when no one pursues, but the righteous are bold as a lion"?
**Proverbs**

Which book instructs "Plans fail for lack of counsel, but with many advisers they succeed"?
**Proverbs**

Which book says "Better is a handful of quietness than two hands full of toil and a striving after wind"?
**Ecclesiastes**

Which Psalm begins "My God, my God, why have you forsaken me?"
**Psalm 22**

Which Psalm opens "The Lord is my light and my salvation; whom shall I fear?"
**Psalm 27**

Which Psalm is the shortest in the Bible, with only two verses?
**Psalm 117**

Which Psalm begins "The Lord is my shepherd, I shall not want"?
**Psalm 23**

Which book says "But he knows the way that I take; when he has tested me, I will come forth as gold"?
**Job**

Which book says "Listen to this, Job; stop and consider God's wonders"?
**Job**

Which book says "You have captivated my heart, my sister, my bride"?
**Song of Solomon**

Which book begins "The words of King Lemuel—an inspired utterance his mother taught him"?
**Proverbs**

Which book says "Train up a child in the way he should go; even when he is old he will not depart from it"?
**Proverbs**

Which Psalm begins "I lift up my eyes to the hills—where does my help come from?"
**Psalm 121**

Which Psalm opens "Sing to the Lord a new song; sing to the Lord, all the earth"?
**Psalm 96**

Which Psalm opens "Out of the depths I cry to you, O Lord!"
**Psalm 130**

Which book says "The fear of the Lord is the beginning of wisdom, but fools despise wisdom and instruction"?
**Proverbs**

Which book opens "There was a man in the land of Uz whose name was Job"?
**Job**

Which book features God's response to a man out of a whirlwind?
**Job**

Which book opens "Vanity of vanities, says the Preacher, vanity of vanities; all is vanity"?
**Ecclesiastes**

Which book says "Wisdom is better than weapons of war, but one sinner destroys much good"?
**Ecclesiastes**

Which book says "Wisdom preserves those who have it"?
**Ecclesiastes**

Which book opens with "Let him kiss me with the kisses of his mouth. For your love is more delightful than wine"?
**Song of Solomon**

Which book ends with "Many waters cannot quench love; rivers cannot sweep it away"?
**Song of Solomon**

Which Psalm opens with "In the Lord I take refuge; how then can you say to me, 'Flee like a bird to your mountain'"?
**Psalm 11**

Which Psalm begins "To you, O Lord, I lift up my soul; in you I trust, O my God"?
**Psalm 25**

Which Psalm says "I waited patiently for the Lord; he turned to me and heard my cry"?
**Psalm 40**

Which Psalm begins "I will extol the Lord at all times; his praise will always be on my lips"?
**Psalm 34**

Which Psalm opens "The Mighty One, God the Lord, speaks and summons the earth"?
**Psalm 50**

Which Psalm begins "My soul finds rest in God alone; my salvation comes from him"?
**Psalm 62**

Which Psalm says "You, God, are my God, earnestly I seek you; I thirst for you"?
**Psalm 63**

Which Psalm opens "Let God arise, let his enemies be scattered; let those who hate him flee before him"?
**Psalm 68**

Which book begins "Then the Lord answered Job out of the whirlwind"?
**Job**

Which book says "Whatever your hand finds to do, do it with your might"?
**Ecclesiastes**

Which book says "A living dog is better than a dead lion"?
**Ecclesiastes**

Which book says "Your garment is fragrant with myrrh and aloes and cassia"?
**Song of Solomon**

Which Psalm begins "Give the king your justice, O God, and your righteousness to a king's son"?
**Psalm 72**

Which Psalm opens "Sing for joy to God our strength; shout aloud to the God of Jacob"?
**Psalm 81**

Which book instructs "Commit to the Lord whatever you do, and your plans will succeed"?
**Proverbs**

Which book says "Though he slay me, yet will I hope in him"?
**Job**

Which book says "My beloved is mine and I am his"?
**Song of Solomon**

Which Psalm begins "My eyes look to the Lord in hope for his word"; in context of watching for deliverance?
**Psalm 130**

Which Psalm opens "Blessed are those who have regard for the weak; the Lord delivers them in times of trouble"?
**Psalm 41**

Which book says "Trust in the Lord with all your heart and lean not on your own understanding"?
**Proverbs**

Which book says "In all your ways acknowledge him, and he will make your paths straight"?
**Proverbs**

Which book begins "There was a man in the land of Uz whose name was Job"?
**Job**

Which book says "'And to man he said, 'Behold, the fear of the Lord, that is wisdom, and to turn away from evil is understanding.'"'?
**Job**

Which book begins with "A person can do nothing better than to eat and drink and find satisfaction in their toil"?
**Ecclesiastes**

Which book says "He has made everything beautiful in its time"?
**Ecclesiastes**

Which book concludes "Fear God and keep his commandments, for this is the whole duty of man"?
**Ecclesiastes**

Which book begins "Let him kiss me with the kisses of his mouth"?
**Song of Solomon**

Which book says "I am a rose of Sharon, a lily of the valleys"?
**Song of Solomon**

Which Psalm says "You make known to me the path of life; in your presence is fullness of joy"?
**Psalm 16**

Which book says "Better is a handful of quietness than two hands full of toil and a striving after wind"?
**Ecclesiastes**

Which book says "A time to be born, and a time to die; a time to weep, and a time to laugh"?
**Ecclesiastes**

Which book warns "Like a gold ring in a pig's snout is a beautiful woman who shows no discretion"?
**Proverbs**

In which book does Job lament "Oh, that I knew where I might find him, that I might come even to his seat"?
**Job**

Which book says "If the iron is blunt, and one does not sharpen the edge, he must use more strength"?
**Ecclesiastes**

Which book contains the line "Catch for us the foxes, the little foxes that spoil the vineyards"?
**Song of Solomon**

Which book says "A gentle answer turns away wrath, but a harsh word stirs up anger"?
**Proverbs**

Which book says "I was once young, and now I am old, yet I have never seen the righteous forsaken or their children begging bread"?
**Job**

Which book states "Wisdom is better than weapons of war, but one sinner destroys much good"?
**Ecclesiastes**

Which book asks "Who is this that comes up from the wilderness, leaning upon her beloved"?
**Song of Solomon**

Which Psalm begins "The heavens declare the glory of God; the skies proclaim the work of his hands"?
**Psalm 19**

Which book says "Commit your work to the Lord, and your plans will succeed"?
**Proverbs**

Which book opens "Naked I came from my mother's womb, and naked shall I return. The Lord gave, and the Lord has taken away; blessed be the name of the Lord"?
**Job**

Which book says "Two are better than one, because they have a good reward for their labor"?
**Ecclesiastes**

Which book likens a beloved's hair to a flock of goats leaping down Mount Gilead?
**Song of Solomon**

Which Psalm opens "Make a joyful noise to the Lord, all the earth"?
**Psalm 100**

Which book warns "The way of fools seems right to them, but the wise listen to advice"?
**Proverbs**

Which book says "Though he slay me, yet will I hope in him; I will defend my ways to his face"?
**Job**

Which book begins "Vanity of vanities! All is vanity"?
**Ecclesiastes**

Which book warns "Pride goes before destruction, and a haughty spirit before a fall"?
**Proverbs**

Which book says "Whoever digs a pit will fall into it"?
**Proverbs**

Which book asks "Who is this who looks forth like the dawn, fair as the moon, bright as the sun"?
**Song of Solomon**

Which Psalm says "He will cover you with his feathers, and under his wings you will find refuge"?
**Psalm 91**

Which book warns "The crucible for silver, and the furnace for gold, but the Lord tests the heart"?
**Proverbs**

Which book asks "But where shall wisdom be found? And where is the place of understanding"?
**Job**

Which book says "Wisdom is better than weapons of war, but one sinner destroys much good"?
**Ecclesiastes**

Which book describes cheeks behind a veil as halves of a pomegranate?
**Song of Solomon**

Which Psalm begins "I lift up my eyes to the hills—where does my help come from"?
**Psalm 121**

Which book says "A word aptly spoken is like apples of gold in settings of silver"?
**Proverbs**

Which book says "My eyes have seen you; I, your redeemer, worship you"?
**Job** *(Job 31:23)*

Which book says "Whoever observes the wind will not sow, and whoever regards the clouds will not reap"?
**Ecclesiastes**

Which book begins "Let him kiss me with the kisses of his mouth; for your love is better than wine"?
**Song of Solomon**

Which Psalm says "You hemmed me in behind and before, and laid your hand upon me"?
**Psalm 139**

Which book says "A merry heart does good like medicine, but a crushed spirit dries up the bones"?
**Proverbs**

Which book declares "Gird up your loins like a man and I will question you"?
**Job**

Which book advises "Cast your bread upon the waters, for after many days you will find it again"?
**Ecclesiastes**

Which book asks "Tell me, you whom I love, where you pasture your flock, where you make it lie down at midday"?
**Song of Solomon**

Which Psalm begins "Be still, and know that I am God"?
**Psalm 46**

Which book says "A good name is to be chosen rather than great riches, and favor is better than silver or gold"?
**Proverbs**

Which book says "Surely I know that you can do all things, and that no purpose of yours can be thwarted"?
**Job**

Which book says "Better is the end of a thing than its beginning, and the patient in spirit is better than the proud in spirit"?
**Ecclesiastes**

Which book begins with "My son, hear the instruction of your father, and forsake not the law of your mother"?
**Proverbs**

Which book says "Lazy hands make for poverty, but diligent hands bring wealth"?
**Proverbs**

Which book says "His left arm is under my head, and his right arm embraces me"?
**Song of Solomon**

Which Psalm proclaims "The Lord is my light and my salvation; whom shall I fear"?
**Psalm 27**

Which book instructs "Whoever loves discipline loves knowledge, but he who hates reproof is stupid"?
**Proverbs**

Which book says "The earth is given into the hand of the wicked; he covers the faces of its judges—if it is not he"?
**Job**

Which book states "There is a time to keep silence, and a time to speak"?
**Ecclesiastes**

Which book says "My beloved is mine, and I am his"?
**Song of Solomon**

Which Psalm says "The Lord is gracious and merciful, slow to anger and abounding in steadfast love"?
**Psalm 145**

Which book warns "Do not say, 'I will repay evil'; wait for the Lord, and he will deliver you"?
**Proverbs**

Which book says "But he knows the way that I take; when he has tried me, I shall come out as gold"?
**Job**

Which book says "For a dream comes with much business, and a fool's voice with many words"?
**Ecclesiastes**

Which book warns "He who spares the rod hates his son, but he who loves him is careful to discipline him"?
**Proverbs**

Which book says "In the multitude of counselors there is safety"?
**Proverbs**

Which book says "Make haste, my beloved, and be like a gazelle or a young stag on the mountains of spices"?
**Song of Solomon**

Which Psalm says "I will praise you, O Lord, with my whole heart; I will tell of all your marvelous works"?
**Psalm 9**

Which Psalm begins "Sing to the Lord a new song, for he has done marvelous things"?
**Psalm 98**

Which Psalm opens "O come, let us worship and bow down; let us kneel before the Lord, our Maker"?
**Psalm 95**

Which Psalm says "You, God, are my God; earnestly I seek you; my soul thirsts for you"?
**Psalm 63**

Which Psalm begins "My times are in your hands; deliver me from the hand of my enemies"?
**Psalm 31**

Which Psalm says "Clap your hands, all peoples! Shout to God with loud songs of joy!"?
**Psalm 47**

Which book warns "Wine is a mocker, strong drink a brawler, and whoever is led astray by it is not wise"?
**Proverbs**

Which book says "There is a time to be silent and a time to speak"?
**Ecclesiastes**

Which book says "God will bring to judgment every deed, including every hidden thing, whether good or evil"?
**Ecclesiastes**

Which book says "The rich and the poor have this in common: the Lord is the Maker of them all"?
**Proverbs**

Which book says "Better to live in a desert land than with a quarrelsome and fretful woman"?
**Ecclesiastes**

Which book warns "All man's labor is for his mouth, yet his appetite is not satisfied"?
**Ecclesiastes**

Which book asks "Who is this who looks forth like the dawn, fair as the moon, bright as the sun"?
**Song of Solomon**

Which book says "Many waters cannot quench love, neither can floods drown it"?
**Song of Solomon**

Which book opens "There was a man in the land of Uz, whose name was Job"?
**Job**

Which book says "Though he slay me, I will hope in him; yet I will argue my ways to his face"?
**Job**

Which book says "Surely God is good to Israel, to those who are pure in heart"?
**Psalms**

Which Psalm begins "Praise the Lord! Praise God in his sanctuary; praise him in his mighty heavens"?
**Psalm 150**

Which Psalm says "He heals the brokenhearted and binds up their wounds"?
**Psalm 147**

Which Psalm opens "The earth is the Lord's and the fullness thereof, the world and those who dwell therein"?
**Psalm 24**

Which Psalm begins "The Lord is slow to anger and great in power; the Lord will not always chide"?
**Psalm 103**

Which Psalm says "Trust in the Lord and do good; dwell in the land and befriend faithfulness"?
**Psalm 37**

Which Psalm begins "Blessed is the man who trusts in the Lord, whose trust is the Lord"?
**Psalm 40**

Which Psalm opens "I will give thanks to the Lord with my whole heart; I will recount all of your wonderful deeds"?
**Psalm 9**

Which Psalm says "He determines the number of the stars; he gives to all of them their names"?
**Psalm 147**

Which book contains the analogy "As a dog returns to its vomit, so fools repeat their folly"?
**Proverbs**

Which book likens cheeks behind a veil to halves of a pomegranate?
**Song of Solomon**

Which book asks "How fair and how pleasant you are, O love, with your delights!"?
**Song of Solomon**

Which book asks "Who can find a virtuous woman?"
**Proverbs**

Which Psalm begins "Have mercy on me, O God, according to your steadfast love; according to your abundant mercy blot out my transgressions"?
**Psalm 51**

Which Psalm says "The Lord is righteous in all his ways and kind in all his works"?
**Psalm 145**

Which Psalm opens "The Lord sits enthroned over the flood; the Lord sits enthroned as king forever"?
**Psalm 29**

Which book says "Blessed is the one whom God reproves, so do not despise the discipline of the Almighty"?
**Job**

Which book says "Naked I came from my mother's womb, and naked shall I return. The Lord gave, and the Lord has taken away; blessed be the name of the Lord"?
**Job**

Which book warns "If you love money, you will never get enough; if you love wealth, you will never be satisfied with your income"?
**Ecclesiastes**

Which book says "It is better to go to the house of mourning than to go to the house of feasting"?
**Ecclesiastes**

Which Psalm begins "Your word is a lamp to my feet and a light to my path"?
**Psalm 119**

Which book says "A friend loves at all times, and a brother is born for a time of adversity"?
**Proverbs**

Which book says "As water reflects the face, so one's life reflects the heart"?
**Proverbs**

Which book describes the mighty creatures Behemoth and Leviathan?
**Job**

# INTERMEDIATE

## Old Testament - The Prophetic Book

Which prophet saw a vision of God seated on a throne high and exalted?
**Isaiah**

Which prophet warned about Judah's coming exile to Babylon?
**Jeremiah**

Which prophet saw dry bones come back to life in a valley?
**Ezekiel**

Which prophet interpreted King Nebuchadnezzar's dream of a statue?
**Daniel**

Which prophet married a woman named Gomer as a sign of Israel's unfaithfulness?
**Hosea**

Which prophet wrote about a locust plague as a warning of the coming Day of the Lord?
**Joel**

Which prophet was a shepherd called to prophesy against Israel's injustice?
**Amos**

Which short prophetic book proclaims doom against Edom?
**Obadiah**

Which prophet was swallowed by a big fish?
**Jonah**

Which prophet predicted the Messiah would be born in Bethlehem?
**Micah**

Which prophet wrote of Nineveh's destruction for its cruelty?
**Nahum**

Which prophet questioned God about the problem of evil and violence?
**Habakkuk**

Which prophet warned of the coming "Day of the Lord" and judgment?
**Zephaniah**

Which prophet encouraged the people to rebuild the temple after exile?
**Haggai**

Which prophet saw a vision of a man with a measuring line for Jerusalem?
**Zechariah**

Which prophet said "I have loved you," but Israel replied, "How have you loved us?"
**Malachi**

Which prophet described a child called Wonderful Counselor, Mighty God?
**Isaiah**

Which prophet was called from his mother's womb to be a prophet?
**Jeremiah**

Which prophet lay on his side 390 days as a sign to Israel's rebellion?
**Ezekiel**

Which prophet survived a night in a den of lions?
**Daniel**

Which prophet's marriage symbolized God's relationship with unfaithful Israel?
**Hosea**

Which prophet called for repentance with a call to "rend your hearts, not your garments"?
**Joel**

Which prophet declared "Let justice roll down like waters, and righteousness like an ever-flowing stream"?
**Amos**

Which prophetic book is just one chapter long?
**Obadiah**

Which prophet's message led a pagan city to repent and be spared?
**Jonah**

Which prophet condemned leaders for hating good and loving evil?
**Micah**

Which prophet described God as a jealous and avenging God?
**Nahum**

Which prophet received a vision written on tablets about the proud?
**Habakkuk**

Which prophet said "I will stretch out my hand against Judah and against all the inhabitants of Jerusalem"?
**Zephaniah**

Which prophet's message ended the exile-induced delay of the temple?
**Haggai**

Which prophet saw four horns representing the nations that scattered Judah?
**Zechariah**

Which prophet predicted the coming messenger to prepare the way for the Lord?
**Malachi**

Which prophet wrote of the suffering servant who was pierced for our transgressions?
**Isaiah**

Which prophet wrote laments following Jerusalem's destruction?
**Jeremiah**

Which prophet saw a vision of wheels within wheels full of eyes?
**Ezekiel**

Which prophet survived a fiery furnace with his friends?
**Daniel**

Which prophet's life included buying his unfaithful wife back for fifteen shekels?
**Hosea**

Which prophet spoke of the sun turning to darkness before the great and terrible day?
**Joel**

Which prophet was a fig farmer before being called to prophesy?
**Amos**

Which prophet depicted a future king called "Prince of Peace"?
**Isaiah**

Which prophet was called "the weeping prophet"?
**Jeremiah**

Which prophet saw a vision of the new temple in great detail?
**Ezekiel**

Which prophet had dreams of beasts representing world kingdoms?
**Daniel**

Which prophet declared "My people are destroyed for lack of knowledge"?
**Hosea**

Which prophet announced the day when worship would be pure and universal?
**Zechariah**

Which prophet asked, "How have you loved us?" after being told of God's love?
**Malachi**

Which prophet said "He has told you, O man, what is good; and what does the Lord require of you but to do justice"?
**Micah**

Which prophet described the lion's den of Nineveh's attackers coming from the hills?
**Nahum**

Which prophet foretold the "valley of dry bones" vision?
**Ezekiel**

Which prophet predicted a messenger like Elijah before the Lord's day?
**Malachi**

Which prophet's book begins "In the year that King Uzziah died"?
**Isaiah**

Which prophet's message involved charging locusts as cavalry?
**Joel**

Which prophet's book is addressed to Edom?
**Obadiah**

Which prophet wrote about the remnant returning to Zion?
**Micah**

Which prophet predicted that a root of Jesse would stand as a banner for the peoples?
**Isaiah**

Which prophet received the vision of the golden lampstand and olive trees?
**Zechariah**

Which prophet called Babylon a cup Jerusalem must drink?
**Jeremiah**

Which prophet's message includes "the just shall live by his faith"?
**Habakkuk**

Which prophet warned that the "day of the Lord is near"?
**Zephaniah**

Which prophet encouraged Zerubbabel by saying "Not by might, nor by power, but by my Spirit"?
**Zechariah**

Which prophet saw the Lord seated on a lofty throne and seraphim calling "Holy, holy, holy"?
**Isaiah**

Which prophet predicted a virgin would conceive and bear a son called Immanuel?
**Isaiah**

Which prophet married Gomer to symbolize Israel's unfaithfulness?
**Hosea**

Which prophet used a vision of a plumb line to pronounce judgment on Jerusalem's leaders?
**Amos**

Which prophetic book is only one chapter long and addresses Edom's fall?
**Obadiah**

Which prophet asked, "What does the Lord require of you but to do justice and love kindness"?
**Micah**

Which prophet was told to buy a field during Jerusalem's siege as a sign of future hope?
**Jeremiah**

Which prophet wrote, "Though the mountains be moved… my steadfast love shall not depart"?
**Isaiah**

Which prophet had a vision of living creatures with four faces and wheels full of eyes?
**Ezekiel**

Which prophet saw dry bones come to life in a valley vision?
**Ezekiel**

Which prophet survived a night in a den of lions?
**Daniel**

Which prophet interpreted the handwriting on Babylon's wall at Belshazzar's feast?
**Daniel**

Which prophet questioned God about injustice, asking "Why do the wicked live on"?
**Habakkuk**

Which prophet foretold the moon would turn to blood before the great Day of the Lord?
**Joel**

Which prophet thundered against Israel for trampling the poor "in the gate"?
**Amos**

Which prophet saw a vision of seven golden lampstands fed by two olive trees?
**Zechariah**

Which prophet proclaimed, "Return to me, and I will return to you, says the Lord of hosts"?
**Malachi**

Which prophet's name means "comforter"?
**Nahum**

Which prophet warned Nineveh of coming destruction?
**Nahum**

Which prophet foresaw a day when "justice shall roll down like waters"?
**Amos**

Which prophet wrote of the "suffering servant" who was pierced for our transgressions?
**Isaiah**

Which prophet told Israel, "I will give you shepherds after my own heart"?
**Jeremiah**

Which prophet's message included buying a linen belt and wearing it without washing or using it, then burying it?
**Jeremiah**

Which prophet's name means "the Lord is salvation"?
**Joel**

Which prophet wrote, "Behold, I will send you Elijah the prophet before the great and awesome day of the Lord"?
**Malachi**

Which prophet lamented, "Woe is me, for I am lost, for I am a man of unclean lips"?
**Isaiah**

Which prophet called for priests to "render true judgments, show kindness and mercy every man to his brother"?
**Zechariah**

Which prophet saw a vision of four chariots coming out between two mountains of bronze?
**Zechariah**

Which prophet wrote, "But who can endure the day of his coming?"
**Malachi**

Which prophet saw the glory of the Lord depart from the temple?
**Ezekiel**

Which prophet foresaw the destruction of Tyre and its merchants?
**Ezekiel**

Which prophet wrote, "Though your sins are like scarlet, they shall be white as snow"?
**Isaiah**

Which prophet was called from his mother's womb to stand as a prophet to the nations?
**Jeremiah**

Which prophet declared, "My soul shall be joyful in the Lord; it shall rejoice in his salvation"?
**Habakkuk**

Which prophet encouraged Zerubbabel with "Not by might, nor by power, but by my Spirit"?
**Zechariah**

Which prophet condemned Israel for worshiping at high places "beyond the Jordan"?
**Jeremiah**

Which prophet predicted the restoration of Israel under a new covenant written on hearts?
**Jeremiah**

Which prophet wrote, "On that day… I will assemble the lame and gather those who have been driven away"?
**Isaiah**

Which prophet wrote, "The nations shall see your righteousness, and all kings your glory"?
**Isaiah**

Which prophet saw a vision of a man with a measuring line to survey Jerusalem?
**Zechariah**

Which prophet wrote, "He has showed you, O man, what is good; and what does the Lord require of you"?
**Micah**

Which prophet used the symbol of a battered loincloth to prophesy Judah's unclean state?
**Jeremiah**

Which prophet announced, "In that day there shall be one Lord, and his name one"?
**Zechariah**

Which prophet wrote, "And I will pour out the Spirit on all flesh"?
**Joel**

Which prophet's name means "my God scorns"?
**Micah**

Which prophet wrote, "I will send the prophet Elijah before the great and awesome day"?
**Malachi**

Which prophet saw "five visions in one night" including four horns and craftsmen?
**Zechariah**

Which prophet wrote, "Behold, the day comes… when I will punish the world for its evil"?
**Zephaniah**

Which prophet wrote, "For the Lord God does nothing without revealing his secret to his servants the prophets"?
**Amos**

Which prophet's book begins "The vision of Obadiah"?
**Obadiah**

Which prophet writes, "Thus says the Lord… though they dig into hell, from there my hand shall take them"?
**Amos**

Which prophet cried, "The grass withers, the flower fades, but the word of our God will stand forever"?
**Isaiah**

Which prophet wrote, "Their heart is deceitful above all things, and desperately sick; who can understand it"?
**Jeremiah**

Which prophet wrote of a time when "the wolf shall dwell with the lamb"?
**Isaiah**

Which prophet wrote, "Behold, I am the Lord, and there is no other"?
**Isaiah**

Which prophet wrote, "And I will restore the fortunes of Judah and Israel who are left"?
**Jeremiah**

Which prophet's book opens with the words "The vision of Isaiah the son of Amoz"?
**Isaiah**

Which prophet predicted that justice would roll on like waters?
**Amos**

Which prophet was a shepherd called from Tekoa to prophesy against Israel's injustice?
**Amos**

Which prophet's book is the shortest in the Old Testament prophets?
**Obadiah**

Which prophet was swallowed by a large fish?
**Jonah**

Which prophet tried to flee God's call by sailing to Tarshish?
**Jonah**

Which prophet's children's names symbolized Israel's punishment and restoration?
**Hosea**

Which prophet used locust-plague imagery to warn of the Day of the Lord?
**Joel**

Which prophet promised, "I will pour out my Spirit on all flesh"?
**Joel**

Which prophet's name means "Who is like Yahweh"?
**Micah**

Which prophet's unfaithful wife was named Gomer?
**Hosea**

Which prophet's name means "comforter"?
**Nahum**

Which prophet predicted Nineveh's destruction for its cruelty?
**Nahum**

Which prophet questioned God about injustice, asking "Why do you make me see iniquity"?
**Habakkuk**

Which prophet concluded, "The righteous shall live by his faith"?
**Habakkuk**

Which prophet saw a vision of the day when the moon would turn to blood?
**Joel**

Which prophet's name means "the Lord has hidden"?
**Zephaniah**

Which prophet warned, "The great day of the Lord is near"?
**Zephaniah**

Which prophet encouraged Zerubbabel to "Be strong, all you people of the land"?
**Haggai**

Which prophet's preaching led the people of Nineveh to repent?
**Jonah**

Which prophet spoke to people who "lived in paneled houses while this house lay in ruins"?
**Haggai**

Which prophet's message included the promise, "I will fill this house with glory"?
**Haggai**

Which prophet saw eight night visions including four horns and craftsmen?
**Zechariah**

Which prophet saw a flying scroll and a woman in a basket among the visions?
**Zechariah**

Which prophet proclaimed, "Behold, I will send you Elijah before the great and awesome day of the Lord"?
**Malachi**

Which prophet ended his book with the words "Remember the law of my servant Moses"?
**Malachi**

Which prophet proclaimed, "Comfort, comfort my people; speak tenderly to Jerusalem"?
**Isaiah**

Which prophet foresaw a time when a shooting star called Wormwood would fall?
**Jeremiah**

Which prophet was told to eat a scroll and then prophesy to the exiles?
**Ezekiel**

Which prophet's friends Shadrach, Meshach, and Abednego accompanied him into a fiery furnace?
**Daniel**

Which prophet wrote, "He shall judge between many peoples and decide for strong nations afar off"?
**Micah**

Which prophet prayed, "O Lord, revive your work in the midst of the years"?
**Habakkuk**

Which prophet described a future time when "they shall beat their swords into plowshares"?
**Micah**

Which prophet's marriage symbolized Israel's spiritual adultery?
**Hosea**

Which prophet asked, "Will a man rob God? Yet you are robbing me"?
**Malachi**

Which book opens with "Hear this, you elders of the people; give ear, all inhabitants of the land"?
**Amos**

Which one-chapter book condemns Edom for violence against Jacob?
**Obadiah**

Which prophet predicted the Messiah's birth in Bethlehem?
**Micah**

Which prophet was sent to Nineveh but spent three days in the fish's belly first?
**Jonah**

Which prophet declared, "He has shown you, O man, what is good; and what does the Lord require of you but to do justice"?
**Micah**

Which prophet declared, "The Lord is slow to anger but great in power"?
**Nahum**

Which prophet questioned God, "How long, O Lord, must I call for help"?
**Habakkuk**

Which prophet warned, "I will utterly sweep away everything from the face of the earth"?
**Zephaniah**

Which prophet used the image of a lion's den to describe Nineveh's downfall?
**Nahum**

Which prophet urged the people to "consider your ways" in rebuilding the temple?
**Haggai**

Which prophet saw visions of horses patrolling the earth from between two mountains of bronze?
**Zechariah**

Which prophet wrote, "Behold, I send my messenger, and he will prepare the way before me"?
**Malachi**

Which prophet's vision included four living creatures each with four faces?
**Ezekiel**

Which prophet foretold that a remnant would return after seventy years?
**Jeremiah**

Which prophet wrote, "Though your sins are like scarlet, they shall be white as snow"?
**Isaiah**

Which prophet ate a scroll that tasted as sweet as honey in his mouth?
**Ezekiel**

Which prophet wrote a one-chapter oracle against Edom?
**Obadiah**

Which prophet's name means "Yahweh is salvation"?
**Isaiah**

Which prophet saw a vision of seraphim with six wings?
**Isaiah**

Which prophet interpreted dreams of four beasts rising from the sea?
**Daniel**

Which prophet's children were named Lo-Ruhamah and Lo-Ammi?
**Hosea**

Which prophet wrote, "Blow the trumpet in Zion; consecrate a fast; call a solemn assembly"?
**Joel**

Which prophet condemned Amos for prophesying in Bethel?
**Amos**

Which prophet declared Nineveh's downfall "like a calf unaccustomed to tread the stall"?
**Nahum**

Which prophet's prayer asked, "Why do you make me see wrongdoing and look at trouble"?
**Habakkuk**

Which prophet saw a vision of Joshua the high priest in filthy garments?
**Zechariah**

Which prophet wrote of a child called Wonderful Counselor, Mighty God?
**Isaiah**

Which prophet lamented, "Woe is me, for I am lost, for I am a man of unclean lips"?
**Isaiah**

Which prophet wrote, "My messenger will prepare the way before me"?
**Malachi**

Which prophet described the "suffering servant" who would bear our sins?
**Isaiah**

Which prophet's book opens, "The word of the Lord that came to Jeremiah the prophet"?
**Jeremiah**

Which prophet preached from the court by the temple, warning of imminent exile?
**Jeremiah**

Which prophet's vision included wheels "full of eyes all around"?
**Ezekiel**

Which prophet's friends were thrown to the lions for refusing to cease praying?
**Daniel**

Which prophet wrote, "It is for the wicked one to oppress, for the righteous to be oppressed"?
**Ezekiel**

Which prophet warned that "the day of the Lord is near, a day of wrath"?
**Joel**

Which prophet urged, "Seek good, and not evil, that you may live"?
**Amos**

Which prophet spoke against the "lewd women" of Jerusalem?
**Micah**

Which prophet planned a fast in the fifth month to avert disaster?
**Zephaniah**

Which prophet saw the seven lampstands and seven stars?
**Zechariah**

Which prophet declared, "I will refine them as silver is refined"?
**Malachi**

Which prophet proclaimed, "I will restore the fortunes of Judah and Israel"?
**Jeremiah**

Which prophet wrote, "They will beat their swords into plowshares"?
**Micah**

Which prophet wrote, "I will pour out my Spirit on all flesh"?
**Joel**

Which prophet was told to lie on his right side for 40 days as a sign?
**Ezekiel**

Which prophet condemned Israel's "high places" where they offered sacrifices?
**Hosea**

Which prophet proclaimed, "Comfort, comfort my people; speak tenderly to Jerusalem"?
**Isaiah**

Which prophet warned, "For behold, the day is coming, burning like an oven"?
**Malachi**

Which prophet's marriage to Gomer illustrated Israel's unfaithfulness?
**Hosea**

Which prophet saw a vision of dry bones coming back to life?
**Ezekiel**

Which prophet wrote, "Not by might, nor by power, but by my Spirit"?
**Zechariah**

Which prophet called for pure worship, saying "Render true judgments and show kindness"?
**Zechariah**

Which prophet thundered, "Let justice roll down like waters, and righteousness like an ever-flowing stream"?
**Amos**

Which prophet wrote, "Blow the trumpet in Zion; consecrate a fast; call a solemn assembly"?
**Joel**

Which prophet's book is one chapter long and condemns Edom?
**Obadiah**

Which prophet predicted that a remnant would seek refuge in the Lord's presence?
**Zephaniah**

Which prophet fled by ship but called Nineveh to repent?
**Jonah**

Which prophet declared, "He has shown you, O man, what is good; and what does the Lord require of you but to do justice"?
**Micah**

Which prophet predicted Nineveh's destruction for cruelty?
**Nahum**

Which prophet asked, "How long, O Lord, must I call for help, and you will not hear?"
**Habakkuk**

Which prophet warned, "The great day of the Lord is near; it is near and hastens quickly"?
**Zephaniah**

Which prophet encouraged Zerubbabel, "Not by might, nor by power, but by my Spirit"?
**Zechariah**

Which prophet rebuked the priests, "You have wearied the Lord with your words"?
**Malachi**

Which prophet wrote, "Sing and rejoice, O daughter of Zion; for behold, I come and I will dwell in your midst"?
**Zechariah**

Which prophet saw creatures with four faces and wheels within wheels?
**Ezekiel**

Which prophet interpreted King Nebuchadnezzar's dream of four beasts?
**Daniel**

Which prophet compared locusts to an invading army?
**Joel**

Which prophet condemned Israel for trampling the poor "in the gate"?
**Amos**

Which prophet wrote, "Though your sins are like scarlet, they shall be as white as snow"?
**Isaiah**

Which prophet's writing begins, "The burden of the word of the Lord to Judah"?
**Jeremiah**

Which prophet predicted a ruler called the Prince of Peace?
**Isaiah**

Which prophet's name means "the Lord is salvation"?
**Jonah**

Which prophet saw a vision of a scroll full of lamentations, mourning, and woe?
**Ezekiel**

Which prophet wrote, "In that day I will make a fountain for sin and uncleanness"?
**Zechariah**

Which prophet used a vision of a plumb line in Jerusalem?
**Amos**

Which prophet wrote, "I will pour out my Spirit on all flesh"?
**Joel**

Which prophet's children were named Lo-Ruhamah and Lo-Ammi?
**Hosea**

Which prophet wrote laments over Jerusalem's destruction?
**Lamentations**

Which prophet saw an eagle with great wings proclaiming judgment?
**Jeremiah**

Which prophet wrote "They will look on me, the one they have pierced"?
**Zechariah**

Which prophet preached under a terebinth tree east of Jerusalem?
**Hosea**

Which prophet predicted, "Behold, days are coming… when I will raise up to David a righteous Branch"?
**Jeremiah**

Which prophet saw a vision of the glory of the Lord depart the temple?
**Ezekiel**

Which prophet's name means "Yahweh is God"?
**Micah**

Which prophet wrote, "Behold, I will send you Elijah the prophet before the great and awesome day of the Lord"?
**Malachi**

Which prophet declared, "You have plowed wickedness; you have reaped injustice"?
**Hosea**

Which prophet asked, "Is not my word like fire, declares the Lord, and like a hammer that breaks the rock in pieces"?
**Jeremiah**

Which prophet predicted, "In the last days… I will pour out my Spirit on all flesh"?
**Joel**

Which prophet lamented, "My soul is weary of my life; I will leave my complaint upon myself"?
**Jeremiah**

Which prophet urged, "Seek good, and not evil, that you may live"?
**Amos**

Which prophet commanded, "Wash yourselves; make yourselves clean"?
**Zechariah**

Which prophet wrote, "I the Lord do not change; therefore you, O children of Jacob, are not consumed"?
**Malachi**

# INTERMEDIATE

# New Testament - The Gospels

Who told Mary she would bear a son named Jesus?
**Gabriel**

In which town did Mary and Joseph live when Jesus was born?
**Bethlehem**

Who visited Jesus first after His birth, tending flocks by night?
**Shepherds**

What did the angels sing to the shepherds?
**"Glory to God in the highest"**

Which foreign visitors brought gifts to the infant Jesus?
**Wise men**

What gift did the magi bring that symbolized Jesus' priesthood?
**Frankincense**

What gift did they bring that symbolized His death?
**Myrrh**

Where did Joseph and Mary flee to keep Jesus safe from Herod?
**Egypt**

In which town did Jesus grow up?
**Nazareth**

Who recognized Jesus as the Messiah when He was presented at the temple?
**Simeon**

Which prophetess also blessed Jesus at the temple and spoke of Him to all?
**Anna**

What special event did Jesus' parents go to every year, where He stayed to teach at age twelve?
**Passover**

What amazed the teachers when twelve-year-old Jesus sat among them?
**His understanding**

Who found Jesus in the temple talking with the teachers?
**His parents**

Which relative of Jesus prepared the way by preaching repentance?
**John the Baptist**

What unusual diet did John the Baptist have in the wilderness?
**Locusts and wild honey**

Where did John baptize people as they confessed their sins?
**Jordan River**

What did John say he baptized with, besides water?
**Holy Spirit**

What did John call Jesus when he saw the Spirit descend?
**The Lamb of God**

What title did Jesus use for Himself when He invited sinners to come?
**The door**

Which "I am" statement called Jesus the one who gives living water?
**Bread of life**

Which "I am" statement described Jesus as the light that cannot be hidden?
**Light of the world**

Which "I am" statement said, "I am the Good Shepherd"?
**Good Shepherd**

Which cousin of Jesus leaped in her mother's womb at His greeting?
**John**

Who was the Roman emperor when Jesus was born?
**Caesar Augustus**

Which king heard of Jesus' birth and sought to kill Him?
**Herod**

What sign did the shepherds see in the sky?
**A great light**

Which prophet had foretold a virgin would bear Immanuel?
**Isaiah**

What does "Immanuel" mean?
**God with us**

Which ancestor of Jesus was a Moabite woman?
**Ruth**

Which ancestor was an Ethiopian eunuch mentioned in tradition?
**Cush** (tradition)

Which prophet spoke of "a voice crying in the wilderness"?
**Isaiah**

Which river banks did John's ministry prepare?
**Jordan**

What did Jesus do immediately after His baptism?
**Went into the wilderness**

For how many days was Jesus tempted by the devil?
**Forty**

Who was the first disciple called by Jesus at the Sea of Galilee?
**Andrew**

Which fisherman left his nets to follow Jesus?
**Peter**

Who was Peter's brother, also called to follow Jesus?
**Andrew**

Which tax collector Jesus invited to be His follower?
**Matthew**

Who brought his brother to Jesus, saying, "We have found the Messiah"?
**Andrew**

Which former fisherman did Jesus nickname "the Rock"?
**Peter**

Which disciple was known as "the twin"?
**Thomas**

Which disciple doubted Jesus' resurrection until he could see and touch Him?
**Thomas**

Which two brothers were sons of Zebedee?
**James and John**

Which disciple wrote a Gospel emphasizing love?
**John**

Who among the twelve were Zealots before following Jesus?
**Simon**

Which disciple was a fisherman named Nathanael?
**Bartholomew**

Which disciple carried a knife in the Garden of Gethsemane?
**Peter**

Which disciple cut off the ear of the high priest's servant?
**Peter**

Which disciple confessed Jesus as "Son of the living God"?
**Peter**

Which disciple said, "Rabbi, where are you staying?"
**Philip**

Which disciple climbed a tree to see Jesus in Jericho?
**Zacchaeus**

Which man did Jesus call "Friend" at the Last Supper?
**Judas Iscariot**

Who sat next to Jesus at the Last Supper and leaned on Him?
**John**

Who asked Jesus, "Lord, show us the Father"?
**Philip**

Which disciple pled, "Lord, increase our faith"?
**The disciples**

Which two disciples walked to Emmaus after the resurrection?
**Cleopas and another**

Who did Jesus appear to first after His resurrection in John's Gospel?
**Mary Magdalene**

Who did Jesus send to declare His resurrection to the disciples?
**Mary Magdalene**

Which two disciples were fishermen who returned to their nets after the resurrection?
**Peter and six others**

Which disciple ran fastest to the empty tomb but waited outside?
**John**

Which disciple entered the empty tomb first?
**Peter**

What was Jesus doing when He called Peter and Andrew?
**Fishing**

Which mountain did the Transfiguration occur on?
**Mount Tabor**

Who appeared with Jesus at the Transfiguration?
**Moses and Elijah**

What did Jesus feed 5,000 people with?
**Five loaves and two fish**

How many baskets of leftovers were gathered in that miracle?
**Twelve**

What miracle later fed 4,000 with seven loaves?
**Feeding of the 4,000**

How many baskets remained after that feeding?
**Seven**

Which storm did Jesus calm?
**A storm on the Sea of Galilee**

What did Jesus walk on during that storm?
**Water**

Who began to sink when he tried walking on water?
**Peter**

Which paralytic did Jesus forgive and heal?
**The man lowered through the roof**

Which synagogue leader's daughter did Jesus raise from the dead?
**Jairus's daughter**

Who did Jesus heal by touching his ears and looking up to heaven?
**A deaf and mute man**

Which blind man did Jesus heal by spitting on his eyes?
**The man at Bethsaida**

What did Jesus cleanse with seven jars of water?
**A woman with a bleeding issue**

Which leper did Jesus heal who later thanked Him?
**One of ten lepers**

What did Jesus use to heal a centurion's servant?
**His word**

Which element did Jesus walk on to meet His disciples?
**Water**

Which parable says, "Everyone…" about new garments on old cloth?
**New cloth on an old garment**

Which parable warns against pouring new wine into old wineskins?
**New wine and old wineskins**

What did Jesus use as a mustard seed illustration?
**Mustard seed**

Which way did Jesus say to enter, wide or narrow?
**Narrow**

Which tree did Jesus call a fig tree?
**Useless fig tree**

What did Jesus do in the Temple courts to drive out merchants?
**Cleansed the Temple**

Which sermon begins with "Blessed are the poor in spirit"?
**Sermon on the Mount**

How many Beatitudes are there?
**Eight**

Which parable follows the Beatitudes in Matthew?
**Salt and light**

What did Jesus say you cannot hide under a bushel?
**A lamp**

Which parable features a house built on rock?
**Wise and foolish builders**

Which tree did Jesus say produces good fruit when healthy?
**A good tree**

Which parable warns that "out of the abundance of the heart…"?
**Good and bad trees**

In which parable does a king forgive a large debt?
**Unmerciful servant**

Which parable warns to forgive "seventy times seven"?
**Unmerciful servant**

Which parable shows a Pharisee and a tax collector praying?
**Pharisee and the tax collector**

Which parable features a lost sheep?
**Lost Sheep**

Which parable features a lost coin?
**Lost Coin**

Which parable features the prodigal son?
**Prodigal Son**

Which parable features the sower scattering seed?
**Sower**

Which parable features ten minas or pounds?
**Ten minas**

Which parable features wedding guests and a king's banquet?
**Wedding Feast**

Which parable features workers in a vineyard?
**Laborers in the Vineyard**

Which parable compares the kingdom of heaven to leaven in dough?
**Leaven**

Which command did Jesus call the greatest?
**Love God and neighbor**

What new commandment did He give at the Last Supper?
**Love one another**

Which prayer begins, "Our Father in heaven"?
**Lord's Prayer**

Which psalm did Jesus quote on the cross, "My God, my God…"?
**Psalm 22**

Which Old Testament prophet's words did Jesus read in Nazareth?
**Isaiah**

Which donkey-ridden entry did Jesus make into Jerusalem?
**Triumphal Entry**

What did people wave on Palm Sunday?
**Palm branches**

Where did Jesus say He would celebrate the Passover with His disciples?
**Upper Room**

What did Jesus do to the bread at the Last Supper?
**Gave thanks and broke it**

What did Jesus do to the cup at the Last Supper?
**Offered it**

Which garden did Jesus pray in before His arrest?
**Gethsemane**

Who betrayed Jesus with a kiss?
**Judas Iscariot**

Which disciple cut off an ear?
**Peter**

What trial did Jesus endure before Pilate?
**Roman trial**

Who washed his hands to show he found no guilt in Jesus?
**Pilate**

Which prisoner did Pilate release instead of Jesus?
**Barabbas**

What title was placed on Jesus' cross?
**King of the Jews**

Who offered Jesus vinegar to drink on the cross?
**A soldier**

What did Jesus say to the repentant thief?
**"Today you will be with me in paradise."**

At what hour did darkness come over the land?
**The sixth hour (noon)**

Who witnessed the tearing of the temple curtain?
**All the people**

Who witnessed Jesus' resurrection?
**The women who came to the tomb**

What did the angel say at the empty tomb?
**"He is not here; He has risen."**

Which two women found the tomb empty?
**Mary Magdalene and Joanna**

Which disciple saw the burial clothes lying there?
**Peter**

Which disciple saw the grave cloth wrapped separately?
**John**

Who met Jesus on the road to Emmaus?
**Two disciples**

Which disciple entered the upper room with Thomas?
**The other disciples**

Which miracle did Jesus perform for doubting Thomas?
**Showed His wounds**

Where did Jesus meet His disciples for breakfast after the resurrection?
**Sea of Galilee**

What did Jesus ask Peter three times?
**"Do you love me?"**

What commission did Jesus give before ascending?
**Make disciples of all nations**

What sign did Jesus say would follow believers?
**Speak in new tongues**

Where did Jesus ascend into heaven?
**Mount of Olives**

Which Old Testament promise did Jesus repeat before ascending?
**"I am with you always."**

Which apostle wrote the first Gospel?
**Matthew**

Which Gospel ends with an empty tomb and fear and great joy?
**Matthew**

Which Gospel emphasizes Jesus as Son of Man?
**Mark**

Which Gospel begins with a hymn of praise to God the Father, Son, and Holy Spirit?
**John**

Which Gospel records the "I am" statements seven times?
**John**

Which Gospel highlights Jesus' compassion for outcasts?
**Luke**

Which Gospel includes the story of Zacchaeus?
**Luke**

At which well did Jesus meet the Samaritan woman?
**Jacob's well**

What word did Jesus use to address the woman who had been bleeding?
**Daughter**

What Aramaic phrase did Jesus say to raise Jairus's daughter?
**Talitha koum**

Where did Jesus heal the royal official's son?
**Cana**

What part of Jesus' garment did people touch to be healed?
**Fringe**

Which Gospel opens with John the Baptist's ministry and contains no birth narrative?
**Mark**

Near which town did Jesus feed 5,000 people?
**Bethsaida**

At which pool did Jesus heal a man who had been an invalid for 38 years?
**Bethesda**

What was Zacchaeus's occupation?
**Tax collector**

What was the name of the high priest's servant whose ear Peter cut off?
**Malchus**

In which town did Jesus teach and heal with authority in Galilee?
**Capernaum**

In the Parable of the Rich Fool, what did the man build to store his surplus grain?
**Barns**

How many times did Peter deny knowing Jesus?
**Three**

Who did Jesus say we must become like to enter the kingdom of heaven?
**Children**

What did Jesus miraculously restore on the Sabbath in the synagogue?
**Hand**

Where did Jesus say we should store up our treasures?
**Heaven**

Which path did Jesus describe as leading to life: narrow or wide?
**Narrow**

Who tempted Jesus in the wilderness?
**Satan**

What did Jesus say He would make His first followers?
**Fishers of men**

In which Gospel does Jesus say, "Come to me, all who are weary and burdened"?
**Matthew**

What did Jesus offer to the Samaritan woman at the well?
**Living water**

Who is the mother of Jesus?
**Mary**

Who is the earthly father of Jesus?
**Joseph**

Where did Jesus eat the Last Supper with His disciples?
**Upper Room**

Which feast was being celebrated at the Last Supper?
**Passover**

What did Jesus say would happen when two or three gather in His name?
**He is there among them**

Which "I am" statement says Jesus is the resurrection and the life?
**Resurrection and the Life**

Which "I am" statement describes Jesus as the True Vine?
**True Vine**

Who rolled away the stone from Jesus' tomb?
**Angel**

Why did the women bring spices to the tomb?
**Anoint Jesus**

Who invited Jesus to dinner, where a sinful woman anointed His feet?
**Simon the Pharisee**

What did Jesus eat to prove He had flesh and bones after the resurrection?
**Fish**

In which Gospel does the story of the Good Samaritan appear?
**Luke**

In which Gospel is the Parable of the Talents found?
**Matthew**

Which part of Jesus' body was pierced on the cross?
**Side**

What did the soldiers cast for Jesus' clothing?
**Lots**

In which Gospel does Mary's Magnificat appear?
**Luke**

Who asked Jesus, "How can a man be born when he is old?" referring to being born again?
**Nicodemus**

Which parable teaches persistence in prayer with a judge and a widow?
**Unjust Judge**

Who spoke from heaven at Jesus' baptism, saying, "This is my Son"?
**God**

Where did Jesus tell Peter to feed His sheep after the resurrection?
**Galilee**

At what time did the women go to the tomb and find it empty?
**Early morning**

What did Jesus call the temple after driving out the money changers?
**Den of robbers**

Who declared, "I am the light of the world"?
**Jesus**

How many stone jars of water did Jesus turn into wine at Cana?
**Six**

How many people did Jesus feed with seven loaves and a few small fish?
**Four thousand**

Which two disciples asked Jesus to call fire down on a Samaritan village?
**James and John**

Who dreamed of an angel telling him to flee to Egypt with Mary and Jesus?
**Joseph**

What did Jesus do before appointing the twelve apostles?
**Prayed**

How many fish did the disciples catch in the net after Jesus' resurrection?
**153**

What did Jesus promise to those who believe in Him?
**Eternal life**

What did the people shout as Jesus rode into Jerusalem on Palm Sunday?
**Hosanna**

What did Jesus say His followers are to the world besides light?
**Salt**

What did people lay on the road before Jesus besides palm branches?
**Cloaks**

How did Jesus respond when asked whether taxes should be paid to Caesar?
**Render unto Caesar**

Who questioned Jesus about the greatest commandment?
**A lawyer**

What did Jesus say is the measure that will be used for you when you judge others?
**The same measure**

Where did Jesus weep over Jerusalem?
**Mount of Olives**

What did Jesus curse for not bearing fruit?
**A fig tree**

Who carried Jesus' cross on the way to Golgotha?
**Simon of Cyrene**

What did Jesus ask to be taken from Him in Gethsemane?
**The cup**

What title was placed above Jesus on the cross?
**King of the Jews**

Which thief crucified next to Jesus rebuked the other thief?
**The repentant thief**

What did Jesus promise to the repentant thief?
**Paradise**

Who rolled the stone away from Jesus' tomb?
**An angel**

What did the angel say to the women at the tomb?
**He is not here; He has risen**

Who was the first person to see the risen Jesus?
**Mary Magdalene**

What did Jesus say to Thomas to prove His resurrection?
**Put your finger here; see my hands**

Where did Jesus meet some disciples after His resurrection for breakfast?
**Sea of Galilee**

How many fish did the disciples catch in the net after breakfast?
**153**

What did Jesus ask Peter three times by the shore?
**Do you love me?**

What commission did Jesus give after His resurrection?
**Make disciples of all nations**

Which festival commemorates the gift of the Holy Spirit?
**Pentecost**

Which Gospel contains the Parable of the Good Samaritan?
**Luke**

In that parable, who helped the man beaten by robbers?
**Samaritan**

Which parable features a man inviting guests to a great banquet?
**Great Banquet**

Which Gospel includes the Parable of the Talents?
**Matthew**

In that parable, how many talents did the man bury?
**One**

Which Gospel records Jesus' conversation with Pilate?
**John**

What did Pilate say when he found no guilt in Jesus?
**I find no basis for a charge against him**

In which river did John baptize Jesus?
**Jordan River**

What happened to the heavens after Jesus was baptized?
**They opened**

Who appeared with Jesus at the Transfiguration?
**Moses and Elijah**

Where did the Transfiguration take place?
**A high mountain**

Which Gospel records the Parable of the Sheep and the Goats?
**Matthew**

In that parable, which group did the king place on his right?
**Sheep**

Which parable tells of a treasure hidden in a field?
**Hidden Treasure**

Which parable compares the kingdom of heaven to yeast?
**Leaven**

Who was healed when he touched the fringe of Jesus' garment?
**A bleeding woman**

Which miracle did Jesus perform on the Sabbath in a synagogue?
**Healed a man's withered hand**

Which Old Testament book did Jesus read in the synagogue?
**Isaiah**

What did He read there?
**"The Spirit of the Lord is upon me"**

Which disciple asked Jesus to increase his faith?
**The disciples**

Which woman did Jesus raise from the dead at Nain?
**A widow's son**

What did Jesus say about children entering the kingdom of God?
**Become like children**

Which parable warns against building on sand?
**Wise and Foolish Builders**

What did Jesus say would happen to the house built on rock?
**It stood firm**

Which gift did Jesus say was the greatest of all?
**Love**

How many days after Jesus' birth was He circumcised?
**Eight**

In which city did Mary and Joseph present Jesus at the temple?
**Jerusalem**

What did the voice from heaven say when Jesus was baptized?
**This is my beloved Son**

At what kind of event did Jesus perform His first miracle?
**A wedding**

What ran out at the wedding in Cana, prompting Jesus' first miracle?
**Wine**

Which "I am" statement describes Jesus as the way, the truth, and the life?
**The Way, the Truth, and the Life**

What rule did Jesus give for treating others?
**Do unto others as you would have them do to you**

Which flower did Jesus mention that grows beautifully without effort?
**Lilies**

What did Jesus say His followers are to the world besides light?
**Salt**

Which parable involves a man who hid his master's money in a field?
**Hidden Treasure**

Which parable compares the kingdom of heaven to yeast in dough?
**Leaven**

How many blind men did Jesus heal as He left Jericho?
**Two**

What did Jesus use to heal a blind man in John chapter 9?
**Mud**

Where did Jesus tell the blind man to wash to receive his sight?
**Siloam**

What natural event occurred when Jesus died?
**Earthquake**

What flowed out when the soldier pierced Jesus' side?
**Blood and water**

Who carried Jesus' cross part of the way to Golgotha?
**Simon of Cyrene**

How many pieces of silver did Judas receive for betraying Jesus?
**Thirty**

What title was placed above Jesus on the cross?
**King of the Jews**

Who rolled the stone away from Jesus' tomb?
**An angel**

What did the angel say at the empty tomb?
**He is not here; He has risen**

Who was the first person to see the risen Jesus?
**Mary Magdalene**

How many days did Jesus appear to His disciples after His resurrection?
**Forty**

Which disciple doubted Jesus' resurrection until he saw His wounds?
**Thomas**

What did Jesus ask Peter three times by the shore?
**Do you love me?**

What commission did Jesus give His disciples after His resurrection?
**Make disciples of all nations**

Which commandment did Jesus call the greatest?
**Love God and neighbor**

What did Jesus say the greatest gift is?
**Love**

Who did Jesus say He would make His followers?
**Fishers of men**

Which miracle saw Jesus feed a crowd with loaves and fish?
**Feeding of the 5,000**

How many baskets of leftovers were gathered after feeding the 5,000?
**Twelve**

Which Beatitude says "Blessed are the merciful"?
**The merciful**

Which Beatitude says "Blessed are the peacemakers"?
**The peacemakers**

Which Beatitude says "Blessed are those persecuted for righteousness"?
**Those persecuted**

Which Gospel begins with the genealogy of Jesus?
**Matthew**

Which Gospel opens with the story of Jesus' birth?
**Luke**

Which Gospel emphasizes Jesus as the Word from the beginning?
**John**

Which Gospel records Jesus washing His disciples' feet?
**John**

Which parable teaches about a manager praised for shrewdness despite dishonesty?
**Unjust Steward**

Which parable involves a fig tree that bore no fruit for three years?
**Barren Fig Tree**

Which parable describes tenants who mistreated the owner's servants and killed his son?
**Wicked Tenants**

How many followers did Jesus send out two by two to every town?
**Seventy-two**

Which parable describes a friend giving bread at midnight?
**Friend at Midnight**

Who was Jesus' earthly father?
**Joseph**

# INTERMEDIATE

## New Testament - The Acts of the Apostles

What feast were the believers celebrating when the Holy Spirit came upon them?
**Pentecost**

What sound filled the house when the Holy Spirit arrived?
**A mighty rushing wind**

What form appeared above each believer's head at Pentecost?
**Tongues of fire**

What did the new believers speak after receiving the Spirit?
**Tongues**

Who preached the first sermon recorded in Acts?
**Peter**

How many people were baptized on the day of Pentecost?
**Three thousand**

What did the early Christians do with their possessions?
**Sold them**

Who lied about the proceeds of a field sale and fell down dead?
**Ananias**

Who died shortly after Ananias for lying to the Holy Spirit?
**Sapphira**

Who sold a field and brought the money to the apostles?
**Barnabas**

Which deacon was the first Christian martyr?
**Stephen**

Who approved Stephen's execution by stoning?
**Saul**

In which region did Philip preach after leaving Jerusalem?
**Samaria**

Who baptized the Ethiopian eunuch?
**Philip**

What was the Ethiopian official's occupation?
**Eunuch**

Who was the first Gentile convert mentioned in Acts?
**Cornelius**

What was Cornelius's rank in the Roman army?
**Centurion**

In which town did Peter receive a vision of a sheet with animals?
**Joppa**

Who was raised from the dead by Peter in Joppa?
**Tabitha**

By what other name is Tabitha known?
**Dorcas**

Which prophet warned believers of a coming famine?
**Agabus**

Who carried the relief gift from Antioch to Jerusalem?
**Judas and Silas**

On which island did Paul and Barnabas begin their first missionary journey?
**Cyprus**

Which sorcerer opposed Paul in Paphos?
**Elymas**

Who was the Roman proconsul that believed Paul's message in Cyprus?
**Sergius Paulus**

In which city did Paul survive being stoned and left for dead?
**Lystra**

What miracle did Paul perform in Lystra?
**Healed a lame man**

What did the crowd call Paul after the miracle at Lystra?
**Hermes**

What did they call Barnabas at the same time?
**Zeus**

Which city became the center of Paul's work on his second missionary journey?
**Philippi**

How were Paul and Silas punished in Philippi?
**Whipped and imprisoned**

What miraculous event freed Paul and Silas from prison?
**Earthquake**

Who was the first European convert when the Philippian jailer believed?
**The jailer**

Where did Paul go to reason with people after leaving Philippi?
**Thessalonica**

What did Paul do on the Sabbath in Thessalonica?
**Reasoned in the synagogue**

Which Berean practice was commended by Luke?
**Examining the Scriptures daily**

Which city did Paul visit next, famous for its idol-filled Acropolis?
**Athens**

On which hill did Paul address the philosophers in Athens?
**Mars Hill**

What altar did Paul refer to that helped him introduce the gospel in Athens?
**The altar to the Unknown God**

Which merchant seller of purple cloth became the first convert in Philippi?
**Lydia**

Which city did Paul stay in for eighteen months teaching the Word?
**Corinth**

Before which proconsul did Paul defend his faith in Corinth?
**Gallio**

Which tentmaking couple hosted Paul in Corinth?
**Aquila and Priscilla**

What did Paul publicly burn in Ephesus to demonstrate his faith?
**Pagan books**

How long did Paul speak daily in the hall of Tyrannus at Ephesus?
**Two years**

Which young man fell from a window during Paul's long sermon?
**Eutychus**

On which island was Paul shipwrecked on his way to Rome?
**Malta**

Which sea did Paul cross when traveling to Rome?
**Mediterranean Sea**

How many days did Jesus remain on earth after His resurrection before ascending?
**Forty**

Who replaced Judas Iscariot as the twelfth apostle?
**Matthias**

Which prophet did Peter quote when explaining the outpouring of the Spirit at Pentecost?
**Joel**

What did the early believers do to help those in need?
**Sold possessions**

Which man tried to buy the power to give the Holy Spirit?
**Simon the Sorcerer**

Through which gate did Peter and John enter the temple to heal the lame man?
**Beautiful Gate**

Who was healed by Peter and John at the temple gate?
**A lame man**

What did the healed man do immediately after he was made whole?
**Walk and praise God**

Where did Peter preach after healing the lame man?
**Solomon's Portico**

Approximately how many people joined the believers after Peter's second sermon?
**About five thousand**

Which prophet predicted a severe famine in the Roman world?
**Agabus**

Who stood with Paul at the Jerusalem Council arguing that Gentiles need not follow the law?
**Barnabas**

Which port city did Paul sail from on his first missionary journey?
**Seleucia**

In which city's synagogue did Paul first preach to Gentiles on his first journey?
**Antioch of Pisidia**

In which city did Paul and Barnabas perform miracles but then flee because of a plot against them?
**Iconium**

Which companion joined Paul at Troas after he had a vision of a man from Macedonia?
**Luke**

Who was baptized along with his entire household after an earthquake in Philippi?
**The jailer**

What was Lydia's business before she was baptized in Philippi?
**Seller of purple**

In which city did Paul speak for three Sabbaths in a synagogue?
**Thessalonica**

Which group of people in Berea were praised for examining the Scriptures daily?
**Bereans**

Which two philosophical schools did Paul address in Athens?
**Epicureans and Stoics**

On which hill did Paul address the philosophers in Athens?
**Mars Hill**

Which proconsul refused to judge Paul's case in Corinth because he was Roman?
**Gallio**

Which goddess's temple sparked a riot against Paul in Ephesus?
**Artemis**

How many sons of Sceva attempted to cast out demons in Ephesus?
**Seven**

What did new believers in Ephesus publicly burn to renounce sorcery?
**Pagan books**

Which young man fell asleep during Paul's sermon in Troas and fell from a window?
**Eutychus**

What animal bit Paul on the island of Malta?
**Viper**

What did the locals on Malta think Paul was after the snake bite?
**A god**

Whose father was healed by Paul on Malta?
**Publius's**

How many missionary journeys did Paul complete before his arrest?
**Three**

Which prophet bound Paul's hands and feet with his own belt as a warning?
**Agabus**

Before which governor did Paul defend his faith in Caesarea?
**Felix**

Who succeeded Felix as governor and heard Paul's appeal?
**Festus**

Which king said, "Almost thou persuadest me to be a Christian"?
**King Agrippa**

Where was Paul taken for safe custody to avoid plots against his life?
**Caesarea**

Which Roman soldier escorted Paul on his journey to Rome?
**Acenturion** (a soldier)

Which sea did Paul cross as he traveled toward Rome?
**Mediterranean**

After arriving in Rome, where did Paul live under house arrest?
**His rented house**

How long did Paul preach in Rome under house arrest?
**Two years**

Which feast marked the beginning of the church in Acts 2?
**Pentecost**

Who was the first Christian martyr?
**Stephen**

Which apostle baptized the Ethiopian eunuch?
**Philip**

Who was the first Gentile convert in Acts?
**Cornelius**

What was Cornelius's occupation?
**Centurion**

Which prophet's vision convinced Peter to eat unclean animals?
**None**—it was a heavenly vision

Which book follows Acts of the Apostles in the New Testament?
**Romans**

Which couple hosted Paul and were fellow tentmakers?
**Aquila and Priscilla**

Who accompanied Paul on his second missionary journey and stayed loyal through trials?
**Silas**

In which city did Paul baptize Lydia?
**Philippi**

Which Jewish council did Paul address first in Jerusalem?
**Sanhedrin**

Who warned the Sanhedrin to leave the apostles alone because if God's work couldn't be stopped?
**Gamaliel**

What gift did Peter and John lay hands on Samaritans to receive?
**Holy Spirit**

Which book records the spread of the gospel through the early church?
**Acts**

Where were the believers when they prayed for Peter's release?
**Mary's house**

How did the disciples choose Matthias as an apostle?
**Casting lots**

Which Jewish sect opposed the apostles and arrested them?
**Sadducees**

Who advised the Sanhedrin to wait and see if the apostles' work was from God?
**Gamaliel**

What action did the apostles take after being miraculously freed from prison?
**Returned to the temple courts**

Which practice characterized the early church's fellowship?
**Breaking bread together**

Who in Acts sold a field and laid the money at the apostles' feet?
**Barnabas**

Which language did the apostles pray in when filled with the Spirit?
**Various languages**

What was the name of the gate where Peter healed the crippled beggar?
**Beautiful Gate**

Who proclaimed that Jesus was "the stone the builders rejected"?
**Peter**

Which Old Testament prophet did Peter quote at Pentecost?
**Joel**

Which church sent Paul and Barnabas on their first missionary journey?
**Antioch**

On Cyprus, which port did Paul and Barnabas arrive at first?
**Salamis**

Which island did Paul and Silas shake off a viper to into the fire?
**Malta**

What did Paul and Silas do in their cell at midnight?
**Sang hymns**

Which silversmith led a riot against Paul in Ephesus?
**Demetrius**

Which harbor did Paul's ship shelter at before the Cretan storm?
**Fair Havens**

Who fell asleep during Paul's sermon and fell out a window?
**Eutychus**

What did Paul say would happen to everyone aboard if they stayed on the ship?
**They would perish**

Which man did Paul leave sick in Miletus when he went to Jerusalem?
**Trophimus**

Who addressed the crowd after Peter healed the lame man?
**John**

What title did the angel use when calling Peter to escape prison?
**"Quick, get up!"**

Which prophet's belt did Agabus use to bind his own hands and feet?
**None—he used his own belt**

What did the Roman centurion's household do after believing in Philippi?
**Was baptized**

Which city's believers were commended for examining the Scriptures daily?
**Berea**

At what location did Paul sermonize in Athens?
**Areopagus (Mars Hill)**

Which altar did Paul cite to introduce the "Unknown God" sermon?
**Altar to an Unknown God**

Who was the synagogue ruler in Corinth that believed Paul's message?
**Crispus**

Which couple in Corinth worked alongside Paul making tents?
**Aquila and Priscilla**

In Ephesus, where did Paul teach for two years?
**School of Tyrannus**

Which young man was restored to life by Paul in Troas?
**Eutychus**

Which governor heard Paul's defense and almost believed?
**Agrippa**

Which sea did Paul cross when traveling toward Rome?
**Mediterranean Sea**

Who escorted Paul from Caesarea to Rome?
**A centurion**

What status did Paul live under while in Rome?
**House arrest**

Which road did Paul walk when he met Jesus?
**Road to Damascus**

What happened to the temple curtain at Jesus' death in Acts?
**Tore in two** (reported in the Gospels, referenced in Acts tradition)

Which prophet did Peter refer to as foretelling Judas's betrayal?
**Psalm 109**

Who sent Paul letters of recommendation to the elders in Jerusalem?
**Antioch church**

Which non-Christian woman did Paul baptize in Philippi?
**Lydia**

Which ruler ordered James, brother of John, to be executed?
**Herod Agrippa I**

Which festival was celebrated when Peter had his vision of the sheet?
**Unspecified, while praying**

Which pagan temple did Paul's Ephesians riot center around?
**Artemis**

What did Paul do when he saw seven sons of Sceva attempting exorcism?
**Overpowered them**

Which prisoner did Paul defend before Felix?
**Himself**

What warning did Paul give the sailors before they threw cargo overboard?
**To keep the ship from breaking up**

What city did Paul write letters to that begins the letters section of the New Testament?
**Rome**

Which follower did Paul leave in Ephesus to support the church there?
**None specifically—he continued on**

Which jail did Paul and Silas occupy when the earthquake struck?
**Philippi jail**

What did the jailer do upon seeing the prison doors open?
**Drew his sword**

Which living creature did Peter see in his vision on the rooftop?
**Unclean animals**

Which practice did new believers keep after Pentecost?
**Fellowship**

Which first-century trade did Luke, author of Acts, practice?
**Physician**

Which region did Paul pass through on his way to Antioch at the end of Acts?
**Phoenicia**

Which companion of Paul is mentioned as a notable writer of Acts?
**Luke**

Which key city did Paul visit to plant a church before returning to Troas?
**Philippi**

What was the final destination of Paul's travels recorded in Acts?
**Rome**

Which Jewish council did Paul face in Jerusalem?
**Sanhedrin**

What vision did Stephen report seeing before he died?
**Jesus standing at the right hand of God**

How did Philip leave the Ethiopian eunuch after baptism?
**The Spirit of the Lord caught him away**

Where did Philip preach after leaving the Ethiopian eunuch?
**Caesarea**

What was Saul doing when he encountered the risen Jesus?
**Traveling to Damascus**

What blinded Saul on the road to Damascus?
**A bright light**

Who restored Saul's sight?
**Ananias**

What did Saul preach in the synagogues after his conversion?
**That Jesus is the Son of God**

How did Saul escape Damascus?
**Lowered in a basket through an opening in the wall**

Which disciple met Saul after his conversion?
**Ananias**

What was Saul's Roman name?
**Paul**

In which city did Cornelius live?
**Caesarea**

Who baptized Cornelius and his household?
**Peter**

What type of person was Cornelius described as?
**God-fearing**

Which young disciple joined Paul and Silas in Derbe and Lystra?
**Timothy**

Who circumcised Timothy before going on mission?
**Paul**

Which Roman commander rescued Paul from a mob in Jerusalem?
**Claudius Lysias**

Which governor succeeded Felix?
**Festus**

Which king visited Festus to hear Paul's defense?
**Agrippa**

What did Festus ask Paul to do instead of go to Jerusalem for trial?
**Appeal to Caesar**

What did the Philippian jailer ask Paul and Silas after the earthquake?
**"What must I do to be saved?"**

Where did Paul visit after Malta on his way to Rome?
**Syracuse**

How long did Paul stay on Malta before setting sail?
**Three months**

What was the name of the centurion who escorted Paul to Rome?
**Julius**

What did the ship's crew decide to do to lighten the load before being shipwrecked?
**Throw cargo overboard**

Who swam to shore after the shipwreck on Malta?
**Everyone aboard**

What did the islanders do for Paul and the survivors after they landed on Malta?
**Showed unusual kindness**

How long did Paul stay in Ephesus on his third missionary journey?
**Three years**

Who accompanied Paul on his second missionary journey and was imprisoned in Philippi?
**Silas**

Who wrote the Acts of the Apostles?
**Luke**

In which city did Paul have a vision of a Macedonian man?
**Troas**

Who went with Paul to Macedonia after his vision?
**Luke**

Which city did Paul sail from to enter Macedonia?
**Troas**

Who brought Eutychus back to life after he fell during Paul's sermon?
**Paul**

Which couple hosted Paul and were fellow tentmakers?
**Aquila and Priscilla**

Which Jewish council did Paul face in Jerusalem?
**Sanhedrin**

Which city's disciples warned Paul not to go to Jerusalem?
**Tyre**

Which companion did Paul leave behind sick at Miletus?
**Trophimus**

Where did the believers sell their property and share with anyone in need?
**Jerusalem**

Who laid hands on the new Samaritan believers to receive the Holy Spirit?
**Peter and John**

In which city did disciples first get called Christians?
**Antioch**

What items did people bring from Paul to the sick in Ephesus for healing?
**Handkerchiefs and aprons**

How many deacons were chosen to serve the early church?
**Seven**

What happened to the believers when Stephen was martyred?
**They scattered**

Who welcomed the scattered believers and preached in Samaria?
**Philip**

What did the apostles do for the Samaritan converts to receive the Holy Spirit?
**Prayed**

What did the jailer do before Paul stopped him after the earthquake?
**Drew his sword**

What did Paul say to the jailer so he would not kill himself?
**"We are all here"**

What profession was Luke?
**Physician**

Who prayed earnestly for Peter while he was in prison?
**The church**

What was their reaction when they realized Peter was at the door?
**They were overjoyed**

Who wrote the Acts of the Apostles?
**Luke**

How many days after His resurrection did Jesus ascend into heaven?
**Forty**

Where were the believers gathered when they prayed for Peter's release from prison?
**Mary's house**

Who was chosen by casting lots to replace Judas Iscariot?
**Matthias**

How many men were appointed as deacons to serve the early church?
**Seven**

Who became the first Christian martyr when he was stoned?
**Stephen**

Which future apostle approved Stephen's execution?
**Saul**

After fleeing Jerusalem, in which city did Philip continue preaching?
**Samaria**

Who baptized the Ethiopian eunuch on the road from Jerusalem to Gaza?
**Philip**

In which port city did Peter have a vision of a sheet with unclean animals?
**Joppa**

Who was the first Gentile convert in the early church?
**Cornelius**

What was Cornelius's rank in the Roman army?
**Centurion**

Who raised Tabitha (also called Dorcas) from the dead in Joppa?
**Peter**

Which prophet bound his own hands and feet with Paul's belt as a warning?
**Agabus**

Which church commissioned Paul and Barnabas for their first missionary journey?
**Antioch**

On which Mediterranean island did Paul and Barnabas first preach the gospel?
**Cyprus**

Who opposed Paul on Cyprus, trying to turn Sergius Paulus from the faith?
**Elymas**

What title did Paul's opponents give Barnabas and Paul after a healing in Lystra?
**Hermes and Zeus**

In which city were Paul and Silas imprisoned and then freed by an earthquake?
**Philippi**

What question did the Philippian jailer ask Paul to learn how to be saved?
**"What must I do to be saved?"**

Which city's believers were commended for examining the Scriptures daily?
**Berea**

On which hill in Athens did Paul address the philosophers?
**Mars Hill**

What altar did Paul point to when telling the Athenians about the "Unknown God"?
**Altar to an Unknown God**

Which tentmaking couple hosted Paul in Corinth?
**Aquila and Priscilla**

Who was the synagogue ruler in Corinth that believed Paul's message?
**Crispus**

How long did Paul remain in Corinth during his second journey?
**Eighteen months**

Which temple riot erupted over the worship of Artemis?
**Ephesus**

What did new believers publicly burn to renounce sorcery in Ephesus?
**Magic books**

How much were the burned magic books worth?
**Fifty thousand pieces of silver**

Which young man fell from a third-story window and was restored by Paul?
**Eutychus**

On which island was Paul shipwrecked on his way to Rome?
**Malta**

What bit Paul on Malta but did him no harm?
**Viper**

Who showed Paul and the shipwreck survivors "unusual kindness" on Malta?
**The islanders**

Whose father did Paul heal of fever and dysentery on Malta?
**Publius's**

Which centurion escorted Paul safely to Rome?
**Julius**

Under what condition did Paul live in Rome while awaiting trial?
**House arrest**

What did Paul do daily while under house arrest in his rented house?
**Preached the gospel**

Which council met in Jerusalem to decide Gentile believers' requirements?
**Jerusalem Council**

Who delivered the Council's decision letter to the Gentile church in Antioch?
**Judas Barsabbas and Silas**

What was the Council's ruling about circumcision for Gentiles?
**Not required**

What gift did Barnabas give after selling a field?
**Relief for the poor**

Which coastal city's disciples warned Paul not to go to Jerusalem?
**Tyre**

Which prophet and evangelist hosted Paul in Caesarea?
**Philip**

What book of the New Testament follows Acts?
**Romans**

Which psalm did Peter quote to describe Judas's betrayal?
**Psalm 109**

Which practice brought the early believers together daily in fellowship?
**Breaking bread**

How many days was Saul blind after encountering Jesus on the road to Damascus?
**Three**

Which city did Paul preach in immediately after escaping Damascus in a basket?
**Damascus**

Who baptized Paul following his conversion?
**Ananias**

In what regions were believers scattered after Stephen's martyrdom?
**Judea and Samaria**

Who did Peter heal in Lydda who had been bedridden for eight years?
**Aeneas**

What was Tabitha (Dorcas) known for making for the poor?
**Clothing**

At whose house was Peter staying when he received the vision of unclean animals?
**Simon the Tanner**

What did Peter see coming down from heaven in his vision?
**A sheet**

Which Roman centurion's household was baptized by Peter?
**Cornelius's**

Who raised Tabitha (also called Dorcas) from the dead in Joppa?
**Peter**

What warning did the prophet Agabus give about a coming famine?
**There would be a famine**

Who escorted the relief gift from Antioch to Jerusalem?
**Judas Barsabbas and Silas**

# INTERMEDIATE

## New Testament - The Epistles (Letters)

Who is traditionally credited with writing the Epistle to the Romans?
**Paul**

How many epistles in the New Testament are traditionally attributed to Paul?
**13**

Which epistle tells believers to put on the full armor of God?
**Ephesians**

Which letter of Paul is the first written to the church in Corinth?
**1 Corinthians**

How many chapters are in Philemon?
**1**

Who wrote the Epistle to the Galatians?
**Paul**

Which epistle emphasizes Christ as the great high priest?
**Hebrews**

How many chapters does 1 Corinthians have?
**16**

To whom did Paul address the epistle that stresses sound doctrine and good works on Crete?
**Titus**

How many chapters does 1 Peter have?
**5**

Which epistle states "Faith without works is dead"?
**James**

How many chapters are in 2 Thessalonians?
**3**

Who is the recipient praised for showing hospitality to traveling teachers in 3 John?
**Gaius**

Which epistle welcomes its readers as "partners in the gospel"?
**Philippians**

How many chapters are in the Epistle to the Romans?
**16**

Which epistle warns believers to contend for the faith once for all delivered to the saints?
**Jude**

Which epistle is written to the church in Colossae?
**Colossians**

How many chapters are there in Colossians?
**4**

Which epistle tells believers to rejoice always, pray without ceasing, and give thanks in all circumstances?
**1 Thessalonians**

How many chapters are there in Galatians?
**6**

Who is the primary recipient of Paul's first pastoral epistle?
**Timothy**

Which epistle contains the "love chapter" often read at weddings?
**1 Corinthians**

How many chapters are in 1 John?
**5**

Which epistle contains the teaching on the fruit of the Spirit?
**Galatians**

To which city is 1 Thessalonians addressed?
**Thessalonica**

Which epistle is the shortest letter written by Paul?
**Philemon**

How many chapters does 2 Timothy have?
**4**

Which epistle calls its recipients "saints in Ephesus"?
**Ephesians**

How many chapters does 2 Corinthians have?
**13**

Which epistle opens with the greeting "Simon Peter, a servant and apostle of Jesus Christ"?
**2 Peter**

How many chapters does the Epistle to Titus contain?
**3**

Which epistle warns against false teachers and predicts scoffers in the last days?
**2 Peter**

Which epistle begins with "James, a servant of God and of the Lord Jesus Christ"?
**James**

How many chapters are in the Epistle of James?
**5**

Which epistle is addressed to Jewish Christians and uses Old Testament examples to explain Christ's supremacy?
**Hebrews**

To whom is 2 John addressed?
**The elect lady and her children**

How many chapters are in 2 John?
**1**

Which epistle opens with the greeting "Jude, a servant of Jesus Christ and brother of James"?
**Jude**

How many chapters are in 3 John?
**1**

Which epistle encourages believers to submit to their masters and do their work heartily?
**Colossians**

Which epistle asks a slave master to welcome back his runaway slave?
**Philemon**

How many chapters does the Epistle to the Hebrews have?
**13**

Which epistle instructs wives to submit to their husbands?
**Ephesians**

Which epistle teaches that hope does not disappoint us?
**Romans**

Which epistle opens with "To all the saints in Christ Jesus who are at Philippi"?
**Philippians**

How many epistles in the New Testament are pastoral epistles?
**3**

Which epistle's author identifies himself as "the brother of James"?
**Jude**

Which epistle urges believers to "consider how to spur one another on toward love and good deeds"?
**Hebrews**

Which epistle tells believers to walk in a manner worthy of the calling to which they were called?
**Ephesians**

How many chapters are in the Epistle to the Philippians?
**4**

Which epistle states "If God is for us, who can be against us"?
**Romans**

How many chapters are in the First Epistle to the Thessalonians?
**5**

Which epistle contains Paul's teaching on spiritual gifts, including prophecy and speaking in tongues?
**1 Corinthians**

How many chapters are in the First Epistle to Timothy?
**6**

Which epistle begins with the greeting "To all the saints in Christ Jesus who are at Philippi"?
**Philippians**

Which epistle instructs believers not to be unequally yoked with unbelievers?
**2 Corinthians**

Which epistle defines faith as "the assurance of things hoped for, the conviction of things not seen"?
**Hebrews**

Who wrote the First Epistle of Peter?
**Peter**

Which epistle famously states "God is love"?
**1 John**

Which epistle instructs children to obey their parents in everything?
**Colossians**

Which epistle includes the "hall of faith" chapter, recounting heroes like Abel and Abraham?
**Hebrews**

Which epistle begins with the greeting "To the saints in Ephesus, the faithful in Christ Jesus"?
**Ephesians**

Which epistle contains the verse "I can do all things through him who strengthens me"?
**Philippians**

Which epistle warns against quarreling about words, saying it leads to ruin rather than success?
**2 Timothy**

Which epistle opens with "To the churches of Galatia"?
**Galatians**

Which epistle contains the famous "love is patient, love is kind" passage?
**1 Corinthians**

Which epistle tells believers to cast all their anxieties on God because he cares for them?
**1 Peter**

Which epistle ends with the admonition "Stand firm, let nothing move you, always give yourselves fully to the work of the Lord"?
**1 Corinthians**

Which epistle instructs men to pray with holy hands without anger or quarreling?
**1 Timothy**

Which epistle instructs believers to address one another in psalms, hymns, and spiritual songs, singing and making melody in your heart to the Lord?
**Ephesians**

How many chapters are in the Epistle of Jude?
**1**

Which epistle contains the statement "The love of money is a root of all kinds of evil"?
**1 Timothy**

Which epistle contains the verse "The wages of sin is death, but the free gift of God is eternal life in Christ Jesus our Lord"?
**Romans**

Which epistle instructs believers to bear one another's burdens?
**Galatians**

Which epistle describes pure and undefiled religion as caring for orphans and widows in their distress?
**James**

Which epistle tells believers to submit to governing authorities because they are instituted by God?
**Romans**

Which epistle warns that not many should become teachers because they will be judged more strictly?
**James**

Which epistle instructs that whatever you do, work heartily, as for the Lord rather than for men?
**Colossians**

Which epistle describes Phoebe as a servant of the church at Cenchreae?
**Romans**

Which epistle declares that Christ is the head of the body, the church?
**Colossians**

Which epistle instructs readers to remember Jesus Christ, risen from the dead and descended from David?
**2 Timothy**

Which epistle instructs elders to shepherd the flock willingly, not for shameful gain?
**1 Peter**

Which epistle encourages believers to speak the truth in love, growing in every way more like Christ?
**Ephesians**

Which epistle begins with "Paul, an apostle of Christ Jesus by the will of God, for the obedience of faith among all nations"?
**Romans**

In which epistle is the church described as built on the foundation of the apostles and prophets, Christ Jesus himself being the cornerstone?
**Ephesians**

Which epistle begins "To Timothy, my beloved child"?
**2 Timothy**

Which epistle instructs that each person should remain in the situation they were in when God called them?
**1 Corinthians**

Which epistle states that Christ redeemed us from the curse of the law by becoming a curse for us?
**Galatians**

Which epistle tells believers to live in harmony with one another, being sympathetic, loving as brothers, and compassionate and humble?
**1 Peter**

Which epistle says that the prayer of a righteous person is powerful and effective?
**James**

Which epistle sets out qualifications for overseers and deacons in the church?
**1 Timothy**

Which epistle contains the phrase "For to me to live is Christ, and to die is gain"?
**Philippians**

Which epistle identifies its author simply as "the elder" and warns about deceivers who do not acknowledge Jesus Christ coming in the flesh?
**2 John**

Which epistle advises believers to test everything and hold fast to what is good?
**1 Thessalonians**

Which epistle instructs servants to submit to their masters with all respect, even to the unjust?
**1 Peter**

Which epistle instructs believers to rejoice in hope, be patient in tribulation, and be constant in prayer?
**Romans**

Which epistle tells that the mystery hidden for ages is now revealed, that Gentiles are fellow heirs?
**Ephesians**

Which epistle says "Do not be conformed to this world, but be transformed by the renewing of your mind"?
**Romans**

Which epistle begins with the greeting "Paul, called by the will of God to be an apostle of Christ Jesus and our brother Sosthenes"?
**1 Corinthians**

Which epistle states "For you were called to freedom, brothers. Only do not use your freedom as an opportunity for the flesh"?
**Galatians**

Which epistle instructs children to obey their parents in the Lord, for this is right?
**Ephesians**

Which epistle says "Do nothing from rivalry or conceit, but in humility count others more significant than yourselves"?
**Philippians**

Which epistle urges believers to set their minds on things above, not on things that are on earth?
**Colossians**

Which epistle says "For this is the will of God, your sanctification: that you abstain from sexual immorality"?
**1 Thessalonians**

Which epistle states "Godliness with contentment is great gain"?
**1 Timothy**

Which epistle instructs that rebellious people must be silenced because they are teaching things they ought not for the sake of dishonest gain?
**Titus**

Which epistle asks Philemon to welcome back Onesimus as a beloved brother?
**Philemon**

Which epistle says "Since we are surrounded by so great a cloud of witnesses"?
**Hebrews**

Which epistle says "Count it all joy when you meet trials of various kinds"?
**James**

Which epistle contains the warning "Certain individuals have secretly slipped in among you, who are ungodly"?
**Jude**

Which epistle calls Christians "aliens and strangers" in the world?
**1 Peter**

Which epistle says "If we confess our sins, he is faithful and just to forgive us our sins"?
**1 John**

Which epistle says "Above all, keep loving one another earnestly, since love covers a multitude of sins"?
**1 Peter**

Which epistle states "For the kingdom of God is not a matter of talk but of power"?
**1 Corinthians**

Which epistle says "Greet Andronicus and Junia, my fellow Jews who are outstanding among the apostles"?
**Romans**

Which epistle instructs believers to regard masters as worthy of all honor, so that the name of God is not reviled?
**1 Timothy**

Which epistle says "Clothe yourselves with humility toward one another, for God opposes the proud but gives grace to the humble"?
**1 Peter**

How many books are classified as the general epistles in the New Testament?
**8**

Which epistle uses the metaphor of the body with many members to illustrate unity in Christ?
**1 Corinthians**

Which epistle contains the teaching "All Scripture is breathed out by God and profitable for teaching, for reproof, for correction, and for training in righteousness"?
**2 Timothy**

Which epistle ends with the doxology "To Him who is able to do far more abundantly than all that we ask or think, according to the power at work within us"?
**Ephesians**

Which epistle states "Love is the fulfilling of the law"?
**Galatians**

Which epistle teaches that believers are justified by faith apart from the works of the law?
**Romans**

Which epistle says "I thank my God in all my remembrance of you"?
**Philippians**

Which epistle warns believers not to quench the Spirit?
**1 Thessalonians**

Which epistle contains the plea "Open your hearts to us"?
**2 Corinthians**

Which epistle tells believers to stand firm in the liberty by which Christ has made them free, and not be entangled again with a yoke of bondage?
**Galatians**

Which epistle declares "We live by faith, not by sight"?
**2 Corinthians**

Which epistle instructs believers to hold fast what is good and abstain from every form of evil?
**1 Thessalonians**

Which epistle says "Submit yourselves for the Lord's sake to every human institution"?
**1 Peter**

Which epistle contains the statement "Great indeed, we confess, is the mystery of our religion"?
**1 Timothy**

How many chapters are in the Second Epistle of Peter?
**3**

Which epistle instructs that older men should be sober-minded, dignified, self-controlled, sound in faith, in love, and in steadfastness?
**Titus**

Which epistle says "Pray for kings and all who are in high positions, that we may lead a peaceful and quiet life"?
**1 Timothy**

Which epistle says "If anyone teaches a different doctrine, let him be accursed"?
**Galatians**

Which epistle contains the verse "The love of money is a root of all kinds of evil"?
**1 Timothy**

Which epistle says "If anyone does not love the Lord, let him be accursed"?
**1 Corinthians**

Which epistle opens with the greeting "To Philemon our beloved and fellow worker"?
**Philemon**

Which epistle refers to its readers as "elect exiles" scattered throughout Pontus, Galatia, Cappadocia, Asia, and Bithynia?
**1 Peter**

Which epistle warns believers to beware of deceivers who do not acknowledge Jesus Christ coming in the flesh?
**2 John**

Which epistle instructs believers to use their spiritual gifts to serve one another as good stewards of God's varied grace?
**1 Peter**

Which epistle says "Preach the word; be ready in season and out of season; reprove, rebuke, and exhort, with complete patience and teaching"?
**2 Timothy**

Which epistle says "The Lord is faithful. He will establish you and guard you against the evil one"?
**2 Thessalonians**

Which epistle warns that "lawless men and impostors will go on from bad to worse, deceiving and being deceived"?
**2 Timothy**

Which epistle urges believers to "test everything; hold fast what is good; abstain from every form of evil"?
**1 Thessalonians**

Which epistle instructs believers to set their minds on things above, not on earthly things?
**Colossians**

Which epistle opens with the words "Paul and Timothy, servants of Christ Jesus, to all God's holy people" in Thessalonica?
**1 Thessalonians**

Which epistle tells readers to let the word of Christ dwell in them richly?
**Colossians**

Which epistle says "Let the elders who rule well be considered worthy of double honor, especially those who labor in preaching and teaching"?
**1 Timothy**

Which epistle says "Christ is the head of the body, the church"?
**Colossians**

Which epistle states "The wages of sin is death, but the free gift of God is eternal life in Christ Jesus our Lord"?
**Romans**

Which epistle describes the fruit of the Spirit?
**Galatians**

Which epistle warns believers to beware of false teachers with destructive heresies?
**2 Peter**

Which epistle instructs believers to "be kind to one another, tenderhearted, forgiving one another, as God in Christ forgave you"?
**Ephesians**

Which epistle says "Do nothing from selfish ambition or conceit, but in humility count others more significant than yourselves"?
**Philippians**

Which epistle says "Since Christ also suffered for you, leave your sins and follow his example"?
**1 Peter**

Which epistle instructs believers to rejoice in hope, be patient in tribulation, and be constant in prayer?
**Romans**

Which epistle says "Let each of you look not only to his own interests, but also to the interests of others"?
**Philippians**

Which epistle warns that the day of the Lord will come like a thief in the night?
**1 Thessalonians**

Which epistle says "Let the word of Christ dwell in you richly, teaching and admonishing one another in all wisdom"?
**Colossians**

Which epistle says "Be on your guard; stand firm in the faith; be courageous; be strong"?
**1 Corinthians**

Which epistle instructs, "Bear with one another and, if one has a complaint against another, forgiving each other; as the Lord has forgiven you, so you also must forgive"?
**Colossians**

Which epistle states "The gospel is the power of God for salvation to everyone who believes"?
**Romans**

Which epistle begins with "To the church of God that is in Corinth, to those sanctified in Christ Jesus, called to be saints"?
**1 Corinthians**

Which epistle says "Rejoice with those who rejoice, weep with those who weep"?
**Romans**

Which epistle says "And now these three remain: faith, hope and love. But the greatest of these is love"?
**1 Corinthians**

Which epistle teaches "Walk by the Spirit, and you will not gratify the desires of the flesh"?
**Galatians**

Which epistle uses the metaphor: "There is one body and one Spirit, just as you were called to one hope"?
**Ephesians**

Which epistle instructs believers to do everything without grumbling or arguing?
**Philippians**

Which epistle opens with "Paul, an apostle of Christ Jesus by the will of God, and Timothy our brother"?
**Colossians**

Which epistle asks believers to pray that the word of the Lord may speed ahead and be honored?
**2 Thessalonians**

Which epistle instructs believers to flee youthful passions and pursue righteousness, faith, love, and peace?
**2 Timothy**

Which epistle says "For the grace of God has appeared, bringing salvation for all people"?
**Titus**

Which epistle opens with "Paul, a prisoner for Christ Jesus, and Timothy our brother, to Philemon our dear friend"?
**Philemon**

Which epistle calls Jesus the author and perfecter of our faith?
**Hebrews**

Which epistle warns that if anyone thinks he is religious but does not bridle his tongue, his religion is worthless?
**James**

Which epistle ends with the exhortation to grow in the grace and knowledge of our Lord and Savior Jesus Christ?
**2 Peter**

Which epistle says "Whoever says 'I know him' but does not keep his commandments is a liar"?
**1 John**

Which epistle exhorts believers to keep themselves in the love of God, waiting for the mercy of our Lord Jesus Christ?
**Jude**

Which epistle says "Beloved, let us love one another, for love is from God"?
**1 John**

Which epistle says "Nothing will be able to separate us from the love of God in Christ Jesus"?
**Romans**

Which epistle says "Now to each one the manifestation of the Spirit is given for the common good"?
**1 Corinthians**

Which epistle compares believers to living stones being built into a spiritual house?
**1 Peter**

Which epistle warns not to neglect to show hospitality, for thereby some have entertained angels?
**Hebrews**

Which epistle begins with "Paul, an apostle—not from men nor through man, but through Jesus Christ and God the Father"?
**Galatians**

Which epistle cites the command "Do not muzzle an ox while it treads out the grain"?
**1 Corinthians**

Which epistle says "Whoever sows to please their flesh will reap destruction, but whoever sows to please the Spirit will reap eternal life"?
**Galatians**

Which epistle instructs believers to put away falsehood and speak the truth to their neighbor?
**Ephesians**

Which epistle instructs believers to admonish the idle, encourage the fainthearted, help the weak, and be patient with everyone?
**1 Thessalonians**

Which epistle says "Be filled with the Spirit"?
**Ephesians**

Which epistle says "The Lord is near"?
**Philippians**

Which epistle instructs believers to clothe themselves with compassion, kindness, humility, meekness, and patience?
**Colossians**

Which epistle instructs believers to put on the Lord Jesus Christ and make no provision for the flesh?
**Romans**

Which epistle says "Above all these put on love, which binds everything together in perfect harmony"?
**Colossians**

Which epistle instructs believers to set their hope fully on the grace that will be brought to them at the revelation of Jesus Christ?
**1 Peter**

Which epistle says "So, whether you eat or drink, or whatever you do, do all to the glory of God"?
**1 Corinthians**

Which epistle says "Have this mind among yourselves, which is yours in Christ Jesus"?
**Philippians**

Which epistle says "Be strong in the Lord and in the strength of his might"?
**Ephesians**

Which epistle says "Let all that you do be done in love"?
**1 Corinthians**

Which epistle says "Therefore encourage one another and build one another up, just as you are doing"?
**1 Thessalonians**

Which epistle says "Without faith it is impossible to please him"?
**Hebrews**

Which epistle says "But be doers of the word, and not hearers only, deceiving yourselves"?
**James**

Which epistle says "Little children, keep yourselves from idols"?
**1 John**

Which epistle says "To him who is able to keep you from stumbling and to present you blameless before the presence of his glory"?
**2 Peter**

Which epistle says "Remind them to be submissive to rulers and authorities, to be obedient, to be ready for every good work"?
**Titus**

Which epistle sends greetings to the household of Stephanas?
**1 Corinthians**

Which epistle states that Christ made the two groups one and broke down the dividing wall of hostility?
**Ephesians**

Which epistle sends greetings to Priscilla and Aquila, fellow workers in Christ Jesus?
**Romans**

Which epistle warns that wrongdoers, the sexually immoral, idolaters, and thieves will not inherit the kingdom of God?
**1 Corinthians**

Which epistle describes hope as an anchor for the soul, firm and secure?
**Hebrews**

Which epistle says no one can say "Jesus is Lord" except by the Holy Spirit?
**1 Corinthians**

Which epistle says through Christ we have redemption, the forgiveness of sins?
**Colossians**

Which epistle teaches that we are seated with Christ in the heavenly places?
**Ephesians**

Which epistle says "Let no one seek his own good but the good of his neighbor"?
**1 Corinthians**

Which epistle calls Epaphroditus a brother, coworker, and fellow soldier?
**Philippians**

Which epistle includes the doxology "But thanks be to God, who gives us the victory through our Lord Jesus Christ"?
**1 Corinthians**

Which epistle states that Christ is our peace, making Jews and Gentiles one?
**Ephesians**

Which epistle uses the analogy of a race, saying "Do you not know that in a race all the runners run, but only one gets the prize"?
**1 Corinthians**

Which epistle says you have died, and your life is hidden with Christ in God?
**Colossians**

Which epistle instructs women to adorn themselves with modest apparel, with shamefacedness and sobriety?
**1 Timothy**

Which epistle teaches that all people are to be convinced of sound doctrine and to rebuke those who contradict it?
**Titus**

Which epistle describes Jesus as the mediator of a better covenant?
**Hebrews**

Which epistle begins "To those who are called, beloved in God the Father and kept for Jesus Christ"?
**Jude**

Which epistle warns that false teachers will secretly bring in destructive heresies?
**2 Peter**

Which epistle says to hold fast what is good and abstain from every form of evil?
**1 Thessalonians**

Which epistle declares that the gospel is the power of God for salvation to everyone who believes?
**Romans**

Which epistle warns believers not to quench the Spirit?
**1 Thessalonians**

Which epistle instructs servants to submit to their masters with all respect, even to those who are unjust?
**1 Peter**

Which epistle says "May the Lord make you increase and abound in love for one another and for all"?
**1 Thessalonians**

Which epistle instructs Timothy to flee youthful passions and pursue righteousness, faith, love, and peace?
**2 Timothy**

Which epistle instructs that rebellious people must be silenced because they are teaching things they ought not, for dishonest gain?
**Titus**

Which epistle calls Onesimus a former slave and now a beloved brother?
**Philemon**

Which epistle warns that "the Lord is near"?
**Philippians**

Which epistle instructs believers to be clothed with compassion, kindness, humility, meekness, and patience?
**Colossians**

Which epistle warns that not many should become teachers because they will be judged more strictly?
**James**

# INTERMEDIATE

# New Testament - The Book of Revelation

Who wrote the book of Revelation?
**John**

On which island was John when he received the visions in Revelation?
**Patmos**

To how many churches did Revelation send messages?
**Seven**

Which church was told to repent and return to their first love?
**Ephesus**

Which church was commended for holding fast in the face of persecution?
**Smyrna**

Which church had a reputation for being alive but was actually dead?
**Sardis**

Which church was praised for keeping Jesus' word and not denying His name?
**Philadelphia**

Which church was rebuked for being neither hot nor cold?
**Laodicea**

How many seals are on the scroll in Revelation?
**Seven**

Who is the rider on the white horse in Revelation 6 often interpreted as?
**Conqueror**

What color was the horse that represented war?
**Red**

What symbol did the rider on the black horse carry?
**Scales**

What did the pale horse represent?
**Death**

Who followed Death on the pale horse?
**Hades**

What was the name of the star that fell from heaven in the third trumpet judgment?
**Wormwood**

How many trumpets sounded after the seventh seal was opened?
**Seven**

How many angels poured out the bowl judgments?
**Seven**

What number is called "the number of the beast"?
**666**

What did the beast require people to have on their right hand or forehead?
**Mark of the beast**

How many servants of God were sealed on their foreheads?
**144,000**

Which animal in Revelation is referred to as a Lamb?
**Lamb**

How many living creatures surround the throne of God?
**Four**

How many elders sit on thrones around God's throne?
**Twenty-four**

What did the elders cast before the throne?
**Crowns**

What flows from the throne of God, bright as crystal?
**River of life**

What kind of tree grows on each side of the river of life?
**Tree of life**

How many gates does the New Jerusalem have?
**Twelve**

How many foundations does the city wall of the New Jerusalem have?
**Twelve**

What is the street of the New Jerusalem made of?
**Pure gold**

What will there be no more of in the new creation?
**Death**

Who is called the Alpha and the Omega in Revelation?
**Jesus**

What does "Alpha and Omega" mean?
**Beginning and End**

Who gave John the message to write?
**An angel**

What did the seven stars in Jesus' right hand represent?
**Angels of the Seven Churches**

What did the seven lampstands represent?
**Seven Churches**

What sound did John hear like many waters?
**Voice**

What was the voice likened to?
**A trumpet**

What did John fall down to do when he saw the vision of Jesus?
**Worship Him**

What was written on the gates of the New Jerusalem?
**Names of the twelve tribes**

What was written on the foundation stones of the city wall?
**Names of the twelve apostles**

What will shine in the New Jerusalem so there's no need for sun or moon?
**God's glory**

Where are the beast and false prophet thrown at the end?
**Lake of fire**

What promise is given to those who conquer in Revelation?
**Right to eat from the tree of life**

What will be excluded from the new city?
**Anything impure**

Who is described as the bright morning star?
**Jesus**

What does John say at the very end of Revelation?
**Amen**

Who said, "Behold, I am coming soon"?
**Jesus**

What instruction does John give readers about the words of this book?
**Write and keep them**

Which "I am" title does Jesus use in Revelation 1 to emphasize His eternality?
**Holy, the True**

What did John see in the midst of the lampstands?
**One like a son of man**

What was His hair described as?
**White as wool**

What were His eyes described as?
**Flame of fire**

What came out of His mouth as he spoke?
**Sharp two-edged sword**

What shining thing did John see on Jesus' feet?
**Bronze like glowing metal**

What did Jesus hold in His right hand when John saw Him?
**Seven stars**

What did the seven horns of the Lamb symbolize?
**Perfect power**

What did the seven eyes of the Lamb symbolize?
**Seven Spirits of God**

What did the living creatures with many eyes say day and night?
**Holy, holy, holy**

What did John see in the city with twelve gates?
**Twelve angels**

What marked each gate of the New Jerusalem?
**Name of a tribe of Israel**

What source of light is in the city?
**The Lamb**

What must no one do to the words of the prophecy in Revelation?
**Add or take away**

Which group is gathered before the throne from every nation?
**Great multitude**

What do they cry out with loud voices?
**"Salvation belongs to our God"**

What does the bright morning star promise?
**I will give to everyone who thirsts**

What does Jesus say He holds in His left hand?
**Seven stars**

What did John see coming down out of heaven from God?
**The New Jerusalem**

What was the wall of the city made of?
**Jasper**

What did the gates of the city not do by day?
**Shut**

What will the nations bring into the city?
**Glory and honor**

Who sits on the great white throne at the final judgment?
**God**

What book is opened at the final judgment?
**Books**

What is the second book opened at judgment?
**Book of life**

What happens to anyone not found in the Book of Life?
**Thrown into the lake of fire**

What is the tree that yields fruit every month?
**Tree of life**

What else does the tree of life provide?
**Leaves for the healing of the nations**

What final invitation does Revelation end with?
**"Come, Lord Jesus"**

Who seals the book until the time of the end?
**No one—it's fully revealed**

What is the main theme of Revelation?
**Jesus' ultimate victory**

Which church was praised for holding fast Jesus' name and not denying faith where Satan's throne is?
**Pergamum**

Which church was rebuked for tolerating a woman named Jezebel who led believers into sin?
**Thyatira**

When the seventh seal was opened, what followed in heaven for half an hour?
**Silence**

What rainbow-like feature surrounded God's throne?
**Emerald rainbow**

What appeared before the throne and looked like glass?
**Sea of glass**

How many stars did John see in Jesus' right hand?
**Seven**

What was written on both sides of the scroll in the Lamb's hand?
**Writing**

Who alone was worthy to open the scroll and its seals?
**The Lamb**

What did the living creatures proclaim about the Lamb?
**"Worthy is the Lamb"**

Who is worshiped by the creatures and elders around the throne?
**God**

How many angels hold trumpets before sounding the judgments?
**Seven**

What instrument did the angels blow to announce the trumpet judgments?
**Trumpets**

Which river dried up to prepare the way for the kings from the east?
**Euphrates**

How many angels poured out bowl judgments on the earth?
**Seven**

What painful affliction came upon those who worshiped the beast when the first bowl was poured?
**Ugly sores**

What happened to the sea when the second bowl was poured?
**It turned to blood**

What happened to rivers and springs when the third bowl was poured?
**They became blood**

Which celestial body scorched people when the fourth bowl was poured?
**Sun**

What covered the beast's kingdom in the fifth bowl?
**Darkness**

Who was bound and thrown into the Abyss for a thousand years?
**Satan**

How long is the thousand-year period described in Revelation?
**One thousand years**

What color robes do the twenty-four elders wear?
**White**

In Revelation 19, what was the rider on the white horse wearing?
**A robe dipped in blood**

What city did John see descending from heaven?
**New Jerusalem**

What are the gates of the New Jerusalem made from?
**Pearl**

What provides light for the New Jerusalem instead of sun or moon?
**God's glory**

What book lists the names of those allowed into the city?
**Book of Life**

How many gates does the New Jerusalem have?
**Twelve**

What are the streets of the New Jerusalem made of?
**Pure gold**

Which creature in Revelation is symbolically called the Lamb?
**Lamb**

What tree yields fruit every month in the New Jerusalem?
**Tree of life**

For whom are the leaves of the tree of life for healing?
**The nations**

What must no one do to the words of this prophecy?
**Add or take away**

Which title does Jesus use for Himself as the beginning and the end?
**Alpha and Omega**

How many living creatures surround God's throne?
**Four**

Which of these creatures has a face like an eagle?
**Eagle**

How many times do the living creatures say "holy"?
**Three**

What flows from the throne and is called the river of life?
**River of life**

What was the sea of glass compared to?
**Crystal**

Will the gates of the New Jerusalem ever be shut?
**No**

What temple is found in the New Jerusalem?
**None**

What invitation concludes the book of Revelation?
**"Come, Lord Jesus"**

What blessing is pronounced on those who read and hear the words of this prophecy?
**Blessed**

Which title refers to Jesus as the Lion of the tribe of Judah?
**Jesus**

Which title calls Jesus the Bright Morning Star?
**Bright Morning Star**

What will God do with every tear in the new creation?
**Wipe away every tear**

Who is thrown into the lake of fire along with the beast?
**False prophet**

Who holds the seven stars representing the churches?
**Jesus**

What spirit does John call "before the throne" in Revelation?
**Seven Spirits**

What did John see standing among the seven golden lampstands?
**One like a Son of Man**

What reward is promised to overcomers in Thyatira?
**Authority over nations**

What did Jesus promise to overcomers in Ephesus?
**Hidden manna**

What promise is given to overcomers in Smyrna?
**Not hurt by the second death**

What will overcomers receive in Pergamum?
**A white stone with a new name**

What promise is given to overcomers in Laodicea?
**Sit with Jesus on His throne**

What is the color of the first horse in the Four Horsemen?
**White**

What calamity follows the opening of the second seal?
**War**

What does the rider on the black horse carry?
**Scales**

What does the pale horse represent?
**Death**

Who follows the pale horse?
**Hades**

How many seals are on the scroll that only the Lamb can open?
**Seven**

After the seventh seal, what sound does John hear?
**Trumpet sound**

Which bowl makes painful sores break out on those worshiping the beast?
**First**

Which bowl turns the sea into blood?
**Second**

Which bowl turns rivers and springs to blood?
**Third**

Which bowl makes the sun scorch people?
**Fourth**

Which bowl plunges the earth into darkness?
**Fifth**

Which bowl dries up the Euphrates River?
**Sixth**

What comes from the mouths of the dragon, the beast, and the false prophet?
**Frogs**

What place is gathered for the battle on the great day of God Almighty?
**Armageddon**

What titles are given on the robe and thigh of the rider on the white horse in Revelation 19?
**King of kings and Lord of lords**

What does the great multitude in white robes cry out before the throne?
**Salvation belongs to our God**

Who will dwell with the redeemed and wipe away every tear?
**God**

What is no longer found in the new heaven and earth?
**Death**

Which river flows from the throne of God?
**River of life**

What is the tree of life used for in Revelation 22?
**Leaves for healing**

Which city needs no temple because its temple is the Lord God Almighty?
**New Jerusalem**

What provides light for the New Jerusalem?
**Glory of God**

What must no one do to the words of the prophecy in Revelation?
**Add or take away**

Who holds the seven stars in His right hand in Revelation 1?
**Jesus**

What are the seven stars symbolic of?
**Angels of the churches**

What sound did John hear like a trumpet when Jesus spoke to him?
**Voice**

What emerges from Jesus' mouth in Revelation 1 when He speaks?
**Sharp two-edged sword**

What do the seven lampstands represent?
**The churches**

How many living creatures surround God's throne?
**Four**

How many elders sit around God's throne?
**Twenty-four**

What do the living creatures and elders cast before the throne?
**Crowns**

What is the sea before God's throne compared to?
**Glass**

Who alone is worthy to open the scroll and its seals?
**The Lamb**

What do the living creatures call the Lamb around the throne?
**Worthy**

In Revelation 5, who joins in worshiping the Lamb?
**Angels**

What appears around God's throne resembling an emerald?
**Rainbow**

What are the gates of the New Jerusalem made of?
**Pearl**

Where are the names of the twelve apostles inscribed in the New Jerusalem?
**On foundation stones**

Who is described as the bright morning star?
**Jesus**

Who falls at Jesus' feet like dead when he sees Him in vision?
**John**

In Revelation 10, what does John do with the little scroll?
**Eats it**

How did the little scroll taste in John's mouth?
**Sweet**

Who is called the dragon in Revelation?
**The devil**

How many heads does the dragon have?
**Seven**

How many horns on the dragon?
**Ten**

What color is the dragon?
**Red**

Who fights the dragon in heaven?
**Michael**

For how long is the dragon bound in Revelation?
**A thousand years**

Where does the dragon persecute the woman after being cast out of heaven?
**Earth**

What does the dragon try to devour?
**The child**

What does the Lamb represent in Revelation?
**Jesus**

Who alone is worthy to open the scroll and its seals?
**The Lamb**

How many seals are on the scroll?
**Seven**

What appears when the first seal is opened?
**A white horse**

What symbol does the rider on the black horse carry?
**Scales**

Which horse represents Death?
**Pale horse**

Who follows the pale horse?
**Hades**

What falls from the sky in the third trumpet judgment?
**A great star**

What is the name of the star that falls?
**Wormwood**

What does the first trumpet bring?
**Hail and fire mixed with blood**

What does the fifth trumpet release from the abyss?
**Locusts**

How many angels are released at the Euphrates in the sixth trumpet?
**Four**

What river is dried up for the kings of the east?
**Euphrates**

How many trumpets announce judgment in Revelation?
**Seven**

What judgment begins with the pouring of the first bowl?
**Ugly sores**

Which bowl turns the seas into blood?
**Second**

Which bowl makes rivers and springs blood?
**Third**

Which bowl makes the sun scorch people with fire?
**Fourth**

What affliction follows the fifth bowl?
**Darkness**

Which bowl dries up the river Euphrates?
**Sixth**

Where do the kings gather for the final battle?
**Armageddon**

Who leads the armies of heaven on a white horse?
**Jesus**

What title is written on His robe and thigh?
**King of kings, Lord of lords**

What emerges from His mouth?
**Sharp sword**

What is the name given to the fallen city in Revelation 18?
**Babylon the Great**

Who mourns Babylon's fall?
**Kings and merchants**

Which message urges God's people to "come out" of Babylon?
**A voice from heaven**

What accompanies the opening of the second seal?
**A red horse**

How many times do the living creatures say "Holy"?
**Three**

What is beneath God's throne that looks like crystal?
**Sea of glass**

What surrounds God's throne like an emerald?
**Rainbow**

How many stars does Jesus hold in His right hand?
**Seven**

What do the seven stars represent?
**Angels of the churches**

What feeds the city in the new heaven and earth?
**River of life**

What tree provides healing in Revelation's new world?
**Tree of life**

How many gates does the New Jerusalem have?
**Twelve**

What are the city's streets made of?
**Pure gold**

What will there be no more of in the new creation?
**Death**

Who will wipe away every tear?
**God**

What warning is given about the words of this prophecy?
**Do not add or take away**

What final invitation ends Revelation?
**"Come, Lord Jesus"**

Who is called the "Alpha and Omega" in Revelation?
**Jesus**

Which island was John exiled to when he received the Revelation?
**Patmos**

How many churches receive letters in Revelation?
**Seven**

Which church is told to "be faithful even to the point of death"?
**Smyrna**

Which church is told that their works are incomplete and to repent?
**Sardis**

Who opens the seven seals of the scroll?
**The Lamb**

What color is the third horse of the Four Horsemen?
**Black**

What does the rider on the black horse carry?
**A pair of scales**

Which trumpet judgment brings locusts from the Abyss?
**Fifth**

How many months do the demonic locusts torment people?
**Five**

What name is given to the woman who rides the scarlet beast?
**Babylon the Great**

How many heads does the beast that the woman rides have?
**Seven**

What river is dried up to prepare the way for the kings of the east?
**Euphrates**

Who is called the "bright Morning Star"?
**Jesus**

What natural feature before God's throne is described as "like jasper and carnelian"?
**A rainbow**

How many living creatures circle the throne worshiping day and night?
**Four**

What did the twenty-four elders cast before the throne?
**Crowns**

What flows from the throne of God like clear crystal?
**A river**

What tree grows on each side of the river of life?
**Tree of life**

How often does the tree of life bear fruit?
**Monthly**

What will there be no more of in the new heaven and earth?
**Death**

Who reigns for a thousand years with Christ?
**The saints**

What happens to Satan at the end of the thousand years?
**He is released**

Which final judgment takes place after the thousand years?
**Great White Throne**

What book is opened at the Great White Throne judgment?
**Book of life**

What happens to those whose names are not found in the Book of Life?
**Thrown into the lake of fire**

Which city is described as coming down out of heaven from God?
**New Jerusalem**

How many gates does the New Jerusalem have?
**Twelve**

What is the material of the city's main street?
**Gold**

Which gemstone is the city wall's foundation stone?
**Jasper**

Who sings the song of Moses and the Lamb in Revelation 15?
**Those victorious over the beast**

Which angel stands at the sea and raises his hand to heaven?
**One of the seven**

What meal is prepared for the wedding of the Lamb?
**Marriage supper**

Who is invited to the wedding supper of the Lamb?
**His called, chosen, faithful**

Which river of Revelation is described as flowing from God's throne?
**River of life**

Which title does Jesus use for Himself in Revelation 1 to emphasize His eternal nature?
**First and Last**

What celestial voice does John hear like in Revelation 4?
**Voice of a trumpet**

What shines like a sardius stone and a ruby around God's throne?
**Rainbow**

Who holds the sharp two-edged sword that comes from Jesus' mouth?
**Jesus**

Which vision shows a scroll sealed with seven seals?
**Revelation 5**

What did the 144,000 on Mount Zion sing?
**New song**

What does the beast from the sea receive from the dragon?
**Authority**

Who is worshiped by the world because of the beast's miraculous signs?
**The beast**

What is written on the gates of the New Jerusalem?
**Names of the twelve tribes**

What is written on the foundations of the city wall?
**Names of the twelve apostles**

What title does Jesus give Himself as both the beginning and the end?
**Alpha and Omega**

Which island was John on when he received the Revelation?
**Patmos**

How many churches does John address in Revelation?
**Seven**

What symbol represents the churches in Revelation 1?
**Lampstands**

What symbol represents the angels of the churches?
**Stars**

Who is described as "clothed with a long robe and golden sash"?
**The Son of Man**

Which creature around God's throne has a lion's face?
**First living creature**

Which creature around God's throne has an ox's face?
**Second living creature**

Which creature around God's throne has a human face?
**Third living creature**

Which creature around God's throne has an eagle's face?
**Fourth living creature**

What do the four living creatures say day and night?
**Holy, holy, holy**

How many elders sit on thrones around God's throne?
**Twenty-four**

What do the elders cast before God's throne?
**Crowns**

What covers the floor around God's throne like sea glass?
**Sea of glass**

What rainbow-like feature surrounds the throne?
**Emerald rainbow**

Who alone is worthy to open the scroll with seven seals?
**The Lamb**

What is the Lamb's other title in Revelation 5?
**Lion of Judah**

What follows each seal when the Lamb opens them?
**Four Horsemen**

What does the rider on the first white horse carry?
**Bow**

What emerges when the fifth seal is opened?
**Souls under the altar**

What question do the martyrs cry out from under the altar?
**"How long, Sovereign Lord?"**

What release follows the opening of the fifth trumpet?
**Locusts from the Abyss**

How long do the locusts torment people?
**Five months**

Which trumpet dries up the Euphrates River?
**Sixth**

Who gathers the kings for the battle of Armageddon?
**Unclean spirits**

What title is written on the rider's robe in Revelation 19?
**King of kings and Lord of lords**

What does the great multitude do in white robes before the throne?
**Worship God**

What does the river flowing from God's throne supply?
**Water of life**

What is on each side of the river of life?
**Tree of life**

How often does the tree of life bear fruit?
**Twelve times a year**

What is the fate of death in the new creation?
**It is no more**

How many gates does the New Jerusalem have?
**Twelve**

What is each gate of the New Jerusalem made of?
**Single pearl**

What does the city's wall of jasper symbolize?
**God's strength**

Which stones adorn the foundations of the city wall?
**Twelve precious stones**

What will never enter the New Jerusalem?
**Anything impure**

What provides the light in the New Jerusalem?
**Glory of God**

Who dwells with His people in the new creation?
**God**

What is written on the gates of the city?
**Names of the twelve tribes of Israel**

What book records the names of those who may enter the city?
**Book of life**

What happens to anyone whose name is not in the Book of Life?
**Thrown into the lake of fire**

Which final invitation in Revelation beckons Jesus?
**"Come, Lord Jesus"**

What blessing is given to those who keep the words of the prophecy?
**Blessed**

What must no one do to the words of this prophecy?
**Add or take away**

Who cried out "Amen! Come, Lord Jesus!" at the end?
**John's readers**

What promise comes with the Revelation?
**Jesus is coming soon**

What does "Alpha" symbolize?
**Beginning**

What does "Omega" symbolize?
**End**

What is the final destiny of the concubine of the beast, Babylon?
**Judgment**

What is the color of the horse in Revelation 19 that the Word of God rides?
**White**

What weapon proceeds from the rider's mouth on the white horse?
**Sharp sword**

What will God wipe away in the new creation?
**Every tear**

What does the harlot hold filled with abominations?
**Cup**

What washes the kings from the earth in chapter 19?
**Wine of God's wrath**

Who sits on the white horse in chapter 19?
**Faithful and True**

What name is written on his robe?
**King of kings and Lord of lords**

# PART 3 – DIFFICULT

## Old Testament - The Law (or Pentateuch)

Which mountain did God give the Ten Commandments on?
**Mount Sinai**

What is the name of Noah's father?
**Lamech**

Who served as Moses' spokesman before Pharaoh?
**Aaron**

Which woman gave birth to twins Perez and Zerah?
**Tamar**

What did God call the darkness He created on the first day?
**Night**

Who built the ark according to God's instructions?
**Noah**

What was the name of Abraham's firstborn son?
**Ishmael**

Which city did God destroy with sulfur and fire?
**Sodom**

What was the sign of the covenant between God and Noah?
**Rainbow**

How many times did Moses lift his rod to bring water from the rock at Horeb?
**Once**

What substance did God provide for the Israelites, described as white like coriander seed?
**Manna**

What was the name of Abraham's wife who laughed at the promise of a son?
**Sarah**

Who worshipped the golden calf?
**Israelites**

What is the Hebrew name for God meaning "I AM WHO I AM"?
**Yahweh**

Which son of Jacob was sold into slavery by his brothers?
**Joseph**

Which ruler appointed Joseph overseer of Egypt?
**Pharaoh**

Which plague turned the Nile into blood?
**Water to blood**

What did Jacob use as a pillow during his dream of a ladder to heaven?
**Stone**

Who is called the "Cushite woman" that Moses married?
**Zipporah**

What did Balaam's donkey see standing in the road?
**Angel**

How old was Abraham when Isaac was born?
**100**

How old was Jacob when he entered Egypt?
**130**

On which day of creation did God create light?
**First**

On which day did God create man and woman?
**Sixth**

Which tree's fruit did God forbid Adam and Eve from eating?
**Tree of knowledge**

How many pairs of clean animals did Noah bring into the ark?
**Seven pairs**

How many days did the floodwaters prevail on the earth?
**150 days**

In Exodus, what did Moses' rod turn into before Pharaoh?
**Serpent**

Who held up Moses' hands during the battle with Amalek?
**Aaron and Hur**

Who succeeded Aaron as high priest after his death?
**Eleazar**

What penalty did Leviticus prescribe for blasphemy?
**Stoning**

What is the Hebrew term for the Day of Atonement?
**Yom Kippur**

On which mountain did Moses view the Promised Land before his death?
**Mount Nebo**

How many spies did Moses send to explore Canaan?
**Twelve**

Who was the chief craftsman appointed to build the Tabernacle?
**Bezalel**

How many cities of refuge were appointed east of the Jordan?
**Three**

What new name did God give Jacob after wrestling all night?
**Israel**

Who was Jacob's firstborn son?
**Reuben**

What did Adam and Eve use to cover themselves before God made garments of skins?
**Fig leaves**

Which commandment prohibits bearing false witness?
**Ninth commandment**

Which commandment requires keeping the Sabbath holy?
**Fourth commandment**

What offering was required for unintentional sins?
**Sin offering**

Which festival commemorates Israel's deliverance from Egypt?
**Passover**

What did Moses place inside the Ark of the Covenant along with the tablets?
**Tablets of the Law**

Who was the father of Miriam, Aaron, and Moses?
**Amram**

What metal were the rings of the Tabernacle's pillars made of?
**Silver**

Which substance symbolized purification when sprinkled on lepers?
**Scarlet yarn**

In what language was the Law originally written?
**Hebrew**

What was the final plague that struck Egypt?
**Death of firstborn**

In which month did the Exodus begin?
**Nisan**

What was Abraham's father's name?
**Terah**

What was the name of Isaac's wife?
**Rebekah**

Who sold his birthright for a meal of stew?
**Esau**

To whom did Jacob flee to escape Canaan?
**Laban**

How many years did Jacob serve Laban?
**Twenty**

Which wife of Jacob died giving birth to Benjamin?
**Rachel**

To which town did Lot flee for safety from Sodom's destruction?
**Zoar**

What ritual sign marked God's covenant with Abraham?
**Circumcision**

Which plague brought gnats upon Egypt?
**Third plague**

Which plague sent frogs to cover the land?
**Second plague**

Which plague struck Egyptian livestock but spared Israelite herds?
**Sixth plague**

Which plague brought hail and fire mixed with blood?
**Seventh plague**

Which plague cloaked Egypt in darkness for three days?
**Ninth plague**

Which plague killed the firstborn of Egypt?
**Tenth plague**

Which sea did God part so Israel could cross on dry ground?
**Red Sea**

What did Moses strike at Rephidim to bring forth water?
**Rock**

Which festival celebrates the giving of the Law seven weeks after Passover?
**Pentecost**

Which harvest festival is also called the Feast of Booths?
**Feast of Tabernacles**

Which holy day begins the civil new year with trumpet blasts?
**Feast of Trumpets**

What cherubic figures overshadow the mercy seat?
**Cherubim**

What filled the Tabernacle by day as God's sign?
**Cloud**

What sign of God's presence appeared by night?
**Fire**

How many spies did Moses send to explore the land of Canaan?
**Twelve**

How many cities of refuge were designated for unintentional killers?
**Six**

How many tribes received their inheritance east of the Jordan River?
**Two**

Which tribe was given no contiguous territory but cities among the other tribes?
**Levites**

How many cities were allotted to the Levites?
**Forty-eight**

How high was the altar of burnt offering in the Tabernacle court?
**Three cubits**

How many stones adorned Aaron's breastpiece?
**Twelve**

How many branches did the golden lampstand have?
**Seven**

How many wooden boards made up each long side of the Tabernacle?
**Ten**

What metal overlaid the interior walls of the Tabernacle?
**Gold**

How many pairs of clean animals did Noah bring into the ark?
**Seven**

Which river did Lot choose to settle near before Sodom's destruction?
**Jordan River**

Who was the father of Shem, Ham, and Japheth?
**Noah**

Which son of Noah is the ancestor of the Israelites?
**Shem**

Which son of Noah is considered the ancestor of many African nations?
**Ham**

Who was the third son of Adam and Eve?
**Seth**

Who committed the first murder by killing his brother?
**Cain**

Which early builder constructed the first city in Genesis?
**Babel**

Who offered the firstfruits of his flock, pleasing God?
**Abel**

Which patriarch "walked with God, and he was not, for God took him"?
**Enoch**

How old was Noah when the floodwaters came?
**Six hundred**

To what place did Jacob flee and set up a pillar after his dream of a ladder to heaven?
**Bethel**

What type of wood formed the Ark of the Covenant?
**Acacia**

Which field did Abraham purchase as a burial site for Sarah?
**Machpelah**

Which member of Lot's family was turned into a pillar of salt?
**Lot's wife**

Which of Jacob's sons remained in Egypt as a hostage?
**Simeon**

Which commandment requires observing the Sabbath day as holy?
**Fourth commandment**

Which commandment forbids coveting your neighbor's property?
**Tenth commandment**

What Hebrew name is given to the book of Leviticus?
**Vayikra**

Which offering required fine flour mixed with oil and frankincense?
**Meal offering**

Who was Moses' father-in-law and advisor on judging Israel?
**Jethro**

What was Jethro's vocation before advising Moses?
**Priest of Midian**

What Hebrew word describes the quail provided in the wilderness?
**Shilshalim**

Which rock did Moses strike at Kadesh to bring forth water the second time?
**Meribah**

What was the name of Aaron's son who offered "unauthorized fire" before the LORD?
**Nadab**

Who was the other son of Aaron involved in the unauthorized offering?
**Abihu**

Who was Moses' sister who watched over him as an infant?
**Miriam**

What did the Israelites carry on poles into the wilderness as God's presence?
**Ark of the Covenant**

What color tassels did God require on the corners of Israelite garments?
**Blue**

What blazing material covered the cherubim above the mercy seat?
**Gold**

What birds could be offered in a purification sacrifice for leprosy?
**Turtle doves**

Which festival immediately follows the Passover feast?
**Feast of Unleavened Bread**

On what day of the seventh month is Yom Kippur observed?
**Tenth**

What Hebrew term means "instruction" or "law," often referring to Torah?
**Torah**

How long did the Israelites live in Egypt before the Exodus?
**Four hundred thirty years**

Which mountain did Abraham offer Isaac on?
**Moriah**

What does the Hebrew name Jehovah-Jireh mean?
**The LORD will provide**

What Hebrew term designates the Nazirite vow?
**Nazir**

Which drink was forbidden for those under a Nazirite vow?
**Wine**

Which mountain's summit did Moses ascend to receive the tablets?
**Sinai**

What type of wood formed the boards of the Tabernacle?
**Acacia**

Which precious metal overlaid the interior walls of the Tabernacle?
**Gold**

Which tribe received no land but cities among the other tribes?
**Levites**

How many cities of refuge were designated east and west of the Jordan?
**Six**

What act merited Moses' disqualification from entering Canaan?
**Striking the rock**

What Hebrew word describes the glory of the LORD that filled the Tabernacle?
**Kavod**

What was placed inside the Ark alongside the tablets to attest to Moses' faithfulness?
**Pot of manna**

What house servant did Abraham send to find Isaac a wife?
**His eldest servant**

At which spring did Abraham's servant find Rebekah?
**Well of Haran**

Who sold his birthright for a lentil stew?
**Esau**

How many years did Jacob serve Laban to marry Rachel?
**Fourteen**

Which daughter of Laban did Jacob marry first by deception?
**Leah**

What was the symbol of God's covenant with Noah after the flood?
**Rainbow**

What Hebrew name did Jacob give to the place of his dream ladder?
**Bethel**

Which boundary element "borders" the Promised Land described in Numbers 34?
**Jordan River**

Which two sons of Aaron died suddenly for offering strange fire?
**Nadab and Abihu**

What was the penalty for blasphemy under Mosaic Law?
**Stoning**

Which incense ingredient was strictly prohibited for personal use?
**Holy incense**

What was Moses' age when he fled Egypt after killing an Egyptian?
**Forty**

Which part of the Tabernacle was veiled to separate the Holy Place from the Most Holy?
**Curtain**

Which Hebrew word means "atonement" and names the annual fast?
**Kippur**

Which day of the new year is marked by trumpet blasts?
**First of Tishri**

What was the Hebrew term for the walls and gate measuring the Tabernacle courtyard?
**Hangings**

Which census in Numbers counted men "from twenty years old and upward"?
**Tribal census**

Which red heifer sacrifice provided water for purification?
**Red heifer**

Which cities did Israel capture after wandering 40 years at the end of Numbers?
**None; Moses died before conquest**

Which patriarch's net worth is described in Genesis 13 in flocks, herds, and servants?
**Abraham**

Which Hebrew term describes "holy convocation" on Sabbath days?
**Mikra**

Who was appointed as the first high priest of Israel?
**Aaron**

What was the Hebrew name for the second son born to Jacob and Leah?
**Simeon**

Which portion of each year's harvest was to be given to the Levites?
**Tithe**

Which patriarch dreamt of stars bowing to him?
**Joseph** *(in Torah)*

Which Hebrew phrase concludes each negative commandment in the Decalogue?
**Lo ya'aseh**

What Hebrew word for "testimony" appears in the Ark alongside the tablets?
**'Edut**

Which tribe was stationed directly south of the Tabernacle encampment?
**Reuben**

What was the width of each gate of the Tabernacle courtyard?
**Five cubits**

Which precious wood comprised the poles of the Ark?
**Acacia**

What Hebrew term describes the "model" of the Tabernacle given on Sinai?
**Tabnit**

Which two items were to be kept inside the Ark of the Covenant?
**Tablets of the Law and jar of manna**

What was the length of the Tabernacle courtyard?
**One hundred cubits**

Which day's offerings in Leviticus required two lambs, a grain offering, and drink offerings?
**Day of Atonement**

Which patriarch's near-sacrifice is recounted again in Deuteronomy as a test?
**Isaac**

What command does Deuteronomy give concerning the vua of the Gibeonites?
**Keep their treaty; do not abhor the Gibeonites**

Which son of Aaron succeeded him as high priest?
**Eleazar**

What instrument accompanied the priests when entering the holy place?
**Trumpets** *(Numbers 10)*

Which tribe carried the Tabernacle's frames and crossbars?
**Reuben, Simeon, and Gad**

What was placed on the altar to designate unintentional sacrifice?
**Blood of the sin offering**

Which covenant name of God appears repeatedly in Deuteronomy?
**Yahweh**

What annual tribute did the Levites receive in lieu of inheritance?
**Tithes**

Which Hebrew phrase begins the Shema in Deuteronomy 6?
**Shema Yisra'el**

What warning does Deuteronomy give against worshiping "when you see the sun, moon, and stars"?
**Do not be enticed to serve them**

Which Levitical festival requires blowing trumpets on the first day of the seventh month?
**Yom Teruah**

Who was to appear before the LORD three times a year according to Exodus 23?
**All males of Israel**

Which deuteronomic law stipulates fairness when appointing weights and measures?
**You shall have honest scales**

What does Moses call the Promised Land in Deuteronomy 11 when urging obedience?
**A good land**

Which book's opening narrative does Deuteronomy recast with Moses addressing the people?
**Exodus**

Which number recurs as Israel's years of wandering before entering Canaan?
**Forty**

What Hebrew term describes the "tabernacle" of meeting?
**Ohel Mo'ed**

Which plague-surviving insect is named in Numbers 11?
**Quail**

What did Israel carry before the Ark to part the Jordan River?
**Priests' feet touching the water's edge**

Which portion of the Law did Israel write on doorposts and gates?
**Words of the Law**

Which Hebrew term means "holy convocation," especially on feast days?
**Miqra'**

What object concealed the mercy seat from unauthorised view?
**Veil**

Which graded sound signaled all camps to break camp during the march?
**Silver trumpets**

What was the Hebrew term for the tabernacle's outer court hangings?
**Me'illat**

Which legal case in Deuteronomy mandates witnesses at a false witness's execution?
**False accusation of a fellow Israelite**

Which river's valley did the Reubenites settle in east of the Jordan?
**Arnon**

Which census command in Numbers distinguishes men "out of the number of names by their polls"?
**Registration by census**

Which sacrificial gift required frankincense from Genub or Galbanum?
**Incense offering** *(Exodus 30)*

The command "Do not muzzle an ox" appears in which book?
**Deuteronomy**

Which portion of every offering was given to Aaron and his sons?
**Breast and right thigh**

What did Moses carve into stone in preparation to enter the land?
**Second set of tablets**

Which death-penalty law in Deuteronomy prescribes stoning for a rebellious son?
**Wayward son law**

Which Hebrew word for "tabernacle" literally means "dwelling"?
**Mishkan**

Which festival in Leviticus requires the trumpets to be sounded over the entire land?
**Feast of Trumpets**

Which number of trumpets were to be blown on the day of rejoicing?
**Two trumpets**

Which Hebrew term denotes the grain offering of fine flour mixed with oil?
**Minchah**

What is the Hebrew name for the new moon festival each month?
**Rosh Chodesh**

On the Day of Atonement, what was the second goat called that was sent into the wilderness?
**Azazel**

According to Deuteronomy, how many witnesses are required to convict someone of a crime?
**Two**

What sabbatical release of debts occurs every seven years?
**Shemitah**

After touching a dead body, for how many days must a priest remain ceremonially unclean?
**Seven days**

What ram's horn instrument was used to call Israel together for assemblies?
**Shofar**

What is the Hebrew name for the Sea of Reeds, often translated as the Red Sea?
**Yam Suph**

Who succeeded Aaron as high priest of Israel?
**Eleazar**

Which dry measure, used for counting manna, was about two quarts?
**Omer**

How wide was the Tabernacle courtyard in cubits?
**Fifty cubits**

At which place did Moses strike the rock to bring forth water in the wilderness?
**Meribah**

What alternative name does Deuteronomy use for Mount Sinai?
**Horeb**

What is the Hebrew name for the fellowship or peace offering?
**Shelamim**

Which Hebrew word describes the unleavened cakes baked in an oven as part of the grain offering?
**Memulot**

What color were the ram skins used to cover the Tabernacle frames?
**Red**

What does the name Judah mean in Hebrew?
**Praise**

What accompaniment of the Passover lamb was strictly required in Exodus?
**Bitter herbs**

What is the Hebrew name for the Feast of Weeks?
**Shavuot**

For how many days and nights did Moses stay on Mount Sinai when receiving the Law?
**Forty days and nights**

What manifestation of God led Israel by day in the wilderness?
**Cloud**

What did the Israelites see on the mountain when God wrote the Law on tablets?
**Finger of God**

During consecration, what part of the priest did Moses apply blood to?
**Right ear**

Which Midianite princess's defilement with an Israelite sparked Moses' wrath and a plague?
**Cozbi**

What amount did each Israelite pay as the census half-shekel tax?
**Half shekel**

Of what metal was the laver made for priestly washing?
**Bronze**

What cubit-based unit measures length in the Tabernacle's structure?
**Cubit**

Which Hebrew term means "dwelling" and refers to the Tabernacle?
**Mishkan**

Which tribe camped directly east of the Tabernacle?
**Judah**

Which clan within Levi was charged with carrying the Tabernacle's most sacred items?
**Kohathites**

Who was the father of Moses, Aaron, and Miriam?
**Amram**

What almond-bearing branch budded on Aaron's rod to confirm his priesthood?
**Almond blossom**

Which Hebrew term describes the "holy convocation" on Sabbath and feast days?
**Miqra'**

What festival releases servants and debts every fifty years?
**Jubilee**

What linen garment did the priest wear under his outer vestments?
**Linen breeches**

Which bitter place name means "bitterness" where the waters were made sweet?
**Marah**

What unit of weight was used for silver offerings, equivalent to about 75 pounds?
**Talent**

What Hebrew word for "law" literally means "instruction" or "teaching"?
**Torah**

What was the fate of Nadab and Abihu after offering unauthorized fire before the LORD?
**Died**

What new name meaning "he who struggles with God" was given to Jacob after wrestling?
**Israel**

What ritual used ashes of a red heifer mixed with water for ceremonial cleansing?
**Purification**

What Hebrew word names the "mercy seat" atop the Ark of the Covenant?
**Kapporet**

Which day of the month begins the civil new year in the Hebrew calendar?
**First of Nisan**

Which commandment is numbered fifth in the Decalogue?
**Honor your father and mother**

What substance was used to anoint the priests and Tabernacle furnishings?
**Olive oil**

Which unclean creeping creature does Leviticus explicitly prohibit?
**Lizard**

Of what metal were the rings of the Tabernacle's poles made?
**Silver**

At what age was a bull considered suitable for sacrifice under the Law?
**One year**

What Hebrew term describes ritual uncleanness contrasted with tahor (clean)?
**Tumah**

Which festival requires all who are able to appear before the LORD three times a year?
**Sukkot**

Which mountain does Deuteronomy identify as the place Moses first spoke to Israel, calling it "the mountain of God"?
**Horeb**

What Hebrew word meaning "I am" does God use to reveal His name to Moses?
**Ehyeh**

What Hebrew term describes the weekly day of rest commanded in the Law?
**Shabbat**

Which tribe's name is rendered "struggles" in Hebrew?
**Naphtali**

Which tribe's name means "blessing" or "happy" in Hebrew?
**Asher**

How many pairs of birds did a leper bring for purification according to Leviticus?
**One pair**

What Hebrew name is given to the new-moon festival each month?
**Rosh Chodesh**

What is the Hebrew term for the meal offering of fine flour, oil, and frankincense?
**Minchah**

Which Hebrew word in Genesis 1 is translated "day" in the creation account?
**Yom**

What Hebrew term is used for the first man created in Genesis?
**Adam**

What Hebrew word describes the creature used to tempt Eve in Genesis 3?
**Nachash**

What Hebrew word in Exodus 25 means "pattern" or "plan," referring to the Tabernacle blueprint?
**Tabnit**

Which Levite clan was charged with carrying the Tabernacle's curtains?
**Gershonites**

Which Levite clan carried the Tabernacle's frames and crossbars?
**Merarites**

Which Levite clan bore the Ark, table, lampstand, and altars?
**Kohathites**

What Hebrew term names the high priest's breastpiece?
**Choshen**

What Hebrew term names the high priest's outer robe?
**Me'il**

What Hebrew term refers to the priestly sash or belt?
**Avnet**

# DIFFICULT

## Old Testament - The Historical Books

Which city's walls collapsed after Israel marched around them for seven days?
**Jericho**

Who was the first judge of Israel following Joshua's death?
**Othniel**

Which left-handed judge delivered Israel by assassinating King Eglon of Moab?
**Ehud**

Which city of Canaan tricked Israel into a peace treaty by feigning distance?
**Gibeon**

Which judge reduced his army to 300 men before defeating the Midianites?
**Gideon**

Which Nazirite judge destroyed a thousand Philistines with a donkey's jawbone?
**Samson**

Which Moabite woman is celebrated for her loyalty to Naomi?
**Ruth**

Who anointed Saul and later David as king over Israel?
**Samuel**

Which prophet rebuked King David for his sin with Bathsheba?
**Nathan**

Who became Israel's second king after Saul?
**David**

At which battle did the Philistines capture the Ark of the Covenant?
**Aphek**

Samson collapsed the temple of which Philistine god?
**Dagon**

Who succeeded Saul's son Ish-bosheth to unite Israel under David?
**David**

Which of Saul's sons died alongside him at Mount Gilboa?
**Jonathan**

Which northern kingdom did Jeroboam I found?
**Israel**

Which king of Israel famously asked for wisdom and built the temple?
**Solomon**

Which king of Judah rediscovered the Book of the Law and led major reforms?
**Josiah**

Which Babylonian monarch destroyed Jerusalem and exiled its king?
**Nebuchadnezzar**

Who was the last king of Judah before the Babylonian conquest?
**Zedekiah**

Under which Persian ruler did Zerubbabel lead the first group of exiles back to Jerusalem?
**Cyrus**

Which priest-scribe led the second wave of returnees and taught the Law?
**Ezra**

Who served as cupbearer to Artaxerxes and later rebuilt Jerusalem's walls?
**Nehemiah**

Which Jewish queen concealed her identity to save her people?
**Esther**

Who was Esther's guardian and cousin in Susa?
**Mordecai**

Which vizier plotted against the Jews and was hung on his own gallows?
**Haman**

Which festival commemorates Mordecai's and Esther's salvation?
**Purim**

Which king of Israel was struck by Jehu's arrow at Ramoth-Gilead?
**Jehoram**

Which king of Judah was thrown from a window by Jehu's men?
**Ahaziah**

Which prophet was taken up to heaven in a whirlwind, leaving his cloak behind?
**Elijah**

Who succeeded Elijah and performed twice as many miracles?
**Elisha**

Which Aramean commander was cleansed of leprosy by washing in the Jordan?
**Naaman**

Which king of Judah saw his army struck down by an angel after mocking Hezekiah's faith?
**Sennacherib** *(Assyrian king)*

Which Babylonian official murdered Governor Gedaliah at Mizpah?
**Ishmael**

Which book concludes with the account of David's death and Solomon's succession?
**2 Samuel**

Which book opens with Solomon's reign and the building of the temple?
**1 Kings**

Which book begins with genealogies from Adam through King Saul?
**1 Chronicles**

Which book records Solomon's temple dedication and the reforms of later Judahite kings?
**2 Chronicles**

Which book narrates Joshua's conquest and division of Canaan?
**Joshua**

Which book recounts Israel's cycles of sin, oppression, and deliverance under leaders?
**Judges**

Which book tells of a Moabite widow's loyalty and her place in David's lineage?
**Ruth**

Which book details Israel's fall under Saul, David's rise, and David's reign?
**1 Samuel**

Which book describes the divided kingdom from Solomon to the exile?
**2 Kings**

Which book follows Israel's history from creation through the exile, with emphasis on David?
**1 Chronicles**

Which governor's prayer of confession opens his memoirs of rebuilding Jerusalem's walls?
**Nehemiah**

Which account records the rebuilding of Jerusalem's temple foundation under Zerubbabel?
**Ezra**

Which book opens with King Ahasuerus' feast and Esther's ascent to queenship?
**Esther**

Which judge vowed to sacrifice his daughter if granted victory over the Ammonites?
**Jephthah**

Which clan member killed 600 Philistines with an oxgoad at a winepress?
**Shamgar**

Which Mesopotamian king oppressed Israel but recognized the LORD after witnessing Israel's God?
**Sennacherib** (acknowledged after defeat; see 2 Kings 19)

Which prophetess and judge led Israel alongside Barak against Sisera?
**Deborah**

Which left-handed judge assassinated King Eglon of Moab?
**Ehud**

Which judge triumphed over the Midianites with just 300 men at the spring of Harod?
**Gideon**

Which judge slew 600 Philistines with an oxgoad at a winepress?
**Shamgar**

Which judge vowed to sacrifice his daughter if he defeated the Ammonites?
**Jephthah**

Which judge's strength lay in his uncut hair, which he lost and later recovered before collapsing a temple?
**Samson**

Which Moabite widow's loyalty led her to Bethlehem and into David's lineage?
**Ruth**

Which kinsman-redeemer married Ruth and restored her family's inheritance?
**Boaz**

Which boy prophet was dedicated by his mother at Shiloh and anointed Israel's first two kings?
**Samuel**

Which Philistine idol fell face-down before the Ark of the Covenant?
**Dagon**

Which city sheltered the Ark in the house of Abinadab for twenty years?
**Kiriath-Jearim**

Which king of Israel built Samaria as his capital?
**Omri**

Which prophet confronted King Ahab at the vineyard of Naboth?
**Elijah**

Which Syrian army commander was cleansed of leprosy by dipping seven times in the Jordan?
**Naaman**

Which king of Judah discovered the Book of the Law during temple renovations under Hilkiah?
**Josiah**

Which official opposed Nehemiah's rebuilding by sending letters filled with lies?
**Sanballat**

Which cupbearer to King Artaxerxes led the rebuilding of Jerusalem's walls?
**Nehemiah**

Which priest-scribe returned from Babylon to teach the Law to the people in Jerusalem?
**Ezra**

Which foreign queen visited Solomon to test his famed wisdom?
**Queen of Sheba**

Which Persian king issued a decree allowing the Jews to rebuild the Jerusalem Temple?
**Cyrus**

Which Jewish queen concealed her identity to risk her life for her people before King Ahasuerus?
**Esther**

Which relative of Esther uncovered a plot to exterminate the Jews and was later honored?
**Mordecai**

Which government official plotted against the Jews but was hanged on his own gallows?
**Haman**

Which feast commemorates the Jews' deliverance from Haman's decree?
**Purim**

Which city's walls tumbled after Israel marched around them for seven days under Joshua's command?
**Jericho**

Which valley became a curse when Achan disobeyed God after the conquest?
**Valley of Achor**

Which tribe's territory included Hebron, Debir, and Libnah?
**Judah**

Which half-tribe received land both east and west of the Jordan with a meeting at Mizpah?
**Manasseh**

Which judge tested God with fleeces made wet and dry on successive nights?
**Gideon**

Which household servant hid Joshua's spies by lowering them through an opening in the city wall?
**Rahab**

Which high priest anointed Solomon as king at the spring of Gihon?
**Zadok**

Which judge's song includes the refrain "the stars in their courses fought against Sisera"?
**Deborah**

Which king of Judah burned incense on the hill of Corazin, provoking prophetic rebuke?
**Hezekiah**

Which king of Israel built golden calves at Bethel and Dan to prevent northern worship in Jerusalem?
**Jeroboam I**

Which general besieged Jerusalem, leading to its fall in 586 BC?
**Nebuchadnezzar**

Which Babylonian official executed the governor Gedaliah at Mizpah?
**Ishmael**

Which priest's sons, Hophni and Phinehas, were struck down for profaning the sacrifices?
**Eli**

Which judge was a Levite from Mount Ephraim whose concubine's murder sparked a civil war?
**Unnamed Levite**

Which commander's rod did Moses use to part the waters of the Red Sea?
**Moses' rod**

Which administrator of Assyria imitated Solomon's glory by building palaces with cedars from Lebanon?
**Shalmaneser** (kings of Assyria)

Which Levite clan carried the frames and bars of the Tabernacle?
**Merarites**

Which Levitical city east of the Jordan served as a city of refuge?
**Bezer**

Which festival in 2 Chronicles does Josiah celebrate after rediscovering the Law?
**Passover**

Which chronicler records David's mighty men, including Jashobeam and Eleazar?
**1 Chronicles**

Which book recounts Rehoboam's reign and the split of Solomon's kingdom?
**2 Chronicles**

Which Amorite king forged a coalition against Gibeon?
**Adoni-Zedek**

At which battle did the sun and moon stand still?
**Battle of Gibeon**

Which valley was cursed after Achan's sin at Jericho?
**Valley of Achor**

Who tricked the people of Gibeon by claiming to be from a distant land?
**The Gibeonites**

Which judge's fleece test involved dew appearing on the fleece but not on the ground?
**Gideon**

Which judge's final act was collapsing a temple by pushing over its pillars?
**Samson**

Who served as priest at Shiloh when Samuel was dedicated?
**Eli**

Which Philistine idol fell before the Ark of the Covenant?
**Dagon**

Which king of Israel built Samaria as his capital city?
**Omri**

Which prophet rebuked Ahab at Naboth's vineyard?
**Elijah**

Which woman anointed David's head with oil in Hebron?
**Abigail**

Who was David's first male heir who died as an infant?
**Amnon**

Which king of Judah removed high places and Asherah poles after finding the Law?
**Josiah**

Which ruler sent Ezra to teach the Law in Jerusalem?
**Artaxerxes**

Who led the people in rebuilding Jerusalem's walls?
**Nehemiah**

Which governor read the Law to all who could understand it on the first day of the seventh month?
**Ezra**

Which orphan from Moab is an ancestor of King David?
**Ruth**

Which foreign woman's grandson became king of Judah?
**Ruth**

What Persian monarch rebuilt the temple in Jerusalem?
**Darius**

Which Babylonian king placed Jehoiachin at his table?
**Evil-Merodach**

Who was the last Jezreelite king of Judah taken to Babylon?
**Zedekiah**

Which city's walls fell after the people shouted and priests blew rams' horns?
**Jericho**

Which judge made an ephod that became a snare to Israel?
**Gideon**

Which city provided refuge where the Levites ministered from age thirty to fifty?
**Kedesh**

Which Assyrian king besieged Jerusalem in Hezekiah's reign?
**Sennacherib**

Who succeeded Elijah after being called in the Jordan's waters?
**Elisha**

Which Syrian general was healed after dipping seven times in the Jordan?
**Naaman**

Which king of Judah rid the land of male cult prostitutes?
**Hezekiah**

Which census under David led to God's judgment on Israel?
**David's numbering**

Which scribe wrote the genealogies in Ezra?
**Shecaniah**

Which Levite helped Ezra distribute the provisions for the exiles?
**Ezra**

Which chronicle records Solomon's riches in horses and chariots?
**1 Kings**

Which book records the deaths of Saul and Jonathan on Mount Gilboa?
**2 Samuel**

Which book opens with Israel crossing the Jordan into Canaan?
**Joshua**

Which book concludes with the declaration of Zerubbabel's temple completion?
**Ezra**

Which book ends with Nehemiah's reforms against mixed marriages?
**Nehemiah**

Which book's final verse sets Esther's feast as an annual decree?
**Esther**

Which place saw lightning and hail following Moses' and Aaron's words?
**Egypt's fields**

Which place name means "smitten," where Moses struck the rock a second time?
**Kadesh**

Which song is recorded in Judges after God's deliverance of Israel?
**Song of Deborah**

Which city's waters were sweetened after Moses threw a tree into them?
**Marah**

Which judge's mother named him "Yahweh saves," and he later defeated the Ammonites?
**Jephthah**

Which city was burned after Israel's first defeat caused by Achan's sin?
**Ai**

Who was the first judge of Israel after Joshua's death?
**Othniel**

Which left-handed judge delivered Israel by assassinating King Eglon?
**Ehud**

Which Moabite king oppressed Israel for eighteen years before his death?
**Eglon**

Which judge's uncut hair was the source of his strength, ending when he collapsed a temple?
**Samson**

Which judge reduced his army to 300 men before defeating the Midianites?
**Gideon**

Which prophet and last judge anointed both Saul and David as kings?
**Samuel**

Under Gideon's command, who used jars and torches in a nighttime attack on the Midianite camp?
**Gideon**

Which Philistine city's gates did Samson drag away to demonstrate his strength?
**Gaza**

In whose house was the Ark of the Covenant kept for twenty years?
**Kiriath-Jearim**

Which Philistine idol repeatedly fell before the Ark of the Covenant?
**Dagon**

Which Philistine king did David serve before returning to Israel?
**Achish**

Which of David's mighty men struck down eight hundred men with his spear?
**Jashobeam**

Which high priest served alongside Zadok during David's reign?
**Abiathar**

Which priest and prophet together anointed Solomon as king?
**Zadok and Nathan**

At which high place did Solomon offer a thousand burnt offerings?
**Gibeon**

Which visiting monarch tested Solomon's wisdom with hard questions?
**Queen of Sheba**

Which king built Samaria as the capital of the northern kingdom?
**Omri**

Which prophet confronted King Ahab over the murder in Naboth's vineyard?
**Elijah**

Who was healed of leprosy after dipping seven times in the Jordan at Elisha's command?
**Naaman**

Which king of Judah rediscovered the Book of the Law during temple renovations?
**Josiah**

Which Samaritan official mocked Nehemiah's rebuilding efforts with slanderous letters?
**Sanballat**

Which Ammonite official opposed the Jerusalem wall project alongside Sanballat?
**Tobiah**

Which cupbearer to King Artaxerxes rebuilt Jerusalem's walls?
**Nehemiah**

Which priest-scribe led exiles back to Jerusalem to teach the Law?
**Ezra**

Which Persian queen risked her life to save the Jewish people in Susa?
**Esther**

Who uncovered Haman's plot against the Jews?
**Mordecai**

Which festival celebrates the Jews' deliverance from Haman's decree?
**Purim**

Which official was hanged on the very gallows he had prepared for Mordecai?
**Haman**

Which king of Judah was taken captive to Babylon in 597 BC?
**Jehoiachin**

Which Babylonian king released Jehoiachin from prison after thirty-seven years?
**Evil-Merodach**

Which of David's mighty men cut off the edge of King Saul's robe at En-gedi?
**Abishai**

Which woman drove a tent peg through Sisera's temple, killing him?
**Jael**

Which Amorite king formed a coalition against Gibeon during Joshua's conquest?
**Adoni-Zedek**

How many years did the Israelites wander in the wilderness before entering Canaan?
**Forty**

Which river did the tribes of Reuben, Gad, and half of Manasseh settle beyond?
**Jordan**

Which Levite clan was responsible for carrying the Tabernacle's boards and bars?
**Merarites**

Which Levite clan bore the most sacred objects, including the Ark and altars?
**Kohathites**

Which king's census led to a plague on Israel as judgment for pride?
**David**

How many youths were mauled by bears for mocking the prophet Elisha?
**Forty-two**

Which prophet rebuked David for his sin with Bathsheba?
**Nathan**

Which king of Judah allied with Aram to resist Israel under King Baasha?
**Asa**

Under which king did the united monarchy split into northern and southern kingdoms?
**Rehoboam**

Which book records the edicts of Cyrus and Darius permitting the temple's reconstruction?
**Ezra**

Who was high priest when Zerubbabel laid the foundation of the second temple?
**Jeshua (Joshua) son of Jozadak**

Which Persian ruler's decree ended the Babylonian exile?
**Cyrus**

Which essential provision did Nehemiah accuse the nobles of extorting from the people?
**Grain**

Which governor prayed, "Remember me, O my God, for good," in his memoirs?
**Nehemiah**

Which book parallels Samuel's reign narratives but focuses on temple worship and genealogies?
**1 Chronicles**

Which prophet poured oil on Jehu's head to anoint him king of Israel?
**Elisha**

Which prostitute hid Israelite spies and helped them escape Jericho?
**Rahab**

Where did Joshua set up twelve stones as a memorial after crossing the Jordan?
**Gilgal**

Which battle saw the sun stand still until Israel defeated its foes?
**Battle of Gibeon**

Which tribe's inheritance included Jerusalem's site?
**Benjamin**

Who was Israel's last judge and first prophet of the monarchy?
**Samuel**

Which Levite's household blessed David after the Ark was returned?
**Obed-Edom**

What city did David burn when its inhabitants sheltered rebels?
**Ziklag**

Which city did David capture to establish his capital?
**Jerusalem**

Which king reigned fifty-five years and saw the fall of Judah to Babylon?
**Manasseh**

Which prophet succeeded Elijah and performed twice as many miracles?
**Elisha**

Which king allied with Ahab at Ramoth-Gilead?
**Jehoshaphat**

Which king of Israel built Samaria on a hill he purchased?
**Omri**

Which king of Israel instituted the worship of golden calves?
**Jeroboam I**

Which Persian palace city was Esther queen of?
**Shushan**

Which king banished Vashti before Esther took her place?
**Ahasuerus**

Who led the exiles back to Jerusalem as high priest under Cyrus?
**Jeshua**

Which leader rebuilt Jerusalem's walls amid opposition from Sanballat?
**Nehemiah**

Who read the Law publicly to the people at the Water Gate?
**Ezra**

Which Jewish festival commemorates deliverance from Haman?
**Purim**

Which official plotted against the Jews and was later executed on his own gallows?
**Haman**

Which Babylonian king released Jehoiachin from prison?
**Evil-Merodach**

Which Egyptian pharaoh opposed Hezekiah but withdrew after a plague?
**Sennacherib**

Which son of Samuel became the first king of Israel?
**Saul**

Who anointed David at Bethlehem to succeed Saul?
**Samuel**

Which fortress did David secure by diverting the water supply?
**City of David**

Which temple did Solomon build on Mount Moriah?
**First Temple**

Which king's wealth and wisdom attracted the Queen of Sheba?
**Solomon**

Which king of Judah instituted major reforms after finding the Book of the Law?
**Josiah**

Which prophetess authenticated Josiah's covenant renewal?
**Huldah**

Which captain of fifty was slain by Joab at a sheep-shearing feast?
**Amasa**

Which prophet rebuked David for his census and foretold the plague's end?
**Gad**

Which valley did Joshua curse after Achan's sin?
**Achor**

Which allied force attacked Gibeon, prompting Israel's miraculous victory?
**Adoni-Zedek's coalition**

Which Gileadite judge delivered Israel by choosing men who lap water with their hands?
**Gideon**

Which Philistine idol fell face-down before the Ark of the Covenant?
**Dagon**

Which judge's uncut hair was the source of his great strength?
**Samson**

Which city of refuge east of the Jordan was named for its oasis?
**Bezer**

Which half-tribe received territory on both sides of the Jordan?
**Manasseh**

Which city did Jephthah destroy after his victory over the Ammonites?
**No specific city named; used judgment**

Which place name means "testing," where Israel quarreled about water?
**Massah**

Which place name means "bitterness," where waters were sweetened?
**Marah**

Which spring did Moses strike to bring forth water in Exodus?
**Meribah**

Which mountain did Moses view from Nebo before his death?
**Mount Nebo**

Which location did David's mighty men bring water from, refusing to drink it?
**Well of Bethlehem**

Which city's gates were burned and replaced by Solomon's laborers?
**Shechem**

Which two mountains did Joshua command Israel to stand upon to renew the covenant and pronounce blessings and curses?
**Gerizim and Ebal**

What scarlet item did Rahab hang from her window to identify her house to the Israelite spies?
**Scarlet cord**

Which Israelite city's walls fell after seven circuits and the sound of ram's horns?
**Jericho**

Where did the Israelites camp after entering Canaan before attacking Ai?
**Gilgal**

Which valley became a curse after Achan's sin at Jericho?
**Achor**

Who was the Moabite king killed by Ehud's concealed dagger?
**Eglon**

Which prophet and judge combated the Canaanite general Sisera alongside Deborah?
**Barak**

Where did Gideon test God with the fleece by morning dew?
**Ophrah**

Which spring of water was narrowed so Gideon could choose men who lapped like dogs?
**Spring of Harod**

What object did Samson use to slay a thousand Philistines?
**Donkey's jawbone**

Which Philistine city's temple did Samson collapse by toppling its pillars?
**Dagon's temple at Gaza**

Which Naomi's relative married Ruth and became her kinsman-redeemer?
**Boaz**

Which town's threshing floor became David's first altar as king in Jerusalem?
**Araunah's (Ornan's) threshing floor**

Which son of David led the rebellion that caused David to flee Jerusalem?
**Absalom**

Which commander carried Joab's armor-bearer's head to David on a platter?
**Benaiah**

Which king of Judah's tunnel diverted water from the spring of Gihon into the city?
**Hezekiah**

What name is given to Hezekiah's tunnel in later tradition?
**Siloam Tunnel**

Which Syrian general was cleansed of leprosy after dipping in the Jordan seven times?
**Naaman**

Which king of Judah removed the bronze serpent Moses had made because people were worshiping it?
**Hezekiah**

Which Aramean king besieged Samaria for three years before its fall?
**Ben-Hadad**

# DIFFICULT

## Old Testament - The Poetic
## (or Wisdom Books)

Which psalm is the longest chapter in the Bible?
**Psalm 119**

Which poetic book is structured largely as dialogues between Job and his three friends?
**Job**

How many chapters are in the book of Job?
**Forty-two**

Which proverb likens a contentious wife to "a continual dripping on a rainy day"?
**Proverbs 27:15**

Which proverb asks, "Who can find a virtuous woman? For her price is far above rubies"?
**Proverbs 31:10**

Which Song of Songs section contains the dialogue of the "Shulamite" bride?
**Song 3**

Which chapter contains God's challenge to Job about the foundations of the earth?
**Job 38**

Which of Job's friends was a Temanite?
**Eliphaz**

Which psalm uses the metaphor "His arrows are sharp in the heart of the king's enemies"?
**Psalm 45:5**

Which proverb affirms, "A person's wisdom yields patience; it is to one's glory to overlook an offense"?
**Proverbs 19:11**

Which proverb states, "As a dog returns to its vomit, so fools repeat their folly"?
**Proverbs 26:11**

Which friend of Job was a Shuhite?
**Bildad**

Which psalm declares, "Create in me a clean heart, O God; and renew a right spirit within me"?
**Psalm 51**

Which psalm proclaims, "The stone that the builders rejected has become the cornerstone"?
**Psalm 118**

Which proverb warns, "Do not muzzle the ox while he is treading out the grain"?
**Proverbs**

Which friend of Job was a Naamathite?
**Zophar**

Which psalm describes, "The righteous flourish like the palm tree; he grows like a cedar in Lebanon"?
**Psalm 92**

Which chapter in Proverbs begins with, "My son, forget not my law; but let thine heart keep my commandments"?
**Proverbs 3**

Which psalm opens with "Great is the Lord and most worthy of praise in the city of our God"?
**Psalm 48**

Which sea-monster does God describe to illustrate His power in Job 41?
**Leviathan**

In which chapter does God begin speaking to Job out of the whirlwind?
**Job 38**

Which verse in Job affirms, "Though he slay me, I will hope in him"?
**Job 13:15**

Which wisdom book begins with the exhortation, "The fear of the Lord is the beginning of knowledge"?
**Proverbs**

Which book is primarily a collection of Solomon's sayings to teach wisdom?
**Proverbs**

Which wisdom book begins, "The words of the Preacher, the son of David, king in Jerusalem"?
**Ecclesiastes**

Which phrase does Ecclesiastes repeat to describe the fleeting nature of life's pursuits?
**Vanity of vanities**

Which psalm ends with the exhortation "Let everything that has breath praise the Lord"?
**Psalm 150**

Which psalm proclaims, "I will extol you, O Lord, for you have drawn me up and have not let my foes rejoice over me"?
**Psalm 30**

Which proverb declares, "Better to meet a bear robbed of her cubs than a fool in his folly"?
**Proverbs 17:12**

Which psalm declares, "Behold, how good and pleasant it is when brothers dwell in unity"?
**Psalm 133**

Which psalm exclaims, "I was glad when they said to me, 'Let us go to the house of the Lord'"?
**Psalm 122**

Which book concludes with, "Fear God, and keep his commandments: for this is the whole duty of man"?
**Ecclesiastes**

Which chapter of Ecclesiastes opens with "To everything there is a season, and a time to every purpose under heaven"?
**Ecclesiastes 3**

Which wisdom poem personifies Wisdom as calling aloud in public squares?
**Proverbs 8**

Which book opens with "The Song of Songs, which is Solomon's"?
**Song of Solomon**

Which psalm opens with "Praise the LORD! For it is good to sing praises to our God"?
**Psalm 147**

Which proverb warns, "Whoever mocks the poor insults his Maker; he who is glad at calamity will not go unpunished"?
**Proverbs 17:5**

Which proverb contrasts "She who is slack in her work" with "a diligent wife"?
**Proverbs 31:27**

Which chapter warns, "Be not quick in your spirit to become angry, for anger lodges in the heart of fools"?
**Ecclesiastes 7**

Which chapter closes Ecclesiastes with the exhortation, "Fear God and keep his commandments, for this is the whole duty of man"?
**Ecclesiastes 12**

Which psalm declares, "Praise the Lord! For it is good to sing praises to our God; for it is pleasant, and a song of praise is fitting"?
**Psalm 147:1**

Which psalmist asks, "God, why have you rejected us forever? Why does your anger smolder against the sheep of your pasture?"
**Psalm 74**

Which proverb contrasts, "A merry heart does good like medicine, but a crushed spirit dries up the bones"?
**Proverbs 17:22**

Which proverb observes, "Iron sharpens iron, and one man sharpens another"?
**Proverbs 27:17**

In which book does the beloved exclaim, "Your hair is like a flock of goats"?
**Song of Solomon**

Which Wisdom book counsels, "A merry heart does good like medicine"?
**Proverbs**

Which proverb warns, "As a dog returns to its vomit, so a fool repeats his folly"?
**Proverbs**

Which Wisdom book refers to life under the sun as ultimately meaningless without God?
**Ecclesiastes**

Which proverb lists seven things that the Lord hates, including "haughty eyes" and "a lying tongue"?
**Proverbs**

Which psalm celebrates, "The heavens declare the glory of God; and the firmament shows his handiwork"?
**Psalm 19**

Which psalm opens, "Blessed is the man who walks not in the counsel of the wicked"?
**Psalm 1**

Which psalm promises, "The Lord upholds all who fall and lifts up all who are bowed down"?
**Psalm 145**

Which psalm, one of the Songs of Ascents, begins, "I was glad when they said to me, 'Let us go to the house of the Lord'"?
**Psalm 122**

Which poetic book uses the refrain "under the sun" in its reflections on life's vanity?
**Ecclesiastes**

Which proverb says, "Better is a dry morsel with quiet than a house full of feasting with strife"?
**Proverbs**

Which psalm refers to the Lord as "a very present help in trouble"?
**Psalm 46**

Which poem includes the exclamation, "Let him kiss me with the kisses of his mouth"?
**Song of Solomon**

Which proverb warns, "The first to present his case seems right, till another comes forward and questions him"?
**Proverbs 18:17**

Which proverb states, "There is a way that seems right to a man, but its end is the way to death"?
**Proverbs 14:12**

Which psalm proclaims, "The earth is the Lord's and the fullness thereof, the world and those who dwell therein"?
**Psalm 24**

Which book records the dialogue of lovers repeatedly using the refrain "I am my beloved's and my beloved is mine"?
**Song of Solomon**

Which book uniquely refers to God raining manna like dust on Israel?
**Psalm 78**

Which book opens, "Blessed is the one who does not walk in step with the wicked"?
**Psalm 1**

Which poetic book records the refrain "his word is very pure; he is a shield to all who take refuge in him"?
**Psalm 18**

Which book's wisdom sections are addressed "to my son" or "to my children"?
**Proverbs**

Which chapter in Psalms is an alphabetical acrostic listing the Torah's statutes?
**Psalm 119**

Which proverb says, "Train up a child in the way he should go; even when he is old he will not depart from it"?
**Proverbs 22:6**

Which poetic book ends with the call, "Drink water from your own cistern"?
**Proverbs**

Which psalm says, "When I consider your heavens, the work of your fingers, the moon and the stars, which you have set in place"?
**Psalm 8**

Which psalm opens "As the deer pants for streams of water, so my soul pants for you, my God"?
**Psalm 42**

Which psalm warns "Unless the Lord watches over the city, the watchman stays awake in vain"?
**Psalm 127**

What precious metal surrounds the golden apple in the simile of fitting words?
**Silver**

Which proverb affirms, "Death and life are in the power of the tongue"?
**Proverbs 18:21**

Which proverb characterizes wisdom as "more precious than jewels, and nothing you desire can compare with her"?
**Proverbs 3:15**

Which chapter of Ecclesiastes notes, "Better is a poor but wise youth than an old but foolish king who no longer knows how to take advice"?
**Ecclesiastes 4**

Which psalm opens with "Praise the Lord! Praise the name of the Lord; give glory to his praise"?
**Psalm 135:1**

According to Proverbs, what effect does a joyful heart have on one's countenance?
**Cheerful face**

Which proverb says, "A friend loves at all times, and a brother is born for adversity"?
**Proverbs 17:17**

Which chapter of Proverbs opens by calling out to simple ones and fools to gain prudence?
**Proverbs 8**

Which psalm proclaims, "I will sing to the Lord as long as I live; I will sing praise to my God while I have being"?
**Psalm 104:33**

Which psalm describes, "Many are the afflictions of the righteous, but the Lord delivers him out of them all"?
**Psalm 34:19**

Which chapter of Ecclesiastes declares, "To everything there is a season, and a time to every purpose under heaven"?
**Ecclesiastes 3**

Which proverb states, "The fear of the Lord is a fountain of life, that one may turn away from the snares of death"?
**Proverbs 14:27**

Which proverb declares, "Pride goes before destruction, and a haughty spirit before a fall"?
**Proverbs 16:18**

Which proverb compares soothing words to a tree of life?
**Soothing tongue**

Which proverb likens an insult to one's mother to tearing down one's own house?
**Proverbs 18:7**

Which psalm opens, "In the day of trouble I call upon you, for you answer me"?
**Psalm 86:7**

Which psalm begins, "Give ear, O Shepherd of Israel; you who lead Joseph like a flock"?
**Psalm 80:1**

Which intense emotion does Proverbs say is too cruel to endure?
**Jealousy**

Which psalm includes, "He brought them out of darkness and the shadow of death, and burst their bonds apart"?
**Psalm 107:14**

Which psalm declares, "To him who rides on the highest heavens, the ancient heavens; behold, he sends out his voice, his mighty voice"?
**Psalm 68:33**

Which proverb warns, "Do not boast about tomorrow, for you do not know what a day may bring forth"?
**Proverbs 27:1**

Which small creature does Proverbs hold up as an example of diligence?
**Ant**

Which psalm attributes "Mercy and truth" meeting together and "righteousness and peace" kissing each other?
**Psalm 85:10**

Which proverb declares, "A rebuke goes deeper into one who has understanding than a hundred blows into a fool"?
**Proverbs 17:10**

Which proverb observes, "Better a poor man who lives with integrity than a rich man who is crooked in his ways"?
**Proverbs 19:1**

What does Proverbs call the fear of the Lord in Proverbs 14:27?
**Fountain of life**

Which psalm opens with "Hear my prayer, O Lord; let my cry come to you"?
**Psalm 102:1**

Which psalm asks, "Who among the gods is like you, O Lord? Who is like you, majestic in holiness"?
**Psalm 86:8**

Which proverb states, "Many are the plans in a person's heart, but it is the Lord's purpose that prevails"?
**Proverbs 19:21**

Which proverb states, "A tranquil heart gives life to the flesh"?
**Tranquil heart**

Which proverb says a continual dripping on a rainy day is like a contentious woman?
**Dripping rain**

Which psalm recounts the ascents pilgrims made to Jerusalem, mentioning "go up to the house of the LORD"?
**Psalm 122**

Which proverb advises, "Look well to the path of your feet, and all your ways will be sure"?
**Proverbs 4:26**

Which proverb says, "Iron sharpens iron, and one man sharpens another"?
**Proverbs 27:17**

Which chapter of Ecclesiastes concludes, "Fear God and keep his commandments, for this is the whole duty of man"?
**Ecclesiastes 12**

Which chapter of Job portrays the terrifying might of Leviathan?
**Job 41**

Which psalm begins, "As the deer pants for streams of water, so my soul pants for you, my God"?
**Psalm 42**

Which proverb states, "The eyes of the Lord are in every place"?
**Eyes of the Lord**

Which Hebrew title does Ecclesiastes use for its author?
**Qoheleth**

Which psalm uses vineyard imagery to lament Israel's unfruitfulness?
**Psalm 80**

Which psalm celebrates God's rescue of David from overwhelming foes, including Goliath?
**Psalm 18**

Which proverb warns, "The way of a sluggard is like a hedge of thorns, but the path of the upright is a level highway"?
**Proverbs 15:19**

According to Ecclesiastes 3:11, what has God put into the human heart?
**Eternity**

In Ecclesiastes 7:3, what does the Preacher say is better than laughter?
**Sorrow**

What phrase does Job use to dismiss his friends as comforters in Job 16?
**Miserable comforters**

Which psalm begins by asking, "Why do the nations rage and the peoples plot in vain?"
**Psalm 2**

Which proverb states, "A soft answer turns away wrath, but a harsh word stirs up anger"?
**Proverbs 15:1**

Which proverb declares, "Wine is a mocker, strong drink a brawler, and whoever is led astray by it is not wise"?
**Proverbs 20:1**

Which proverb affirms, "Even a fool who keeps silent is considered wise; when he closes his lips, he is deemed intelligent"?
**Proverbs 17:28**

Which chapter of Ecclesiastes warns, "Be not quick in your spirit to become angry, for anger lodges in the heart of fools"?
**Ecclesiastes 7**

Which psalm opens, "How long, O Lord? Will you forget me forever?"
**Psalm 13**

Which simile does Job use to describe the fleeting nature of his days in Job 7?
**Weaver's shuttle**

What Hebrew word meaning "vanity" begins Ecclesiastes?
**Hevel**

Which psalm calls God "my rock and my fortress and my deliverer"?
**Psalm 18**

Which proverb states, "Correct your son, for there is hope; do not set your heart on putting him to death"?
**Proverbs 19:18**

Which proverb affirms, "The righteous care for the needs of their animals, but the kindest acts of the wicked are cruel"?
**Proverbs 12:10**

In which chapter of Ecclesiastes does it say "To everything there is a season"?
**Ecclesiastes 3**

Which phrase describes life's pursuits without God in Ecclesiastes?
**Under the sun**

What animal does the bride compare the eyes of her beloved to in Song of Solomon 1:15?
**Doves**

What fragrant spice does the bride anoint her beloved with in Song of Solomon 1:3?
**Spikenard**

How is the beloved's hair described in Song of Solomon 5:11?
**Black as a raven**

Which psalm declares, "The Lord is my shepherd; I shall not want"?
**Psalm 23**

Under which tree does the bride say her beloved feeds his flock in Song of Solomon 2:3?
**Apple tree**

Which symbol describes an enclosed space in Song of Solomon 4:12?
**Garden locked**

Which psalm celebrates, "The earth is the Lord's and the fullness thereof"?
**Psalm 24**

Which proverb says, "A friend loves at all times, and a brother is born for adversity"?
**Brother**

Which proverb warns, "The sluggard buries his hand in the dish"?
**Sluggard**

Which psalm begins, "My God, my God, why have you forsaken me?"
**Psalm 22:1**

Which proverb declares, "The one who gets wisdom loves life; the one who cherishes understanding will soon prosper"?
**Proverbs 19:8**

Which proverb warns, "He who trusts in his riches will fall, but the righteous will thrive like a green leaf"?
**Proverbs 11:28**

Which proverb declares, "The wicked flee when no one pursues, but the righteous are bold as a lion"?
**Lion**

Which proverb states, "Hope deferred makes the heart sick"?
**Hope deferred**

Which chapter of Ecclesiastes concludes, "Fear God and keep his commandments, for this is the whole duty of man"?
**Ecclesiastes 12**

Which chapter of Job describes God's control over the constellations Pleiades and Orion?
**Job 38**

Which psalm contains the declaration, "Your word is a lamp to my feet and a light to my path"?
**Psalm 119:105**

Which proverb warns, "The beginning of strife is like letting out water"?
**Strife**

Which proverb says, "As water reflects the face, so one's life reflects the heart"?
**Water**

Which psalm begins, "My flesh and my heart may fail, but God is the strength of my heart and my portion forever"?
**Psalm 73**

Which psalm of Asaph asks, "O God, why do you cast us off forever?"
**Psalm 74**

Which proverb warns, "A fool's lips walk into a fight, and his mouth invites a beating"?
**Fool's lips**

Which proverb contrasts a soft answer with a harsh word in resolving anger?
**Soft answer**

Which psalm proclaims, "The earth is the LORD's and the fullness thereof, the world and those who dwell therein"?
**Psalm 24**

Which proverb observes, "Hope deferred makes the heart sick, but a desire fulfilled is a tree of life"?
**Proverbs 13:12**

Which chapter of Ecclesiastes opens with "Vanity of vanities, says the Preacher, vanity of vanities! All is vanity"?
**Ecclesiastes 1**

In which chapter of Job does he lament his birth, asking, "Why did I not die at birth"?
**Job 3**

Which book says "Your love is better than wine" in its opening?
**Song of Solomon**

Which psalm declares, "He makes grass grow for the cattle, and plants for people to cultivate"?
**Psalm 104**

Which psalm recounts Israel's rebellion at the waters of Meribah and prays for God's steady guidance?
**Psalm 95**

Which proverb declares, "The fear of the LORD is a fountain of life, that one may turn away from the snares of death"?
**Proverbs 14:27**

Which proverb states, "Whoever spares the rod hates his son, but he who loves him is diligent to discipline him"?
**Proverbs 13:24**

Which chapter of Ecclesiastes begins, "Vanity of vanities, says the Preacher, vanity of vanities! All is vanity"?
**Ecclesiastes 1**

Which chapter of Ecclesiastes declares, "Two are better than one, because they have a good reward for their toil"?
**Ecclesiastes 4**

Which psalm begins, "Why do the nations rage and the peoples plot in vain"?
**Psalm 2**

Which psalm is attributed to Moses and begins, "Lord, you have been our dwelling place in all generations"?
**Psalm 90**

Which line in Ecclesiastes says, "For everything there is a season, and a time for every matter under heaven"?
**Ecclesiastes 3:1**

Which book opens with "The words of Job, a man who was blameless and upright"?
**Job**

Which of Job's friends was from Teman, known for wisdom?
**Eliphaz**

Which of Job's friends reproaches him with arguing against God in Job 15?
**Bildad**

Which poetic book contains the line, "Your teeth are like a flock of shorn sheep"?
**Song of Solomon**

Which proverb declares, "Pride goes before destruction, and a haughty spirit before a fall"?
**Proverbs 16:18**

Which psalm's superscription reads "A Maskil of Asaph" and begins, "God, be merciful to me through your name"?
**Psalm 79**

Which creature described in Job 40 has "strong scales" and "fearsome teeth"?
**Leviathan**

In Job, who declares, "I know that my redeemer lives"?
**Job**

Which chapter in Job responds to Job's longing for days that ceased?
**Job 10**

Which book of Wisdom closes with the assertion that "the end of the matter; all has been heard. Fear God and keep his commandments"?
**Ecclesiastes**

Which psalm recounts Israel's testing of God at Meribah, pleading, "Today, if you would hear his voice, do not harden your hearts"?
**Psalm 95**

Which psalm describes the "voice of the Lord" thundering over the waters, powerful and majestic?
**Psalm 29**

Which proverb warns, "Pride goes before destruction, and a haughty spirit before a fall"?
**Proverbs 16:18**

Which proverb states, "The heart of the discerning acquires knowledge, for the ears of the wise seek it out"?
**Proverbs 18:15**

Which chapter of Ecclesiastes begins, "Vanity of vanities, says the Preacher, vanity of vanities! All is vanity"?
**Ecclesiastes 1**

Which chapter of Ecclesiastes declares, "To everything there is a season, and a time for every matter under heaven"?
**Ecclesiastes 3**

Which chapter of Job opens with Job's lament, "Why did I not die at birth, and expire as I came from the womb"?
**Job 3**

Which chapter of Job describes God's challenge about the foundations of the earth and control over the sea?
**Job 38**

Which proverb says, "Better is a dry morsel with quiet than a house full of feasting with strife"?
**Proverbs 17:1**

Which psalm celebrates, "Let everything that has breath praise the Lord"?
**Psalm 150**

Which psalm opens, "Great is the Lord and most worthy of praise in the city of our God"?
**Psalm 48**

Which wisdom poem begins, "The words of the Preacher, the son of David, king in Jerusalem"?
**Ecclesiastes**

Which Ecclesiastes chapter opens, "Vanity of vanities, says the Preacher, vanity of vanities! All is vanity"?
**Ecclesiastes 1**

Which proverb counsels, "Trust in the Lord with all your heart, and do not lean on your own understanding"?
**Proverbs 3:5**

Which proverb warns, "A soft answer turns away wrath, but a harsh word stirs up anger"?
**Proverbs 15:1**

Which Song of Songs verse likens the beloved's cheeks to halves of a pomegranate?
**Song 4:3**

Which psalm is a lament that begins, "Out of the depths I cry to you, O Lord"?
**Psalm 130**

Which proverb states, "Iron sharpens iron, and one man sharpens another"?
**Proverbs 27:17**

Which acrostic chapter of Proverbs praises the attributes of a virtuous wife?
**Proverbs 31**

Which Song of Songs chapter celebrates "My beloved is mine, and I am his"?
**Song 2**

Which poetic book begins, "The words of Job, the man who was blameless and upright"?
**Job**

Which chapter records Job's assertion, "For I know that my Redeemer lives, and at the last he will stand upon the earth"?
**Job 19**

Which Job friend declares, "Should we accept good from God, and not trouble?"
**Bildad**

Which chapter of Ecclesiastes observes, "This also is vanity and a striving after wind"?
**Ecclesiastes 4**

Which chapter of Ecclesiastes warns, "Be not quick in your spirit to become angry, for anger lodges in the heart of fools"?
**Ecclesiastes 7**

Which psalm likens those who trust in the Lord to Mount Zion, which cannot be moved?
**Psalm 125:1**

Which wisdom poem exhorts, "Above all else, guard your heart, for everything you do flows from it"?
**Proverbs 4:23**

Which Book of Psalms is structured into five distinct collections, mirroring the Torah?
**Psalms**

Which Song of Songs image describes the beloved's hair as "a flock of goats, leaping down from Gilead"?
**Song 4:1**

Which Psalm of Ascents begins, "I lift up my eyes to the hills. From where does my help come"?
**Psalm 121**

Which psalmist sings, "Mercy and truth have met together; righteousness and peace have kissed each other"?
**Psalm 85**

Which Poet calls wisdom "more precious than jewels; and nothing you desire can compare with her"?
**Proverbs 8**

Which psalm begins "Sing to the Lord a new song, for he has done marvelous things"?
**Psalm 98**

Which psalm begins "How long, O Lord? Will you forget me forever?"
**Psalm 13**

Which psalm opens "Praise the Lord! Praise, O servants of the Lord, praise the name of the Lord"?
**Psalm 113**

Which psalm exclaims, "Be still, and know that I am God"?
**Psalm 46**

Which psalm opens, "The Lord is my light and my salvation; whom shall I fear"?
**Psalm 27**

Which psalm describes God as "my rock and my fortress and my deliverer"?
**Psalm 18**

Which psalm begins, "O come, let us worship and bow down"?
**Psalm 95**

Which psalm personifies the earth and all its inhabitants giving praise, saying "For he spoke, and it came to be"?
**Psalm 148**

Which psalm describes a mighty king in war with chariots and horses but exalts God's sovereignty?
**Psalm 20**

Which psalm is an acrostic that celebrates the righteous flourishing "like the palm tree"?
**Psalm 92**

Which psalm declares, "My heart is steadfast, O God, my heart is steadfast"?
**Psalm 57**

Which psalm opens with "Behold, how good and pleasant it is when brothers dwell in unity"?
**Psalm 133**

Which psalm, attributed to David, pleads, "Deliver me from my enemies; I flee to you for refuge"?
**Psalm 7**

Which proverb declares, "Hatred stirs up strife, but love covers over all wrongs"?
**Proverbs 10:12**

Which proverb warns, "The craving of a sluggard kills him, for his hands refuse to labor"?
**Proverbs 21:25**

Which proverb says, "A gift opens the way for the giver and ushers him into the presence of the great"?
**Proverbs 18:16**

Which psalm opens Book V of the Psalter with the refrain "Oh give thanks to the Lord, for he is good; for his steadfast love endures forever"?
**Psalm 107**

Which psalm recounts Israel's testing of God at Meribah, warning "Today, if you hear his voice, do not harden your hearts"?
**Psalm 95**

Which psalm of Asaph begins, "God, why do you cast us off forever? Why does your anger smoke against the sheep of your pasture?"
**Psalm 74**

# DIFFICULT

## Old Testament - The Prophetic Book

Which psalm recounts Israel's testing of God at Meribah and warns, "Do not harden your hearts as at Meribah"?
**Psalm 95**

Which psalm personifies the heavens declaring, "The heavens declare the glory of God, and the sky above proclaims his handiwork"?
**Psalm 19**

Which chapter of Proverbs begins, "The proverbs of Solomon, son of David, king of Israel"?
**Proverbs 1**

Which proverb warns, "Pride goes before destruction, and a haughty spirit before a fall"?
**Proverbs 16:18**

Which chapter of Ecclesiastes opens with "Vanity of vanities, says the Preacher, vanity of vanities! All is vanity"?
**Ecclesiastes 1**

Which chapter of Ecclesiastes declares, "To everything there is a season, and a time for every matter under heaven"?
**Ecclesiastes 3**

Which book begins, "The words of Job, a man who was blameless and upright"?
**Job**

Which chapter of Job portrays the terrifying might of Leviathan?
**Job 41**

Which friend of Job is a Temanite?
**Eliphaz**

Which friend of Job is a Shuhite?
**Bildad**

Which friend of Job is a Naamathite?
**Zophar**

Which prophetic book opens, "The vision of Isaiah the son of Amoz, which he saw concerning Judah and Jerusalem"?
**Isaiah**

Which chapter of Isaiah contains the call of the seraphim with six wings?
**Isaiah 6**

Which chapter of Jeremiah contains the potter's house allegory?
**Jeremiah 18**

Which chapter of Jeremiah delivers the "Temple Sermon," condemning empty sacrifices?
**Jeremiah 7**

Which chapter of Lamentations contains the refrain "Great is your faithfulness"?
**Lamentations 3**

Which chapter of Ezekiel features the vision of wheels within wheels full of eyes?
**Ezekiel 1**

Which chapter of Ezekiel records the valley of dry bones coming to life?
**Ezekiel 37**

Which chapter of Daniel records the handwriting on the wall at Belshazzar's feast?
**Daniel 5**

Which chapter of Daniel contains the vision of the four beasts rising from the sea?
**Daniel 7**

Which book opens with "The word of the Lord that came to the prophet Hosea"?
**Hosea**

Which chapter of Joel describes a locust plague as God's army?
**Joel 2**

Which chapter of Amos pronounces judgment on the nations with visions of a plumb line?
**Amos 7**

Which chapter of Obadiah condemns Edom for violence against Jacob?
**Obadiah 1**

Which chapter of Jonah records the city of Nineveh repenting at Jonah's word?
**Jonah 3**

Which chapter of Micah prophesies that the Messiah will be born in Bethlehem?
**Micah 5**

Which chapter of Nahum opens with "A jealous and avenging God is the Lord, the Lord avenging and wrathful"?
**Nahum 1**

Which chapter of Habakkuk ends with the declaration, "Though he slay me, I will hope in him"?
**Habakkuk 3**

Which chapter of Zephaniah announces, "The great day of the Lord is near"?
**Zephaniah 1**

Which chapter of Haggai calls on the people to "consider your ways" and rebuild the temple?
**Haggai 1**

Which chapter of Zechariah depicts a flying scroll twenty cubits long and ten cubits wide?
**Zechariah 5**

Which chapter of Zechariah shows two olive trees and a lampstand sustaining oil for Judah's leaders?
**Zechariah 4**

Which chapter of Malachi concludes the Old Testament with the promise, "Behold, I will send you Elijah the prophet before the great and awesome day of the Lord comes"?
**Malachi 4**

Which chapter of Isaiah depicts the prophet's vision of seraphim and the call "Holy, holy, holy, is the Lord of hosts"?
**Isaiah 6**

Which valley is called the "Valley of Decision" in Joel's prophecy?
**Valley of Jehoshaphat**

Which two northern tribes does Hosea pair with Gomer to illustrate unfaithfulness?
**Israel and Judah**

Which locust plague in Joel is described as the "strong locust, without number"?
**Second swarm**

Which vision in Amos presents a plumb line used to test Israel's wall?
**Amos 7**

Which chapter of Obadiah pronounces the prophecy against Edom?
**Obadiah 1**

Which prophet is swallowed by a "great fish" after fleeing to Tarshish?
**Jonah**

How many days did Jonah spend in the belly of the fish?
**Three days and three nights**

Which chapter of Micah foretells the ruler of Israel coming from Bethlehem?
**Micah 5**

Which city does Nahum predict will be "exposed to the sun" and "burn like a cedar"?
**Nineveh**

Which prophet questions God's justice by asking "Why do you make me see iniquity and why do you idly look at wrong"?
**Habakkuk**

Which king of Judah does Zephaniah specifically warn about in his opening oracle?
**Josiah**

Which two-year fast anniversary does Haggai use to rebuke God's people for neglecting the temple rebuild?
**Two years**

Which vision in Zechariah features two olive trees and a golden lampstand?
**Zechariah 4**

Which prophetic book ends with the promise, "Behold, I will send you Elijah the prophet before the great and awesome day of the Lord comes"?
**Malachi**

Which chapter of Jeremiah contains the allegory of the potter's house?
**Jeremiah 18**

Which Babylonian ruler does Isaiah name as Cyrus, God's anointed, sent to rebuild Jerusalem?
**Cyrus**

Which prophet's book begins with "The word of the Lord came to Jeremiah"?
**Jeremiah**

Which Ezekiel chapter recounts the vision of the valley of dry bones?
**Ezekiel 37**

Which prophet sees "wheels within wheels" full of eyes in a vision beside the river Chebar?
**Ezekiel**

Which chapter of Daniel records King Belshazzar's feast and the writing on the wall "Mene, Mene, Tekel, Upharsin"?
**Daniel 5**

Which prophet compares Israel to "a leafy olive tree" that bears no fruit?
**Hosea**

Which prophet is instructed to write the vision plainly on tablets so a runner can read it easily?
**Habakkuk**

Which chapter of Zephaniah announces, "The great day of the Lord is near, near and hastens fast"?
**Zephaniah 1**

Which prophet laments, "O Lord, you have deceived me, and I was deceived; you overpowered me and prevailed"?
**Hosea**

Which book opens, "The word of the Lord that came to Hosea son of Beeri"?
**Hosea**

Which prophet sees the glory of the Lord depart from the temple in Jerusalem?
**Ezekiel**

Which chapter of Amos denounces Amaziah, the priest at Bethel, calling him a "cow's dung"?
**Amos 7**

Which minor prophet foretells locusts invading like a mighty army at the "Day of the Lord"?
**Joel**

Which chapter of Nahum declares, "The Lord is good, a stronghold in the day of trouble; he knows those who take refuge in him"?
**Nahum 1**

Which prophet's message includes "let justice roll down like waters, and righteousness like an ever-flowing stream"?
**Amos**

Which book portrays a dialogue between God and the lamenting prophet about Judah's sin and restoration?
**Ezekiel**

Which chapter of Jeremiah prophesies the new covenant with Israel written on the heart?
**Jeremiah 31**

Which prophet's vision includes a flying scroll measuring twenty cubits by ten that goes over the whole land?
**Zechariah**

Which prophet is forbidden to marry or mourn at the death of any relative as a sign to Judah?
**Ezekiel**

Which prophet calls Israel "treacherous wife" for pursuing other gods?
**Hosea**

Which prophetic book begins, "The vision of Obadiah"?
**Obadiah**

Which prophet's last message is "Return to me, and I will return to you"?
**Zechariah**

Which prophet's vision in Daniel features four beasts representing successive empires?
**Daniel**

Which book opens, "The words of the prophet Micah of Moresheth"?
**Micah**

Which prophet repeatedly asks, "How long, O Lord, must I cry for help" in his opening chapter?
**Habakkuk**

Which prophetic book includes a judgment oracle against Tyre describing her as merchant of the peoples?
**Ezekiel**

Which prophet's vision shows the LORD riding on a swift cloud and coming to punish Assyria?
**Isaiah**

Which chapter of Isaiah contains the "Suffering Servant" songs (four distinct sections)?
**Isaiah 52–53**

Which prophetic book ends with the exhortation "Behold, I send my messenger, and he will prepare the way before me"?
**Malachi**

Which title in Isaiah 9:6 follows "Wonderful Counselor"?
**Mighty God**

Which chapter of Isaiah prophesies that on that day people will "beat their swords into plowshares"?
**Isaiah 2**

Which chapter of Isaiah contains the prophet's vision of the Lord seated on a high and lofty throne?
**Isaiah 6**

Which chapter of Jeremiah uses the potter's house allegory to illustrate God's sovereignty over nations?
**Jeremiah 18**

Which chapter of Jeremiah contains the promise of a "new covenant" written on the heart?
**Jeremiah 31**

Which chapter of Ezekiel begins with the prophet's vision of four living creatures and "wheels within wheels"?
**Ezekiel 1**

Which chapter of Ezekiel describes the valley of dry bones coming to life?
**Ezekiel 37**

Which chapter of Daniel recounts the fiery furnace trial of Shadrach, Meshach, and Abednego?
**Daniel 3**

Which chapter of Daniel contains the handwriting on the wall at Belshazzar's feast?
**Daniel 5**

Which chapter of Hosea opens with the LORD commanding, "Go, take for yourself a wife of harlotry"?
**Hosea 1**

Which chapter of Joel warns that "the day of the Lord is great and very terrible"?
**Joel 2**

Which chapter of Amos contains the vision of locusts described as the first of the Lord's judgments?
**Amos 7**

Which chapter of Amos depicts the vision of a basket of summer fruit, saying "the end is near"?
**Amos 8**

Which chapter of Obadiah pronounces the oracle against Edom's violence toward Jacob?
**Obadiah 1**

Which chapter of Jonah records the city of Nineveh repenting at the prophet's warning?
**Jonah 3**

Which chapter of Micah declares, "He has told you, O man, what is good; and what does the Lord require of you but to do justice, and to love kindness"?
**Micah 6**

Which chapter of Micah foretells the ruler of Israel coming from Bethlehem Ephrathah?
**Micah 5**

Which chapter of Nahum opens by describing the LORD as "a jealous and avenging God"?
**Nahum 1**

Which chapter of Habakkuk concludes, "Though the fig tree should not blossom… yet I will rejoice in the Lord"?
**Habakkuk 3**

Which chapter of Zephaniah proclaims, "The great day of the Lord is near, near and hastens fast"?
**Zephaniah 1**

Which chapter of Haggai chides the people for living in paneled houses while the LORD's house lay in ruins?
**Haggai 1**

Which chapter of Zechariah presents two olive trees flanking a golden lampstand?
**Zechariah 4**

Which chapter of Zechariah features a flying scroll that brings curses on thieves and swearers?
**Zechariah 5**

Which chapter of Malachi issues the challenge, "Bring the full tithe into the storehouse"?
**Malachi 3**

Which prophet was commanded to lie on his left side for 390 days and on his right side for 40 days?
**Ezekiel**

Which prophet's symbolic act involved wearing a yoke on his neck to signify Judah's subjection?
**Jeremiah**

Which prophet's message begins, "Thus says the Lord: 'Cursed is the man who trusts in man'"?
**Jeremiah**

Which prophet was instructed to marry a woman of harlotry as a sign of Israel's unfaithfulness?
**Hosea**

Which prophet questions God, "Why do you make me see iniquity and why do you idly look at wrong"?
**Habakkuk**

Which prophet laments, "How the faithful city has become a harlot!"?
**Nahum**

Which prophet sees water flowing from Jerusalem to heal the Dead Sea?
**Ezekiel**

Which prophet writes of a "remnant" returning with singing and everlasting joy?
**Isaiah**

Which prophet describes the "beautiful on the mountains" bringing good news of peace?
**Isaiah**

Which prophet exclaims, "I hate, I despise your feast days and your solemn assemblies"?
**Amos**

Which prophetic book opens with the words, "The vision of Obadiah"?
**Obadiah**

Which minor prophet's opening line is "The word of the Lord that came to Joel son of Pethuel"?
**Joel**

Which prophet addresses the people as "lost sheep of the house of Israel"?
**Ezekiel**

Which prophet tells of a future shepherd over God's flock who will be called "Prince of Peace"?
**Isaiah**

Which prophet proclaims, "Behold, the days are coming, declares the Lord, when I will make a new covenant"?
**Jeremiah**

Which chapter of Isaiah depicts the wolf lying down with the lamb and a little child leading them?
**Isaiah 11**

Which chapter of Isaiah begins, "Ho, everyone who thirsts, come to the waters; and you who have no money, come, buy and eat"?
**Isaiah 55**

Which chapter of Jeremiah describes God commanding the prophet to buy a linen loincloth and bury it as a sign?
**Jeremiah 13**

Which chapter of Jeremiah uses the potter's house to illustrate God's sovereign right to reshape nations?
**Jeremiah 18**

Which chapter of Ezekiel opens with the prophet lying on his side for 390 days as a sign?
**Ezekiel 4**

Which chapter of Ezekiel sees the glory of the Lord depart the temple by the eastern gateway?
**Ezekiel 10**

Which chapter of Daniel records Daniel and his friends refusing the king's delicacies and thriving on vegetables?
**Daniel 1**

Which chapter of Daniel depicts Nebuchadnezzar's dream of a four-metal statue and God's rock smashing it?
**Daniel 2**

Which chapter of Hosea begins, "The word of the Lord that came to Hosea, son of Beeri"?
**Hosea 1**

Which chapter of Hosea opens, "Come, let us return to the Lord; for he has torn us, that he may heal us"?
**Hosea 6**

Which chapter of Joel calls Judah to "rend your hearts and not your garments"?
**Joel 2**

Which chapter of Joel depicts the Valley of Jehoshaphat where God will judge the nations?
**Joel 3**

Which chapter of Amos contains a vision of a plumb line testing Israel's wall?
**Amos 7**

Which chapter of Amos depicts the vision of a basket of summer fruit, saying "The end has come"?
**Amos 8**

Which chapter of Obadiah pronounces the oracle against Edom for violence toward Jacob?
**Obadiah 1**

Which chapter of Jonah describes the Ninevites' repentance and God's relenting?
**Jonah 3**

Which chapter of Micah opens with a judgment oracle against Samaria and Jerusalem?
**Micah 1**

Which chapter of Micah foretells a ruler coming from Bethlehem who shepherds Israel in the last days?
**Micah 5**

Which chapter of Nahum begins, "A jealous and avenging God is the Lord"?
**Nahum 1**

Which chapter of Nahum portrays Nineveh's merchants mourning her ruin and lamenting her trade?
**Nahum 3**

Which chapter of Habakkuk begins, "How long, O Lord, must I call for help, and you will not hear"?
**Habakkuk 1**

Which chapter of Habakkuk declares, "But the righteous shall live by his faith"?
**Habakkuk 2**

Which chapter of Zephaniah announces, "The great day of the Lord is near, near and hastens fast"?
**Zephaniah 1**

Which chapter of Haggai rebukes the people for living in paneled houses while God's house was in ruins?
**Haggai 1**

Which chapter of Haggai proclaims, "The glory of this latter house shall be greater than the former"?
**Haggai 2**

Which chapter of Zechariah features Joshua the high priest in filthy garments made clean?
**Zechariah 3**

Which chapter of Zechariah presents a flying scroll that curses thieves and perjurers?
**Zechariah 5**

Which chapter of Malachi warns, "I will send the curse upon your blessings; indeed I have cursed them"?
**Malachi 3**

Which chapter of Malachi concludes with "Behold, I will send you Elijah the prophet before the great and awesome day of the Lord comes"?
**Malachi 4**

Which Hebrew term in Isaiah 14:12 is translated "morning star, son of the dawn"?
**Heilel**

Which winged beings cry "Holy, holy, holy, is the LORD of hosts" in Isaiah 6?
**Seraphim**

In Isaiah 37:36, what does the angel of the LORD do to the Assyrian army?
**Strike down**

What does God promise to give Cyrus as spoil in Isaiah 45:3?
**Treasures**

In Jeremiah 9:1, what does the prophet say he would do all day if he could?
**Weep**

Which town does Rachel weep for her children in Jeremiah 31:15?
**Ramah**

What does the LORD say He has for Israel's future in Jeremiah 29:11?
**Plans**

Which chapter of Ecclesiastes concludes, "Fear God and keep his commandments, for this is the whole duty of man"?
**Ecclesiastes 12**

Which chapter of Job contains God's first speech out of the whirlwind, challenging Job's understanding?
**Job 38**

Which chapter of Isaiah prophesies the coming of Immanuel, "God with us"?
**Isaiah 7**

In Ezekiel 24:3, what vessel does the LORD command the prophet to set on fire?
**Pot**

According to Ezekiel 36:28, where will God put His people to live?
**Their land**

What kind of trees beside the river of life in Ezekiel 47 bear fruit every month?
**Trees of life**

What did the angel tell Daniel to do with the mysterious words in Daniel 12:4?
**Shut up**

To which wilderness does Hosea say God will allure Ephraim in Hosea 2:14?
**Wilderness of Judah**

What will be poured out on all flesh in Joel 2:28?
**Spirit**

Which chapter of Isaiah names Cyrus by name as the LORD's anointed?
**Isaiah 45**

Which chapter of Jeremiah prophesies the "new covenant" written on the heart?
**Jeremiah 31**

Which chapter of Ezekiel prophesies Gog and Magog invading Israel from the north?
**Ezekiel 38**

Which chapter of Daniel describes the fiery furnace trial of Shadrach, Meshach, and Abednego?
**Daniel 3**

What should "roll down like waters" in Amos 5:24?
**Justice**

How is Edom described when judgment comes in Obadiah 1:4?
**Drunken**

How long did Jonah spend in the belly of the great fish in Jonah 1:17?
**Three days and three nights**

What does Micah say the LORD requires of you besides justice and kindness in Micah 6:8?
**Walking humbly**

What does Nahum call the LORD to those who take refuge in Him in Nahum 1:7?
**Good**

What is the vision to be written plainly on tablets so a runner can read it in Habakkuk 2:2?
**Tablet**

Which chapter of Isaiah names Cyrus as God's "anointed," the one who will rebuild Jerusalem?
**Isaiah 45**

Which chapter of Jeremiah depicts the boiling pot tilting away from the north as a symbol of impending judgment?
**Jeremiah 1**

Which chapter of Ezekiel prophesies the attack of Gog of the land of Magog against Israel?
**Ezekiel 38**

What does Zephaniah say the LORD will do for His people in Zephaniah 3:17?
**Joy**

What will "fill this house with glory greater than the former" in Haggai 2:9?
**Glory**

What "Branch" title does Zechariah bestow on the future king in Zechariah 6:12?
**Branch**

How does Zechariah 9:9 describe the coming king of Zion's mount?
**On a donkey**

What will the LORD be over all the earth in Zechariah 14:9?
**King over all the earth**

What are the people instructed to bring into the storehouse in Malachi 3:10?
**Tithe**

What will rise with healing in its wings according to Malachi 4:2?
**Sun**

Which wild animal lies down with the young goat in Isaiah 11:6?
**Leopard**

In Isaiah 19:1, who descends like a swift cloud with noise like a host?
**The Lord**

Who is like a tree planted by water in Jeremiah 17:8?
**Water**

What sprout from David's line will be "our righteousness" in Jeremiah 23:5?
**Righteous Branch**

What appears like a rainbow around God's throne in Ezekiel 1:28?
**Rainbow**

Which chapter of Daniel presents the vision of four beasts rising from the sea?
**Daniel 7**

Which chapter of Hosea begins, "Come, let us return to the Lord; for he has torn, that he may heal us"?
**Hosea 6**

Which chapter of Zechariah prophesies that God will pour out a spirit of grace and supplication on the house of David?
**Zechariah 12**

Which chapter of Isaiah opens with "Comfort, comfort my people, says your God"?
**Isaiah 40**

What did the LORD give Ezekiel that was "full of lamentations, mourning, and woe" in Ezekiel 2:10?
**Scroll**

Where does the LORD say He will place His name in Ezekiel 48:35?
**Heaven**

From which country did God say, "Out of Egypt I called my son" in Hosea 11:1?
**My son**

What does Amos say the LORD will do before revealing His secret in Amos 3:7?
**Without revealing**

Which chapter of Isaiah includes the "Servant Song" in which the servant is "exalted and lifted up"?
**Isaiah 52**

Which chapter of Jeremiah contains the "Temple Sermon," beginning, "Amend your ways and your deeds"?
**Jeremiah 7**

What will the house of Jacob "possess" on Edom's judgment in Obadiah 1:17?
**Possess the land**

What did Jonah vow to give to the LORD in Jonah 2:9?
**Sacrifice**

What will people beat into plowshares in Micah 4:3?
**Swords**

Which chapter of Isaiah promises, "Behold, I create new heavens and a new earth, and the former things shall not be remembered"?
**Isaiah 65**

Which chapter of Jeremiah opens with a vision of a boiling pot tilting away from the north?
**Jeremiah 1**

Which judgment in Nahum 2:4 likens chariots to flickering torches?
**Torches**

Who is declared "my strength" in Habakkuk 3:19?
**God my strength**

What does Zephaniah say will be silent before the LORD in Zephaniah 2:11?
**Mountains**

What two things will the LORD shake according to Haggai 2:6?
**Heavens and earth**

Which chapter of Ezekiel prophesies the invasion of Gog of the land of Magog against Israel?
**Ezekiel 38**

Which chapter of Daniel portrays the vision of a ram with two horns and a male goat breaking its horns?
**Daniel 8**

What city does Zechariah promise will be a "wall of fire" around it in Zechariah 2:5?
**Jerusalem**

Who is described as "a brand plucked from the fire" in Zechariah 3:8?
**A brand plucked from the fire**

How many people from many nations will take hold of a Jew's robe in Zechariah 8:23?
**Ten**

Which patriarch does God say He loved in Malachi 1:2?
**Jacob**

Which brothers are named in Malachi 1:2 as God's?
**Jacob and Esau**

Which chapter of Daniel promises "many shall purify themselves and make themselves white, and be refined"?
**Daniel 12**

Which chapter of Zechariah prophesies that God will pour out a spirit of grace and supplication on the house of David?
**Zechariah 12**

What is to be "finished" at the seventy weeks' end in Daniel 9:24?
**Transgression**

How does Joel describe the "day of the Lord" in Joel 2:1?
**Darkness**

Which psalm opens Book V of the Psalter with the refrain "Oh give thanks to the Lord, for he is good; for his steadfast love endures forever"?
**Psalm 107**

Which psalm of ascent begins, "I was glad when they said to me, 'Let us go to the house of the Lord'"?
**Psalm 122**

Which penitential psalm opens, "Have mercy on me, O God, according to your steadfast love"?
**Psalm 51**

Which psalm declares, "The Lord is my light and my salvation; whom shall I fear?"
**Psalm 27**

Which psalm contains the imagery "Your hands have made and fashioned me; give me understanding that I may learn your commandments"?
**Psalm 119:73**

Which psalmist sings, "Many are the afflictions of the righteous, but the Lord delivers him out of them all"?
**Psalm 34:19**

Which psalm opens, "Great is the Lord and most worthy of praise in the city of our God"?
**Psalm 48**

Which proverb compares the power of words to the power of life and death?
**Proverbs 18:21**

Which proverb states, "As iron sharpens iron, so one man sharpens another"?
**Proverbs 27:17**

Which proverb counsels, "Trust in the Lord with all your heart, and do not lean on your own understanding"?
**Proverbs 3:5**

Which proverb declares, "Hope deferred makes the heart sick, but a desire fulfilled is a tree of life"?
**Proverbs 13:12**

Which proverb advises, "A soft answer turns away wrath, but a harsh word stirs up anger"?
**Proverbs 15:1**

Which chapter of Ecclesiastes warns, "Be not quick in your spirit to become angry, for anger lodges in the heart of fools"?
**Ecclesiastes 7**

Which chapter of Isaiah contains the "Suffering Servant" song, "He was wounded for our transgressions"?
**Isaiah 53**

# DIFFICULT

## New Testament - The Gospels

Which Aramaic word does Jesus use to address God in prayer?
**Abba**

On what occasion does Jesus quote "My God, my God, why have you forsaken me?" in Aramaic?
**Crucifixion**

What Aramaic term does Jesus speak to Mary Magdalene after His resurrection?
**Rabboni**

Which Gospel uniquely records the Parable of the Unmerciful Servant?
**Matthew**

In which Gospel does Jesus declare, "I am the bread of life"?
**John**

Which Old Testament scroll does Jesus read from in the Nazareth synagogue?
**Isaiah**

On which hill did Jesus deliver the Sermon on the Mount according to Matthew?
**Mount of Beatitudes**

Which disciple does Jesus name "Petros," meaning rock?
**Peter**

In which town did Jesus perform His first public miracle according to John?
**Cana**

What sign does Jesus give to identify His betrayer in the Garden of Gethsemane?
**A kiss**

Which Gospel contains Jesus' high priestly prayer?
**John**

Which Gospel tells the story of the Good Samaritan?
**Luke**

What collective name is given to Jesus' teachings in John chapters 14–16?
**Farewell Discourse**

In which Gospel does Jesus say the Son of Man "did not come to be served but to serve"?
**Matthew**

At which pool beside the Sheep Gate does Jesus heal a paralyzed man?
**Pool of Bethesda**

Which Gospel traces Jesus' genealogy through Mary back to Adam?
**Luke**

What title does Jesus use in John 10 to describe Himself as sacrificing for the sheep?
**Good Shepherd**

Which king orders the massacre of the infants in Bethlehem?
**Herod**

What was Matthew's occupation before following Jesus?
**Tax collector**

Who visits Jesus at night in John 3 to discuss being born again?
**Nicodemus**

In which Gospel does Jesus describe the Parable of the Sheep and the Goats?
**Matthew**

What does Jesus say is the greatest commandment?
**Love God**

What does He name as the second, like the first?
**Love your neighbor**

Which Gospel records the Transfiguration on a "high mountain"?
**Matthew**

Who appears with Jesus at the Transfiguration?
**Moses and Elijah**

How many days does Jesus fast during His temptation in the wilderness?
**Forty**

Which Gospel is the shortest in the New Testament?
**Mark**

Which Gospel begins with a poetic hymn about the Word?
**John**

To whom did Jesus say, "I will give you the keys of the kingdom of heaven"?
**Peter**

Near which town did Jesus feed the 5,000 in John 6?
**Bethsaida**

Which two creatures does Jesus compare Pharisees' hypocrisy to straining?
**Gnat and camel**

In the Parable of the Talents, how many talents does the unfaithful servant bury?
**One**

How many pieces of silver does Judas receive for betraying Jesus?
**Thirty**

Which Gospel notes that Jesus wept over Jerusalem?
**Luke**

To whom does Jesus say, "Feed my lambs" after His resurrection?
**Peter**

After the resurrection breakfast, how many fish do the disciples catch?
**153**

By tradition, on which mountain did the Transfiguration take place?
**Mount Tabor**

Which Gospel immediately follows its resurrection appearances with the Ascension?
**Luke**

Who does Jesus say is greatest in the kingdom, lifted up like a child?
**Child**

In which Gospel is the Parable of the Talents found?
**Matthew**

On which shore does Jesus cook fish for the disciples after His resurrection?
**Sea of Tiberias**

Which Gospel describes an earthquake at the moment of Jesus' resurrection?
**Matthew**

Who is the first person to see the risen Jesus at the tomb?
**Mary Magdalene**

Which Gospel uniquely includes the account of the woman caught in adultery?
**John**

What is the shortest verse in the entire Bible?
**Jesus wept**

In which Gospel does the Spirit descend like a dove at Jesus' baptism?
**Matthew**

Which Gospel portrays Jesus' sweat like drops of blood in Gethsemane?
**Luke**

Who declares, "Truly this man was the Son of God" at the cross?
**The centurion**

Which Gospel records Jesus healing a centurion's servant from a distance?
**Matthew**

In which town did Jesus grow up?
**Nazareth**

Which two disciples did Jesus nicknamed "Sons of Thunder"?
**James and John**

Which Gospel contains the Parable of the Wicked Tenants?
**Matthew**

Which Gospel includes the Parable of the Persistent Widow?
**Luke**

Which Old Testament prophet did Jesus quote regarding a messenger preparing the way?
**Malachi**

In which Gospel is the Parable of the Friend at Midnight found?
**Luke**

Which Gospel records the conversation with the Samaritan woman at Jacob's well?
**John**

In which Gospel does Jesus say, "No one can serve two masters"?
**Matthew**

Which Gospel includes the Temple cleansing at the beginning rather than at the end?
**John**

Which Gospel emphasizes Jesus' ministry in Galilee with frequent "immediately"?
**Mark**

Which Gospel begins with a genealogy tracing Jesus back to Abraham?
**Matthew**

Which Gospel records Jesus' words, "I am the resurrection and the life"?
**John**

Which Gospel places the Parable of the Good Samaritan within a lawyer's question?
**Luke**

Which Gospel uniquely mentions Jesus weeping at Lazarus's tomb?
**John**

Which Gospel records the commissioning of the seventy-two disciples?
**Luke**

Which Gospel records Jesus' statement, "Foxes have holes, and birds of the air have nests, but the Son of Man has nowhere to lay his head"?
**Matthew**

Which Gospel records the diagnosis of John the Baptist's doubts in prison?
**Matthew**

In which Gospel does Jesus heal a woman with a hemorrhage simply by her touching his garment?
**Mark**

Which Gospel includes the Parable of the Great Banquet where invitees make excuses?
**Luke**

Which Gospel records Peter's denial in the courtyard with a rooster crowing?
**Matthew**

Which Gospel shows Jesus calming the storm with the rebuke "Peace! Be still!"?
**Mark**

Which Gospel begins with John the Baptist calling out in the wilderness, "Repent, for the kingdom of heaven is at hand"?
**Matthew**

Which Gospel records Jesus' ascension from Bethany?
**Luke**

In which Gospel does Jesus speak the "High Priestly Prayer"?
**John**

Which Gospel includes the detailed healing of the blind man Bartimaeus at Jericho?
**Mark**

Which Gospel mentions Zacchaeus the tax collector climbing a sycamore tree?
**Luke**

Which Gospel records the phrase "It is finished" on the cross?
**John**

Which Gospel mentions the sudden appearance of an angel rolling back the tomb stone?
**Matthew**

Which Gospel records Jesus' post-resurrection walk to Emmaus?
**Luke**

Which Gospel mentions Simon of Cyrene carrying Jesus' cross?
**Mark**

Which Gospel records Jesus healing a centurion's servant whose faith He praises as "great"?
**Luke**

Which Gospel includes the story of the widow's mite?
**Mark**

Which Gospel opens with the Greek poetic prologue "In the beginning…"?
**John**

Which Gospel uniquely records Jesus' command to "Occupy till I come"?
**Luke**

Which council was Joseph of Arimathea a member of?
**Sanhedrin**

At what hour does Mark say Jesus was crucified?
**Third hour**

What Greek word for "good news" appears in each Gospel's theme?
**Euangelion**

In which town did Jesus heal a blind man using spittle and laying on of hands?
**Bethsaida**

At what time of day did Nicodemus visit Jesus?
**Night**

Which city did Jairus lead as synagogue ruler?
**Capernaum**

Which Gospel opens by addressing "most excellent Theophilus"?
**Luke**

Who asked Jesus, "What is truth?" during His trial?
**Pilate**

In which Gospel does Jesus wash His disciples' feet?
**John**

Which Gospel records Jesus healing a centurion's servant from a distance?
**Matthew**

Who carried water in a bowl in the wilderness narrative?
**Naaman** *(he dipped in the Jordan)*

Which Gospel emphasizes immediacy with the word "immediately" over 40 times?
**Mark**

Which disciple did Jesus rename "Cephas," meaning rock?
**Peter**

Which Gospel traces Jesus' lineage through Mary back to Adam?
**Luke**

Which Gospel uses "Kingdom of Heaven" rather than "Kingdom of God"?
**Matthew**

Which miracle is described in all four Gospels?
**Feeding of the 5,000**

What does Jesus call the coin used to pay the temple tax?
**Stater**

In which Gospel does Jesus walk on the Sea of Galilee and rebuke the wind?
**Matthew**

Who climbed a sycamore tree to see Jesus as He passed?
**Zacchaeus**

Which Gospel records the "I am the resurrection and the life" discourse?
**John**

In which Gospel does Jesus promise the Holy Spirit as the Spirit of truth?
**John**

What Aramaic term does Jesus use to address His risen mentor?
**Rabboni**

Which Gospel uniquely notes Jesus saying, "Foxes have holes, but the Son of Man has nowhere to lay his head"?
**Matthew**

In which Gospel does Jesus sweat "great drops of blood" in Gethsemane?
**Luke**

Which Gospel includes the Parable of the Rich Fool?
**Luke**

What title does Jesus use for Himself in John 10 to describe His care for believers?
**Good Shepherd**

Which Gospel mentions Joseph of Arimathea wrapping Jesus' body in linen?
**John**

In which Gospel does an earthquake roll back the tomb stone at Jesus' resurrection?
**Matthew**

Which Gospel records the post-resurrection breakfast of fish and bread on the shore?
**John**

Which Gospel uniquely mentions two Marys at the empty tomb?
**Matthew**

Which Gospel is the only one to record the Parable of the Talents?
**Matthew**

Which Gospel begins with John the Baptist's wilderness proclamation?
**Mark**

Which Gospel begins with the poetic "In the beginning was the Word"?
**John**

Which Gospel includes the Parable of the Persistent Widow?
**Luke**

Who did Jesus commend for having "great faith" from afar?
**Centurion**

Which Gospel places the Lord's Prayer before "Your kingdom come"?
**Matthew**

Which Gospel records Jesus' declaration, "I thirst," on the cross?
**John**

Which Gospel notes that the resurrected Jesus showed His hands and feet to Thomas?
**Luke**

Which Gospel records Jesus telling Peter three times, "Do you love me?…Feed my sheep"?
**John**

Which Gospel uniquely describes the cleansing of the temple twice—at the start and end?
**John**

Which Gospel records the commission to make disciples of all nations?
**Matthew**

Which Gospel records Jesus' benediction, "Blessed are the peacemakers"?
**Matthew**

Which council was Joseph of Arimathea a member of?
**Sanhedrin**

At what hour does Mark record Jesus' crucifixion?
**Third hour**

What Greek term for "good news" is the root of our word "Gospel"?
**Euangelion**

In which town did Jesus restore sight to a blind man by spitting and laying on of hands?
**Bethsaida**

What time of day did Nicodemus come to Jesus by night?
**Night**

Which town was Jairus ruler of the synagogue?
**Capernaum**

Which Gospel opens by addressing "most excellent Theophilus"?
**Luke**

Who asked Jesus "What is truth?" at His trial?
**Pilate**

Which Gospel alone records Jesus washing His disciples' feet?
**John**

Which Gospel uniquely tells of the woman caught in adultery?
**John**

Which Gospel records Jesus healing a centurion's servant from afar?
**Matthew**

Which Gospel emphasizes "immediately" over forty times in describing Jesus' actions?
**Mark**

Which disciple does Jesus rename "Peter," meaning "rock"?
**Peter**

Which Gospel traces Jesus' ancestry all the way back to Adam?
**Luke**

Which Gospel consistently uses the phrase "kingdom of heaven" instead of "kingdom of God"?
**Matthew**

What miracle—feeding a multitude with loaves and fish—appears in all four Gospels?
**Feeding of the 5,000**

What coin does Jesus ask to see to pay the temple tax?
**Stater**

Which Gospel is the only one to name the man born blind whom Jesus healed?
**John**

Which Gospel begins with a genealogy of Jesus through Abraham?
**Matthew**

In which Gospel does Mary anoint Jesus' feet with expensive perfume at Bethany?
**Matthew**

Which Gospel records Jesus' declaration "I am the resurrection and the life"?
**John**

Which Gospel places the Good Samaritan parable in response to a lawyer's question?
**Luke**

Which Gospel alone mentions Jesus weeping at Lazarus's tomb?
**John**

Which Gospel records Jesus sending out seventy-two disciples two by two?
**Luke**

Which Gospel contains the Parable of the Rich Fool?
**Luke**

Which Gospel records Jesus' lament "Foxes have holes, and birds of the air have nests, but the Son of Man has nowhere to lay his head"?
**Matthew**

Which Gospel alone names Bartimaeus as the blind beggar by Jericho?
**Mark**

Which Gospel introduces John the Baptist with the words "In those days came John the Baptist"?
**Matthew**

Which Gospel opens with the poetic hymn "In the beginning was the Word"?
**John**

Which Gospel places Jesus' teaching on the vine and branches in a lengthy discourse?
**John**

Which Gospel uniquely tells of the Parable of the Growing Seed?
**Mark**

Which Gospel records Jesus' prayer for His disciples immediately before His arrest?
**John**

Which Gospel mentions a young man wearing only a linen cloth fleeing naked at Jesus' arrest?
**Mark**

Which Gospel alone records the Parable of the Two Sons (one says yes but doesn't go; the other says no but goes)?
**Matthew**

Which Gospel includes the Parable of the Ten Virgins?
**Matthew**

Which Gospel records Jesus' promise to the penitent thief, "Today you will be with me in Paradise"?
**Luke**

In which Gospel does Jesus use the Aramaic word "Talitha cumi" to raise a girl from the dead?
**Mark**

Which Gospel records a miraculous catch of 153 fish after Jesus' resurrection?
**John**

Which Gospel uniquely includes the healing of a servant's ear by Jesus touching it?
**Luke**

Which Gospel records Peter's threefold restoration question, "Do you love me?" and "Feed my sheep"?
**John**

Which Gospel records Jesus' trial before Herod Antipas?
**Luke**

Which Gospel alone calls the fish breakfast by the shore after the resurrection?
**John**

Which Gospel begins its passion narrative with Judas's decision to betray?
**Mark**

Which Gospel alone records the Parable of the Friend at Midnight?
**Luke**

Which Gospel records Jesus' vision of the sign of Jonah as the only sign given?
**Matthew**

Which Gospel records the declaration "My God, my God, why have you forsaken me?" in Aramaic?
**Mark**

Which servant's ear did Jesus heal after Peter cut it off?
**Malchus**

Which Gospel names the high priest's servant whose ear was cut off?
**John**

In which Gospel does Jesus tell Peter, "Put your sword back into its place"?
**Luke**

What sign did Jesus say would be given instead of a sign, pointing to Jonah?
**Sign of Jonah**

Which Gospel records Jesus asking, "Father, forgive them, for they know not what they do"?
**Luke**

What did Jesus place the bitter wine vinegar on to give him a drink?
**Hyssop**

Which Gospel alone records the detail of a hyssop stalk at the crucifixion?
**John**

Which term does Jesus use for hypocrites straining out a gnat and swallowing a camel?
**Brood**

Which Gospel depicts Jesus quoting Isaiah's prophecy about the "poor having good news preached to them"?
**Luke**

Who did Jesus call a "son of peace" sent to a village?
**A disciple**

Which Gospel illustrates Jesus sending disciples "two by two" ahead of Him?
**Luke**

What made Jesus weep in the shortest recorded verse?
**Lazarus's tomb**

Which Gospel records Jesus' lament over Jerusalem: "Would that you, even you, had known…"?
**Luke**

Which Gospel notes that Jesus saw Nathanael coming under the fig tree?
**John**

Which disciple did Jesus call "Cephas," meaning "rock"?
**Peter**

Which Gospel is the only one to record the Parable of the Dragnet?
**Matthew**

What gift did Jesus say a prophet receives for living in peace in His name?
**A prophet's reward**

Which Gospel contains the Parable of the Two Debtors?
**Luke**

Which Gospel notes that Jesus healed blind Bartimaeus by asking, "What do you want me to do for you?"
**Mark**

Which Gospel uniquely includes the healing of a mute man by feeding him a tongue loosed?
**Mark**

What Old Testament figure does Jesus liken the sign of Jonah to?
**Jonah**

Which Gospel tells of Jesus being anointed by a sinful woman at Simon the Pharisee's house?
**Luke**

Which Gospel records Peter's confession "You are the Christ, the Son of the living God"?
**Matthew**

Which Gospel shows Jesus saying that John the Baptist is the Elijah who was to come?
**Matthew**

What specific tree's fruit did Jesus curse for not being in season?
**Fig tree**

Which Gospel records the disciples plucking grain on the Sabbath?
**Matthew**

Which Gospel records Jesus declaring, "I am the bread of life"?
**John**

Which Gospel says Jesus is the "light of the world"?
**John**

Which Gospel alone includes the Parable of the Hidden Treasure?
**Matthew**

Which Gospel records Jesus saying, "You strain out a gnat but swallow a camel"?
**Matthew**

Which Gospel shows Jesus sending out the twelve apostles, giving them authority over unclean spirits?
**Mark**

Which Gospel depicts Jesus' agony with sweat "like great drops of blood"?
**Luke**

Which Gospel records the Parable of the Barren Fig Tree?
**Luke**

Which Gospel notes that Jesus charged the healed leper to show himself to the priest and offer for cleansing?
**Mark**

Which Gospel alone mentions Jesus blessing the children by laying on of hands?
**Mark**

Which Gospel contains the Parable of the Pharisee and the Tax Collector?
**Luke**

Which Gospel records Jesus saying, "No one knows that day or hour"?
**Matthew**

Which Gospel records Jesus' teaching on the narrow and hard way that "leads to life"?
**Matthew**

Which Gospel alone includes Jesus' statement "I am the good shepherd"?
**John**

Which Gospel opens with Zechariah's prophecy about John the Baptist's coming?
**Luke**

Which Gospel includes Jesus' first miracle at a wedding in Cana?
**John**

Which Gospel records Jesus telling Jairus, "Do not fear, only believe"?
**Mark**

Which Gospel alone mentions the sixty-ninth verse of chapter 9 as "Jesus' heartbeat" of compassion?
**Luke**

Which Gospel records Jesus' prediction that Elijah must come first?
**Matthew**

Which Gospel depicts the coin found in a fish's mouth used to pay the temple tax?
**Matthew**

Which servant's ear did Jesus heal after Peter cut it off?
**Malchus**

Which Gospel names the high priest's servant whose ear was cut off?
**John**

In which Gospel does Jesus tell Peter, "Put your sword back into its place"?
**Matthew**

What sign did Jesus give to point to His resurrection, alluding to Jonah?
**Sign of Jonah**

Which Gospel records Jesus praying, "Father, forgive them, for they know not what they do"?
**Luke**

What plant did the soldiers use to lift a sponge of sour wine to Jesus on the cross?
**Hyssop**

Which Gospel alone mentions the hyssop at the crucifixion?
**John**

Which harsh term does Jesus use for hypocrites who strain out gnats but swallow camels?
**Brood**

Which Gospel quotes Jesus reading, "The Spirit of the Lord is upon me" from Isaiah?
**Luke**

Which disciple did Jesus entrust His mother to at the cross?
**John**

After which miracle does Jesus say, "Follow me, and leave the dead to bury their own dead"?
**Calling of Matthew**

Which Gospel records Jesus weeping over Jerusalem with the lament "If you had known…"?
**Luke**

Who did Jesus describe as an "Israelite indeed, in whom there is no deceit"?
**Nathanael**

Which Gospel uniquely calls Jesus "the bread of life"?
**John**

Which Gospel opens its genealogy of Jesus with Abraham?
**Matthew**

Which Gospel records Jesus calling a Syrophoenician woman a "dog" in order to teach faith?
**Mark**

At which body of water did Jesus calm a storm by rebuking wind and waves?
**Sea of Galilee**

Which Gospel names the demon-possessed man healed in the region of the Gerasenes as having many?
**Mark**

What Greek command does Jesus use to open the ears of the deaf man?
**Ephphatha**

Which Gospel mentions Jesus' sweat "like drops of blood" in Gethsemane?
**Luke**

Which Gospel alone records the Parable of the Rich Fool?
**Luke**

Which Gospel states "No one lights a lamp and puts it under a bushel"?
**Mark**

Which Gospel records Jesus receiving a coin in a fish's mouth to pay the temple tax?
**Matthew**

Which Gospel notes that the centurion at the cross proclaimed, "Truly this man was the Son of God"?
**Mark**

Which Gospel begins its passion narrative with Judas conspiring to betray Jesus?
**Mark**

Who asked Jesus, "What is the great commandment?" and heard "Love God… love neighbor"?
**Lawyer**

Which Gospel records Jesus declaring "I am the light of the world"?
**John**

Which Gospel alone calls Jesus "the good shepherd"?
**John**

Which Gospel records Jesus' Parable of the Growing Seed?
**Mark**

Which Gospel records Jesus' blessing "Blessed are those who mourn"?
**Matthew**

Which Gospel describes the Transfiguration as occurring "six days" after Peter's confession?
**Matthew**

Which Gospel includes Jesus' high-priestly prayer, "Sanctify them in the truth; your word is truth"?
**John**

Which Gospel names the two on the road to Emmaus as Cleopas and an unnamed companion?
**Luke**

# DIFFICULT

# New Testament - The Acts of the Apostles

Which prophet's belt did Agabus use to bind his own hands and feet?
**Agabus**

In whose house did the early believers pray for Peter's release from prison?
**Mary**

Who was chosen by lot to replace Judas Iscariot?
**Matthias**

Which deacon baptized the Ethiopian eunuch?
**Philip**

What Old Testament scroll was the Ethiopian eunuch reading when Philip approached him?
**Isaiah**

What accusation did the Sadducees bring against Peter and John before the Sanhedrin?
**Teaching in Jesus' name**

Who was struck dead alongside his wife for lying to the Holy Spirit?
**Ananias**

How many men were appointed as deacons to serve tables in the Jerusalem church?
**Seven**

Which synagogue official did Paul confront in Paphos for opposing the gospel?
**Elymas**

What Roman proconsul believed after witnessing Paul's miracle on Cyprus?
**Sergius Paulus**

Which disciple baptized Cornelius and his household?
**Peter**

Who delivered the prophecy of a severe famine during Claudius's reign?
**Agabus**

Which prison were Paul and Silas held in when an earthquake freed them?
**Philippi jail**

What did Paul and Silas sing at midnight while imprisoned?
**Hymns**

Which jailer asked, "What must I do to be saved?"
**Philippi jailer**

Which woman seller of purple became Paul's first convert in Europe?
**Lydia**

At which location did Paul preach in Athens, referring to an altar to an unknown god?
**Areopagus**

What translation of "Areopagus" is commonly used in English Bibles?
**Mars Hill**

Which city's believers were commended for examining the Scriptures daily?
**Bereans**

Who accompanied Paul on his second missionary journey until Berea?
**Silas**

Which young disciple joined Paul and Silas at Lystra?
**Timothy**

What trade did Paul and Aquila share, making tents for a living?
**Tentmaking**

Which proconsul refused to judge Paul's case in Corinth, citing Roman law?
**Gallio**

Which two companions did Paul leave in Miletus on his way to Jerusalem?
**Trophimus and Sopater**

What was the name of the island where Paul was shipwrecked on the way to Rome?
**Malta**

Which Roman centurion escorted Paul to Rome?
**Julius**

At what Eastern shape-shifting pagan gods' temple did Demetrius incite a riot in Ephesus?
**Artemis**

How many people in Berea were described as noble for receiving the word with eagerness?
**Many**

Which prophet's image did Paul quote to explain the gospel's advance "from Jerusalem to Illyricum"?
**None; it's Paul's own summary**

Which port city did Paul sail from to embark on his first missionary journey?
**Seleucia**

On which island did Paul and Barnabas first preach the gospel to pagans?
**Cyprus**

Which word did Paul use to describe the men who "always go about from house to house" teaching contrary doctrines?
**Tyrannical**

What vision did Paul have in Troas prompting him to cross to Macedonia?
**A man of Macedonia pleading, "Come over to Macedonia and help us."**

Which person from Jerusalem joined Paul at Troas after this vision?
**Luke**

Which city did Paul visit where he reasoned in the synagogue three Sabbaths about Christ?
**Thessalonica**

Which Old Testament woman did Paul compare the Corinthians' immorality to in 1 Corinthians (though not Acts)?
**None; Acts has no Corinthians immorality**

Which group accused Paul of defiling the temple because he brought Trophimus into it?
**Jews from Asia**

Which Roman tribune rescued Paul from being flogged in Jerusalem?
**Claudius Lysias**

Who escorted Paul down to Caesarea for safe custody?
**Roman soldiers under Claudius Lysias**

Before which governor did Paul make his first defense in Caesarea?
**Felix**

Who succeeded Felix and heard Paul's appeal to Caesar?
**Festus**

Which king did Paul appear before after Festus consulted him?
**Agrippa II**

Who was Agrippa II's sister present at Paul's hearing?
**Bernice**

What was Festus's response after hearing Paul's appeal to Caesar?
**"You have appealed to Caesar; to Caesar you shall go."**

Which prophecy did Paul quote in AG's hearing when pressed to whom he testified?
**None; he summarized the prophets**

Which prophet does Peter quote to explain the outpouring of the Holy Spirit at Pentecost?
**Joel**

At Pentecost, Peter addressed the crowd as "Men of Judea and all who dwell where"?
**Jerusalem**

Who was chosen to serve tables and later became the first Christian martyr?
**Stephen**

Which crowd dragged Stephen outside the city to stone him?
**Men of Israel**

To which region did Philip go and preach after Stephen's martyrdom?
**Samaria**

Who offered money to buy the power to impart the Holy Spirit?
**Simon Magus**

In Joppa, whose death and resurrection caught Peter's attention?
**Tabitha**

What other name is Tabitha known by?
**Dorcas**

Which centurion's vision led Peter to visit Caesarea?
**Cornelius**

What food did Peter see in the sheet lowered from heaven?
**All kinds of animals**

What event convinced Jewish believers that the Gentiles should receive the Holy Spirit?
**Gentiles speaking in tongues**

Which couple lied about selling property and died as a result?
**Ananias and Sapphira**

Who was jailed for proclaiming Jesus as Lord and freed by an angel after prayers?
**Peter**

Which apostle was the first to be martyred, whose death is recorded in Acts?
**James**

Who reported Peter's escape to the assembled believers?
**Rhoda**

Which town did Peter travel to when he stayed with Simon the Tanner?
**Joppa**

What feast marked the outpouring of the Holy Spirit on believers?
**Pentecost**

Which emperor's decree led to the Jews being expelled from Rome?
**Claudius**

On his second journey, Paul traveled through Phrygia and which other province?
**Galatia**

At Lystra, what did the crowd call Paul and Barnabas after a healing?
**Hermes and Zeus**

Who accompanied Paul on his first missionary journey as his cousin?
**Mark**

What did Paul warn would happen if sailors abandoned the ship during his voyage?
**They would perish**

In which jail were Paul and Silas beaten and imprisoned?
**Philippi jail**

At what time did the earthquake occur that opened the prison doors?
**Midnight**

Who became the first European convert after hearing Paul in Philippi?
**Lydia**

Where did Paul preach in Athens at an altar "To an unknown god"?
**Areopagus**

In what language was the Ethiopian eunuch reading Scripture when Philip met him?
**Greek**

Who restored Saul's sight on the road to Damascus?
**Ananias**

How many days was Saul blind after his encounter with Jesus?
**Three**

What miraculous sign did Paul perform to quell a riot in Lystra?
**Healed a lame man**

What method did Paul's friends use to help him escape Damascus?
**Lowered him in a basket through an opening in the wall**

From which port in Lycia did Paul board an Alexandrian grain ship bound for Italy?
**Myra**

Which harbor on Crete did Paul advise against wintering at?
**Fair Havens**

Which harbor did Paul propose instead as more hospitable for winter?
**Phoenix**

What cargo was thrown overboard to lighten Paul's ship?
**Grain**

Which silversmith incited a riot in Ephesus over lost idol trade?
**Demetrius**

Who exclaimed, "Paul, you are insane; much learning is driving you mad"?
**Festus**

Which disease did Publius's father suffer from on Malta?
**Fever and dysentery**

Which centurion escorted Paul to Rome?
**Julius**

What condition of custody did Paul live under in Rome?
**House arrest**

Which community did Paul describe as noble for examining the Scriptures daily?
**Bereans**

Which Pharisee in the Sanhedrin advised leaving the apostles alone to see if their work was from God?
**Gamaliel**

Which envoy accompanied Paul back to Antioch with the Jerusalem Council's letter?
**Judas Barsabbas**

Who served alongside Judas Barsabbas as bearer of the Council's letter?
**Silas**

Which slave girl in Philippi, possessed with a spirit of divination, followed Paul and Silas crying out?
**Spirit of divination**

Which seven sons attempted to invoke Jesus' name over evil spirits in Ephesus?
**Sons of Sceva**

In which city was Jason arrested for hosting Paul and Silas?
**Thessalonica**

Which magistrate calmed the Ephesian riot over the worship of Artemis?
**Town clerk**

Which disciple from Lystra was circumcised so he could accompany Paul?
**Timothy**

Which Roman governor heard Paul appeal to Caesar?
**Felix**

Which king visited Festus to hear Paul's defense?
**Agrippa II**

Who sat beside King Agrippa during Paul's defense?
**Bernice**

In his final recorded speech, what did Paul say he was not disobedient to?
**Heaven's vision**

Which harbour on Malta did Paul's ship run aground?
**Melita**

Which word describes the early church's shared life in Acts 2?
**Koinonia**

Who was the first city official to invite Paul and Silas into his home after the Philippian earthquake?
**Jailer**

At which gate of the Jerusalem temple did Peter heal a lame man?
**Beautiful Gate**

Which port did Paul sail from when he left Corinth on his second journey?
**Cenchrea**

Who carried the new believers' relief gift from Antioch to Jerusalem?
**Judas Barsabbas**

Which silversmith incited a riot in Ephesus over idol-making?
**Demetrius**

Which Lewite family did Apollos belong to?
**Alexandrian**

Which Alexandrian Jew taught accurately about Jesus?
**Apollos**

In which province did Paul briefly teach at Iconium?
**Lycaonia**

Which fortress did the Romans use to guard Paul in Jerusalem?
**Antonia**

Who stood up in the Sanhedrin to suggest leaving the apostles alone?
**Gamaliel**

Which festival does Acts 12 say James was martyred just before?
**Passover**

What word does Luke use when the Spirit "fell" on the Gentiles at Cornelius's house?
**Epipipto**

Which Freetown in Acts welcomed Paul without hesitation?
**Cyprus**

Who fell from a window during Paul's long sermon at Troas?
**Eutychus**

Which town did Peter visit when he raised Tabitha?
**Joppa**

Who prophesied that Paul would be bound in Rome?
**Agabus**

Which sea do Acts writers refer to as "Adriatic"?
**Ionian Sea**

What is the Greek term Luke uses for the "mighty wind" at Pentecost?
**Seismos**

Who sold land but secretly kept part of the price, bringing judgment on himself?
**Ananias**

Which one of the seven deacons was from Cyrene?
**Nicolas**

In what city did Paul find a group of about twelve men who had only John's baptism?
**Ephesus**

Which agora did Paul preach in at Philippi?
**Marketplace**

Who baptized about twelve men in Ephesus who had only John's baptism?
**Paul**

Which goddess's temple was the center of civic identity in Ephesus?
**Artemis**

Which river did Lydia meet Paul and the others beside in Philippi?
**Gangites**

Who joined Paul in Macedonia after his Troas vision?
**Luke**

Which city's recharge of the gospel was hindered by a riot over "the Way"?
**Thessalonica**

Which Roman commander rescued Paul from a murderous crowd in Jerusalem?
**Claudius Lysias**

Who warned Paul not to go to Jerusalem, saying "the Jews will not let you go"?
**Spirit**

Which tree-tender in Acts 21 fell sick and was left behind at Miletus?
**Trophimus**

Whose daughter fell into a trance and prophesied Paul's trip to Rome was God's will?
**Philip**

Which soldier challenged Paul to prove he was a Roman citizen by a fine via birth?
**None; Paul declared**

Better: Which proconsul ordered Paul to be brought before him in Caesarea?
**Felix**

Which procurator did Paul appeal to after his trial before Felix?
**Caesar**

Which sister of Agrippa II was present at Paul's hearing?
**Bernice**

What natural phenomenon blinded Saul?
**Bright light**

Which port on Crete did Paul choose for winter lodging?
**Phoenix**

Who resolved the dispute about Gentile circumcision at the Jerusalem Council?
**James**

Which gift did Paul's Ephesians convert buy up and burn publicly?
**Magic books**

Which Old Testament psalm does Peter quote in Acts 2:27 about "neither will his flesh see corruption"?
**Psalm 16**

Which psalm does Peter cite in Acts 2:34 to prove Christ's exaltation at God's right hand?
**Psalm 110**

After Stephen's martyrdom, believers were scattered throughout which region?
**Judea**

The court official Candace, whose treasurer Philip baptized, reigned over which land?
**Ethiopia**

What did Peter see descending from heaven in a vision while at Joppa?
**A sheet with unclean animals**

In Joppa, Peter stayed in the house of Simon, whose trade was what?
**Tanner**

Who ran in when she heard Peter at the gate and announced his miraculous escape?
**Rhoda**

How many lashes did Paul say a man may receive under the law before he's deemed overall righteous?
**Thirty-nine**

Which harbour on Crete did Paul advise against wintering at before the storm?
**Fair Havens**

Which harbour did Paul suggest as more suitable for winter after Fair Havens?
**Phoenix**

What word does Luke use in Acts 10:44 to describe the Spirit's coming on the Gentiles?
**Epipipto**

Who offered money to the apostles in exchange for the Spirit's power to lay hands?
**Simon Magus**

Which couple lied about selling land and both fell dead when confronted by Peter?
**Ananias and Sapphira**

Which apostle used his shadow to heal the sick as they were carried into the streets of Jerusalem?
**Peter**

Who was chosen to replace Judas Iscariot by casting lots?
**Matthias**

Which deacon baptized the Ethiopian eunuch?
**Philip**

What scroll was the Ethiopian eunuch reading when Philip met him on the road?
**Isaiah**

Which city's synagogue ruler named Sergius Paulus believed after Elymas was struck blind?
**Paphos**

Which two companions did Paul leave in Miletus when he went to Jerusalem?
**Trophimus and Sopater**

Whose daughter fell from a third-story window during Paul's long sermon at Troas?
**Eutychus**

Who was the first to welcome Paul into Rome under house arrest?
**The centurion Julius**

Which Roman official accompanied Paul on his journey to Caesarea for his safety?
**Claudius Lysias**

Which host in Thessalonica was punished because he sheltered Paul?
**Jason**

Which goddess's temple merchants incited the riot in Ephesus against Paul?
**Artemis**

Who calmed the Ephesian assembly by warning them that the city's guild would answer them?
**Town clerk**

Which governor of Judea sent Paul to Rome after he appealed to Caesar?
**Festus**

Before Festus, which governor held Paul in custody for two years?
**Felix**

In Caesarea, before which king did Paul present his defense and almost persuade him to become a Christian?
**Agrippa II**

Which sister of Agrippa II sat beside him during Paul's defense?
**Bernice**

The Bereans were praised for what?
**Examining the Scriptures daily**

Which occupation did Luke mention for both Aquila and Priscilla, Paul's hosts in Corinth?
**Tentmakers**

What price was the burned magic books collected and thrown into the fire in Ephesus?
**Fifty thousand pieces of silver**

Which island's inhabitants showed "unusual kindness" to Paul after he was bitten by a viper?
**Malta**

Whose father did Paul heal of fever and dysentery on Malta?
**Publius's**

Which centurion escorted Paul safely to Rome after the shipwreck?
**Julius**

Who led the Jerusalem Council that decided Gentile believers need not be circumcised?
**James**

Which two leaders delivered the Council's letter to the Gentile church in Antioch?
**Judas Barsabbas and Silas**

Which port did Paul sail from at the start of his second missionary journey?
**Troas**

What Macedonian city's jailer asked Paul, "What must I do to be saved?"
**Philippi jailer**

Which seller of purple cloth in Philippi became Paul's first European convert?
**Lydia**

Which marketplace did Paul reason in at Philippi, leading to the jailer's conversion?
**Marketplace (Agora)**

Which harbour on Crete did Paul's ship first reach before the storm struck?
**Fair Havens**

Which harbour did Paul recommend as more suitable for wintering after Fair Havens proved unsafe?
**Phoenix**

Which porch of the Jerusalem temple is named as the place where Peter healed a man lame from birth?
**Solomon's Portico**

Which official's daughter fell into a trance and was raised by Peter's prayer?
**Tabitha**

Which Ethiopian official was returning from worship in Jerusalem when Philip met him?
**Candace's treasurer**

Who prophesied that Paul would be bound by the Jews and delivered to the Gentiles?
**Agabus**

Which prison was shaken by an earthquake that freed Paul and Silas?
**Philippi jail**

Which believer's home became the gathering place for believers praying for Peter's release?
**Mary, mother of John Mark**

Which Roman centurion escorted Paul safely to Rome?
**Julius**

At which city did Paul encounter a group of devout Greeks and some of the leading women worshipping God?
**Thessalonica**

Who in Berea was commended for examining the Scriptures daily?
**The Berean Jews**

Where did Paul meet Aquila and Priscilla after his escape from Athens?
**Corinth**

Which judge at Philippi released Paul and Silas after the earthquake?
**Philippi jailer**

Which proconsul did Paul convert on Cyprus after condemning Elymas?
**Sergius Paulus**

What was the trade of Aquila and Priscilla, which Paul shared?
**Tentmaking**

Which prophet's scroll was the Ethiopian eunuch reading?
**Isaiah**

Who asked, "What must I do to be saved?" after seeing the prison doors open?
**Philippi jailer**

Which marketplace in Ephesus became a center of Paul's teaching, leading to Demetrius's riot?
**The theatre**

Which silversmith led a protest against Paul in Ephesus?
**Demetrius**

Which Roman governor interrupted the Ephesian riot by reminding the crowd of Roman law?
**Town clerk**

Which Jewish sect did Paul debate with in the synagogue at Pisidian Antioch?
**Jews and God-fearers**

What title did Paul claim for himself when defending his mission to the Gentiles before Agrippa?
**A servant of the gospel**

Which two companions did Paul leave at Miletus to oversee the Ephesian church?
**Trophimus and Sopater**

Which prisoner's appeal led to Paul's journey to Rome?
**Paul himself**

Which island's inhabitants showed "unusual kindness" when Paul was shipwrecked?
**Malta**

Who was bit by a viper on Malta but suffered no harm?
**Paul**

Which official's father did Paul heal of fever and dysentery on Malta?
**Publius**

On what hill did Paul address Athenians about their altar to an "unknown god"?
**Areopagus**

Which tribal group in Jerusalem accused Paul of bringing Trophimus into the temple?
**Jews from Asia**

Which commander rescued Paul from being flogged in Jerusalem by invoking Paul's citizenship?
**Claudius Lysias**

Which governor ordered Paul to stand before Festus after his release by Lysias?
**Felix**

Who succeeded Felix and heard Paul's case before Festus?
**Festus**

Which king heard Paul's defense at Caesarea and almost persuaded him to become a Christian?
**Agrippa II**

Which Jewish leader in Jerusalem opposed Peter's preaching about Jesus' resurrection?
**Sanhedrin**

Which magistrate released Paul and Silas after finding no grounds for charges in Philippi?
**Magistrates of Philippi**

Which assembly in Ephesus debated formulating charges against Paul for heresy?
**The town assembly**

Which official saved Paul from a mob by ordering him into the barracks?
**Roman tribune**

Which jailer was baptized after seeing Paul and Silas unbound by the earthquake?
**Philippi jailer**

Which prophecy did Peter cite in Jerusalem's temple to argue that Jesus must ascend?
**Psalm 110**

Which city did Paul first sail to on his third missionary journey?
**Ephesus**

Which Christian teacher in Ephesus argued "more accurately" about Jesus after meeting Aquila and Priscilla?
**Apollos**

Which group interrupted Paul's sermon in Thessalonica by stirring a mob in the marketplace?
**Jews**

Which region did Philip the evangelist go to after leaving Jerusalem?
**Samaria**

Which route did Paul take from Troas to Macedonia after vision at night?
**Sea route to Neapolis**

Which prophet did Peter quote in his Pentecost sermon to explain the outpouring of the Spirit?
**Joel**

In which part of the Jerusalem temple did Peter and John heal the lame man?
**Beautiful Gate**

Which phenomenon appeared above the disciples' heads at Pentecost?
**Tongues of fire**

Which foreign region's people heard the gospel in their own language at Pentecost?
**Parthia**

Who rebuked Simon Magus for trying to buy the Spirit's power?
**Peter**

Which sorcerer opposed Paul and was struck blind on Cyprus?
**Elymas**

Which deacon baptized the Ethiopian eunuch?
**Philip**

What scroll was the Ethiopian eunuch reading?
**Isaiah**

Which Roman centurion became the first recorded Gentile convert in Caesarea?
**Cornelius**

Which vision taught Peter that he should not call any person impure or unclean?
**Sheet with animals**

What Greek word does Luke use for being filled suddenly at Pentecost (Acts 10:44)?
**Epipipto**

Who was the first apostle killed by martyrdom in Acts?
**James**

Which ruler arrested Peter in Acts 12?
**Herod Agrippa I**

How did Herod Agrippa I die after accepting the crowd's praises?
**Eaten by worms**

Who opened the doors of Paul and Silas's cell in Philippi?
**Angel**

What song did Paul and Silas sing at midnight in prison?
**Hymns**

Who asked, "Sirs, what must I do to be saved?"
**Philippi jailer**

Which seller of purple cloth in Philippi became a believer?
**Lydia**

Which tribunal heard Paul's defense when he stood on the Areopagus?
**Athenian council**

What altar did Paul point to when addressing the Athenians?
**Altar to an unknown god**

Which group of Jews in Berea were praised for verifying Paul's message?
**Bereans**

Who was Gallio's famous brother mentioned in Acts?
**Seneca**

What was Paul's trade, which he shared with Aquila in Corinth?
**Tentmaking**

Which proconsul in Cyprus believed after Paul rebuked Elymas?
**Sergius Paulus**

Which silversmith led the riot in Ephesus?
**Demetrius**

In which city did Paul leave off his letters on church organization, leading to a riot in the theatre?
**Ephesus**

Which seven sons of a Jewish high priest tried—and failed—to cast out demons in Ephesus?
**Sons of Sceva**

# DIFFICULT

## New Testament - The Epistles (Letters)

Which epistle begins "Paul, a servant of Christ Jesus, called to be anostle and set apart for the gospel of God"?
**Romans**

Which epistle contains the "Christ Hymn" describing Christ as existing in the form of God but emptying Himself?
**Philippians**

Which letter quotes Psalm 8:6 ("You made him to have dominion over the works of your hands") to exalt Christ's rule?
**Hebrews**

Which epistle addresses "the household of God, which is the church of the living God, a pillar and buttress of the truth"?
**1 Timothy**

Which letter teaches the doctrine of one new man, reconciling Jew and Gentile into one body?
**Ephesians**

Which epistle warns against building on the foundation with wood, hay, or straw instead of gold, silver, and precious stones?
**1 Corinthians**

Which letter instructs believers not to swear at all, but let "yes" be yes and "no" be no?
**James**

Which epistle lists the Fruit of the Spirit as love, joy, peace, patience, kindness, goodness, faithfulness, gentleness, and self-control?
**Galatians**

Which letter includes the passage on putting on the full armor of God?
**Ephesians**

Which epistle begins by praising God for "every spiritual blessing in the heavenly places in Christ"?
**Ephesians**

Which letter names Euodia and Syntyche and urges they "agree in the Lord"?
**Philippians**

Which epistle warns that if you accept circumcision, "Christ will be of no advantage to you"?
**Galatians**

Which letter opens with "Rejoice in the Lord always. I will say it again: Rejoice!"?
**Philippians**

Which epistle says "Work out your own salvation with fear and trembling"?
**Philippians**

Which letter calls its author a "prisoner for Christ Jesus"?
**Philemon**

Which epistle proclaims Christ as "the firstborn from the dead, that in everything he might be preeminent"?
**Colossians**

Which letter warns Christian people "Do not quench the Spirit"?
**1 Thessalonians**

Which epistle urges believers to pray "at all times in the Spirit, with all prayer and supplication"?
**Ephesians**

Which letter speaks of the mystery once hidden but now revealed to the saints, that Gentiles are fellow heirs?
**Ephesians**

Which epistle gives household codes instructing wives, husbands, children, and slaves?
**Colossians**

Which letter warns that "the love of money is a root of all kinds of evil"?
**1 Timothy**

Which epistle instructs its young leader, "Let no one despise you for your youth"?
**1 Timothy**

Which letter asserts "faith without works is dead"?
**James**

Which epistle quotes the prophecy of Enoch as the seventh from Adam?
**Jude**

Which letter begins "Paul, a servant of Christ Jesus, called to be an apostle, set apart for the gospel of God"?
**Romans**

Which epistle instructs elders to "shepherd the flock of God that is among you"?
**1 Peter**

Which letter says, "Him we proclaim, warning everyone and teaching everyone with all wisdom"?
**Colossians**

Which epistle prays that believers might attain "to the unity of the faith and of the knowledge of the Son of God"?
**Ephesians**

Which letter declares, "The blood of Jesus his Son cleanses us from all sin"?
**1 John**

Which epistle urges "having put on the new self, created after the likeness of God in true righteousness and holiness"?
**Ephesians**

Which letter instructs, "Bear one another's burdens, and so fulfill the law of Christ"?
**Galatians**

Which epistle calls the church "the body, the fullness of him who fills all in all"?
**Ephesians**

Which letter refers to the Law as "our guardian until Christ came, that we might be justified by faith"?
**Galatians**

Which epistle teaches the resurrection body is "sown perishable; raised imperishable"?
**1 Corinthians**

Which letter opens with the greeting, "Grace to you and peace from God our Father and the Lord Jesus Christ"?
**Romans**

Which epistle is addressed to "the elect lady and her children"?
**2 John**

Which letter closes with the warning, "Little children, keep yourselves from idols"?
**1 John**

Which epistle promises, "To him who is able to keep you from stumbling and to present you blameless"?
**Jude**

Which letter names Silvanus as a co-author alongside the main writer?
**1 Thessalonians**

Which epistle greets "the beloved Gaius, whom I love in truth"?
**3 John**

Which letter concludes with the doxology, "Now to him who is able to do far more abundantly than all that we ask or think"?
**Ephesians**

Which epistle warns of "scoffers in the last days, following their own ungodly passions"?
**2 Peter**

Which letter encourages, "Building yourselves up in your most holy faith and praying in the Holy Spirit"?
**Jude**

Which epistle ends with the doxology, "To him be glory both now and to the day of eternity"?
**Romans**

Which letter begins "Jude, a servant of Jesus Christ and brother of James"?
**Jude**

Which epistle points out, "You believe that God is one; you do well. Even the demons believe—and shudder!"?
**James**

Which letter warns that believers "were ransomed… not with perishable things but with the precious blood of Christ"?
**1 Peter**

Which epistle exhorts, "For to me to live is Christ, and to die is gain"?
**Philippians**

Which letter teaches that Christ "has delivered us from the domain of darkness and transferred us to the kingdom of his beloved Son"?
**Colossians**

Which Old Testament prophet does Paul cite in Romans 11:9 about God's word becoming "a snare and a trap"?
**David**

In Romans 5, Paul contrasts Adam with whom, calling one the "type" of the one to come?
**Christ**

Which Greek term does Paul use in Romans 3:23 to describe all have sinned?
**Hamartō ō**

To which city does Paul send Phoebe as a deaconess according to Romans 16?
**Cenchreae**

Which amanuensis does Paul mention as writing Romans alongside him?
**Tertius**

In 1 Corinthians 7, Paul permits what marital concession to avoid burning with passion?
**Self-denial by mutual agreement**

Which man does Paul commend in 1 Corinthians 9 for going to war at his own expense?
**A soldier**

In 1 Corinthians 12, Paul compares the body of Christ to which athletic event?
**Race**

Which prideful act in 1 Corinthians 11 prompted Paul to instruct women to cover their heads?
**Eating the Lord's Supper unworthily**

In 1 Corinthians 15, Paul quotes "O death, where is your victory?" from which prophet?
**Hosea** *(via Isaiah citation)*

Which commander's servant's handkerchief did Paul mention in 2 Corinthians as a sign?
**Trophimus**

In 2 Corinthians 3, Paul contrasts the old covenant and the new using what translucent object?
**A veil**

Which church had "many members, but one body" according to 1 Corinthians 12?
**Corinthian church**

In 2 Corinthians 12, Paul speaks of a thorn in the flesh given by whom?
**Satan**

Which Old Testament account does Paul invoke in Galatians 3:17 to illustrate promise before law?
**Abraham and Isaac**

In Galatians 5, Paul warns against the works of the flesh and lists contrasting what?
**Fruit of the Spirit**

Which Gentile ally does Paul call "his fellow worker in Christ Jesus" in Philippians 4:3?
**Clement**

In Philippians 2, Paul quotes an early Christian hymn using "form of God" and "form of a servant." What two "forms" are contrasted?
**Morphē Theou / Morphē doulou**

Which city's church does Paul urge to "stand fast in one spirit, with one mind" in Philippians 1?
**Philippi**

In Colossians 1, Paul refers to Christ as the image of the invisible God and firstborn of whom?
**Creation**

Which false teaching does Paul warn against in Colossians 2, calling it "philosophy"?
**Human tradition**

In Colossians 4, Paul instructs believers to devote themselves to prayer, being what?
**Watchful and thankful**

Which household code in Colossians instructs servants to obey earthly masters not with eye-service?
**Slaves**

Which city's church does Paul commend for "waiting for his Son from heaven"?
**Thessalonica**

In 1 Thessalonians 4, Paul teaches that the dead in Christ will rise first at what event?
**The Lord's return**

Which of Paul's journeys does he reference when reminding Thessalonians of how he preached among them?
**His first missionary journey**

Which word does Paul use in 2 Thessalonians 2 to describe the man of lawlessness?
**Anthrōpos anomias**

In 1 Timothy 3, Paul lists qualifications for overseers, including being above what?
**Reproach**

Which epistle calls godliness with contentment "great gain"?
**1 Timothy**

In Titus 2, Paul instructs older women to teach younger women to love their what?
**Husbands**

Which letter does Paul address to "my beloved son in the faith"?
**1 Timothy**

Which runaway slave is named in Paul's shortest epistle?
**Onesimus**

Which epistle instructs that elders who rule well be considered worthy of double what?
**Honor**

Which letter quotes "Faith without works is dead"?
**James**

Which letter refers to Abraham's faith being counted as righteousness before his circumcision?
**Romans**

In James 5, believers are urged to pray using the prayer of which Old Testament figure?
**Elijah**

Which Petrine epistle calls believers to "humble yourselves under the mighty hand of God"?
**1 Peter**

Which epistle warns that false teachers will privately bring in destructive heresies, denying what?
**Master (Lord) who bought them**

Who does Peter call a "shepherd of God's flock" in his first letter?
**Elders**

Which letter names the elect lady and her children?
**2 John**

Which epistle declares that Jesus Christ is the faithful witness, the firstborn of the dead, and what else?
**Ruler of the kings of the earth**

In 1 John 4, what test does John give to discern the spirits?
**Confession that Jesus Christ has come in the flesh**

Which letter includes the doxology "to him be glory both now and to the day of eternity"?
**Romans**

Which epistle concludes with "to him who is able to keep you from stumbling"?
**Jude**

In 2 Peter 1, believers are reminded that God's promises through God's own what?
**Divine power**

Which epistle contrasts the elders' shepherding by being examples to the flock rather than lording it over them?
**1 Peter**

Which letter addresses the sin of partiality in the assembly, warning against showing favor to the rich?
**James**

Which epistle contains the earliest Christian confession: "Christ died for our sins…"?
**1 Corinthians**

Which letter warns that "love covers a multitude of sins" and is greater than prophecy?
**1 Peter**

Which epistle mentions "the unfruitful works of darkness" and instructs to expose them?
**Ephesians**

Which letter admonishes believers to welcome one another as Christ welcomed them?
**Romans**

Which epistle notes that believers are "strangers and exiles" in the world?
**1 Peter**

Which letter calls the high priest forever "after the order of Melchizedek"?
**Hebrews**

Which epistle warns that if we deliberately keep sinning after receiving the knowledge of the truth, nothing remains but what?
**A fearful expectation of judgment**

Which letter describes running with endurance the race set before us, looking to Jesus?
**Hebrews**

Which epistle says "God opposes the proud but gives grace to the humble"?
**James**

Which letter calls its readers to "grow in the grace and knowledge of our Lord and Savior Jesus Christ"?
**2 Peter**

Which epistle refers to God's household as having "builders, not only hearers"?
**Hebrews**

Which letter instructs believers to "spur one another on toward love and good deeds"?
**Hebrews**

Which Old Testament prophet's question "Who has known the mind of the Lord?" does Paul cite to show God's inscrutable judgments?
**Isaiah**

What Greek word does Paul use in Romans 1:17 for "righteousness" received by faith?
**Dikaiosynē**

To which house church does Paul send Phoebe as a deacon in Romans 16?
**Cenchreae**

Who does Paul say in Romans 11:4 God preserved as a "remnant" by grace?
**Seven thousand**

Which co-worker does Paul commend in Romans 16 as having "labored much" for him?
**Rufus**

By what Greek term does Paul in 1 Corinthians 8:1 say "knowledge puffs up"?
**Gnosis**

Which Corinthian speaker does Paul accuse in 1 Corinthians 11 of "tempting Christ" by eating the Lord's Supper unworthily?
**Some among you**

In 1 Corinthians 12, Paul compares the body to a race course and calls the goal a what?
**Prize**

Which household code bookends Paul's argument in Ephesians 5–6?
**Ephesians** *(the epistle itself frames it)*

Which letter instructs that overseers be "above reproach, the husband of one wife, sober-minded"?
**1 Timothy**

Which city's church does Paul urge to "stand firm and hold to the traditions" taught by him and Timothy?
**Corinth**

What term does Paul use in Galatians 3:28 to describe the oneness of believers in Christ?
**One**

Which Greek phrase does Paul quote in Philippians 2:6 to describe Christ's equality with God?
**Ischōnôn Theon**

Which epistle uniquely calls Mark "my son" in ministry?
**Philemon**

In Colossians 1, Paul calls Christ the "firstborn of everything" as sign of what?
**Preeminence**

Which letter warns "everyone who competes as an athlete does not receive the victor's crown unless he competes according to the rules"?
**2 Timothy**

Which early Christian in 1 Thessalonians 5 is commended for "turning from idols to serve the living and true God"?
**The Thessalonians**

What metaphor does Paul in 2 Thessalonians 2 use for the restrainer of the man of lawlessness?
**What now restrains**

Which epistle instructs widows to "enroll only those who are at least sixty years old"?
**1 Timothy**

Which letter warns that some have "erred concerning the faith" and who does it name first?
**Jude**

In Hebrews 2, Jesus is described as "not ashamed to call them brothers" after suffering death. What term is given to this shared fellowship?
**Koinōnia**

Which epistle contrasts "living by faith" with "the deadness of the law"?
**Galatians**

Which letter cites Psalm 110:1 ("Sit at my right hand") to prove Christ's superiority to angels?
**Hebrews**

Which epistle calls believers "aliens and exiles" scattered abroad?
**1 Peter**

Which letter instructs slaves to "do the will of God from the heart, rendering service to the Lord and not to man"?
**Ephesians**

Which New Testament figure does James reference in James 5 as an example of patience?
**Job**

Which epistle contains the high-priestly exhortation "Let us draw near with a true heart in full assurance of faith"?
**Hebrews**

Which letter warns against "despising heavenly things" by turning back from Christ?
**Hebrews**

In 1 John 4, what test does John give for discerning the Spirit?
**Confession that Jesus Christ has come in the flesh**

Which letter counsels believers to "rejoice in hope, be patient in tribulation, be constant in prayer"?
**Romans**

Which epistle names "Nympha and the church in her house"?
**Colossians**

Which letter uses the image of running a race and looking to Jesus as the "founder and perfecter of our faith"?
**Hebrews**

Which epistle advises that elders "shepherd the flock of God" and "exercise oversight willingly"?
**1 Peter**

Which letter states that "faith apart from works is useless"?
**James**

Which epistle refers to the "ministering spirits sent to serve those who will inherit salvation"?
**Hebrews**

Which epistle ends with the benediction "to him who is able to keep you from stumbling and to present you blameless"?
**Jude**

Which letter criticizes believers for requiring milk and not solid food because they are unskilled?
**Hebrews**

Which letter greets "the elect lady and her children" and warns her to "watch out for the dogs"?
**2 John**

Which epistle associates the "first fruits of the Spirit" with a down payment of our inheritance?
**Ephesians**

Which letter calls its readers to "grow in the grace and knowledge of our Lord and Savior Jesus Christ"?
**2 Peter**

Which epistle admonishes, "Do not quench the Spirit, do not despise prophecies, test everything"?
**1 Thessalonians**

Which letter describes Christ as "the Apostle and High Priest of our confession"?
**Hebrews**

Which letter commands Christians to "submit yourselves one to another in the fear of God"?
**Ephesians**

Which epistle refers to "the Lord's bondservant" in its opening greeting?
**Philemon**

Which letter states that "to set the mind on the flesh is death, but to set the mind on the Spirit is life and peace"?
**Romans**

Which epistle admonishes to "let brotherly love continue"?
**Hebrews**

Which letter ends with a description of those who "have erred" and should be mercifully snatched from fire?
**Jude**

Which epistle calls the church "God's household, built on the foundation of the apostles and prophets"?
**Ephesians**

Which letter instructs women to adorn themselves with good works rather than elaborate hairstyles?
**1 Timothy**

Which epistle declares that "there is one body and one Spirit, just as you were called to the one hope"?
**Ephesians**

Which letter warns that if anyone corrupts the gospel, "let him be accursed"?
**Galatians**

Which epistle mentions that the "eyes of your hearts" may be enlightened to know hope in God's calling?
**Ephesians**

Which letter calls believers "no longer strangers and sojourners, but fellow citizens with the saints"?
**Ephesians**

Which epistle warns that believers should not "go beyond what is written" but hold fast to sound words?
**1 Corinthians**

Which letter refers to "the church of the firstborn who are enrolled in heaven"?
**Hebrews**

Which epistle admonishes to "keep your life free from love of money and be content with what you have"?
**Hebrews**

Which letter describes false teachers as "spots in your love feasts"?
**Jude**

Which epistle commends "bearing fruit in every good work and increasing in the knowledge of God"?
**Colossians**

Which letter closes with the reminder to "do all in the name of the Lord Jesus, giving thanks to God the Father"?
**Colossians**

Which epistle notes that believers were "ransomed… not with perishable things but with the precious blood of Christ"?
**1 Peter**

Which letter warns not to "stiffen your necks" but to obey God's voice as at Sinai?
**Hebrews**

Which epistle instructs church leaders to "not be domineering over those in your charge"?
**1 Peter**

Which letter states that "we do not wrestle against flesh and blood, but against…" what?
**Spiritual hosts of wickedness**

Which epistle instructs believers to "put on the new self, created after the likeness of God"?
**Ephesians**

Which letter urges believers to "rejoice always, pray without ceasing, give thanks in all circumstances"?
**1 Thessalonians**

Which epistle defines love as "patient and kind, not jealous or boastful, not arrogant or rude"?
**1 Corinthians**

Which letter mentions that to those who love God, "all things work together for good"?
**Romans**

Which epistle instructs that elders should not be "lover of money"?
**1 Timothy**

Which letter names "Archippus" and urges him to "fulfill the ministry" given him?
**Philemon**

Which letter refers to the "hope laid up for you in heaven"?
**Colossians**

Which epistle describes Christ as "the only wise God, through Jesus Christ, to whom be glory forever"?
**Jude**

Which letter instructs us to "abstain from the passions of the flesh, which wage war against your soul"?
**1 Peter**

Which epistle warns that false teachers will secretly bring in destructive heresies, even denying whom?
**Christ** (Jude warns denying our only Master and Lord…)

Which letter opens with the declaration that "if anyone imagines that he knows something, he does not yet know as he ought to know"?
**1 Corinthians**

Which epistle lists "faith, hope, and love" as abiding virtues, with love being the greatest?
**1 Corinthians**

Which letter commends "God's household, a pillar and buttress of the truth"?
**1 Timothy**

Which epistle notes that Jesus "has been manifested to destroy the works of the devil"?
**1 John**

Which letter instructs believers to "not be conformed to this world, but be transformed by the renewal of your mind"?
**Romans**

Which epistle urges submission to every human institution for the Lord's sake, including kings?
**1 Peter**

Which letter warns that unrepentant sin "hardens" the sinner, like in the Exodus?
**Hebrews**

Which epistle contains the verse "For freedom Christ has set us free; stand firm therefore"?
**Galatians**

Which letter speaks of a "hope that does not put us to shame, because God's love has been poured into our hearts"?
**Romans**

Which epistle teaches that "the word of God is living and active, sharper than any double-edged sword"?
**Hebrews**

Which letter describes how we are "fellow citizens with the saints and members of the household of God"?
**Ephesians**

Which epistle instructs believers to "abhor what is evil; hold fast to what is good"?
**Romans**

Which Old Testament prophet's question "Who has known the mind of the Lord?" does Paul cite in Romans 11:34?
**Isaiah**

What Greek word does Paul use in Romans 1:17 for "righteousness" received by faith?
**Dikaiosynē**

To which city does Paul send Phoebe as a deacon in Romans 16?
**Cenchreae**

Who does Paul say in Romans 11:4 God preserved as a "remnant" by grace?
**Seven thousand**

Which co-worker does Paul commend in Romans 16 as having "labored much" for him?
**Rufus**

Which epistle instructs believers to "remain in the condition in which you were called"?
**1 Corinthians**

Which letter commends the Thessalonians for "turning from idols to serve the living and true God"?
**1 Thessalonians**

Which epistle states "there is neither Jew nor Greek, slave nor free, male nor female; for you are all one in Christ Jesus"?
**Galatians**

Which epistle begins with "Grace to you and peace from God our Father and the Lord Jesus Christ"?
**Romans**

Which letter instructs elders to "shepherd the flock of God among you" and "exercise oversight willingly"?
**1 Peter**

Which epistle defines "faith as the assurance of things hoped for, the conviction of things not seen"?
**Hebrews**

Which letter warns of "the man of lawlessness" being revealed before the Lord's coming?
**2 Thessalonians**

Which epistle includes the "Christ Hymn" about Christ's preexistence, equality with God, and humility?
**Philippians**

Which letter instructs younger widows to remarry so they avoid idleness?
**1 Timothy**

Which epistle quotes Psalm 110:1 to demonstrate Christ's superiority over angels?
**Hebrews**

Which letter teaches "work out your own salvation with fear and trembling"?
**Philippians**

Which epistle warns that "knowledge puffs up, but love builds up"?
**1 Corinthians**

Which letter calls Christ "the firstborn of all creation, that in everything he might be preeminent"?
**Colossians**

Which epistle warns that "the love of money is a root of all kinds of evil"?
**1 Timothy**

Which letter instructs slaves to obey their earthly masters "not with eye-service, as people-pleasers"?
**Colossians**

Which epistle contains the analogy of the body having many members, each indispensable?
**1 Corinthians**

Which letter instructs wives to submit to their own husbands as to the Lord?
**Colossians**

Which epistle contrasts works of the flesh with the fruit of the Spirit?
**Galatians**

Which letter warns that "if we deliberately keep on sinning after we have received the knowledge of the truth, no sacrifice for sins remains"?
**Hebrews**

Which epistle calls believers "sojourners and exiles" scattered abroad?
**1 Peter**

Which letter instructs church leaders to "pray without ceasing, give thanks in all circumstances"?
**1 Thessalonians**

Which epistle calls Jesus "the Apostle and High Priest of our confession"?
**Hebrews**

Which letter declares that "to set the mind on the flesh is death, but to set the mind on the Spirit is life and peace"?
**Romans**

Which epistle admonishes that "if Christ has not been raised, your faith is worthless"?
**1 Corinthians**

Which letter instructs believers to "submit yourselves to every human institution for the Lord's sake"?
**1 Peter**

Which epistle states "faith without works is dead"?
**James**

Which letter reminds its readers that "faith comes from hearing, and hearing through the word of Christ"?
**Romans**

Which epistle instructs widows to be enrolled only if they are at least sixty years old?
**1 Timothy**

Which letter warns that "knowledge puffs up, but love builds up"?
**1 Corinthians**

**DIFFICULT**

**New Testament - The Book of Revelation**

Which island was John exiled to when he received the Revelation?
**Patmos**

How many churches are addressed in Revelation chapters 2–3?
**Seven**

What symbol represents the churches in Revelation 1?
**Lampstands**

What do the seven stars represent in Revelation 1?
**Angels of the churches**

Who is called the "Alpha and Omega" in Revelation?
**Jesus**

Which creature takes the scroll from God's right hand in Revelation 5?
**Lamb**

How many seals are on the scroll in Revelation 5?
**Seven**

Which horse appears when the first seal is opened?
**White horse**

Which horse is named War in the Four Horsemen vision?
**Red horse**

Which seal summons Death and Hades riding a pale horse?
**Fourth seal**

How many trumpets announce the judgments after the seals?
**Seven trumpets**

What plague follows the first trumpet in Revelation 8?
**Hail and fire mixed with blood**

What is the name of the star that falls and makes the waters bitter?
**Wormwood**

How many angels are released to bind Satan for a thousand years?
**One angel**

Who reigns with Christ for a thousand years?
**The saints**

What number is the beast from the sea given in Revelation 13?
**666**

Which river is dried up in preparation for the kings of the east?
**Euphrates**

Which beast enforces worship of the first beast and performs signs?
**Second beast**

How many bowls of God's wrath are poured out in Revelation 16?
**Seven bowls**

What affliction is poured out in the first bowl?
**Ugly and painful sores**

Which bowl turns the sea into blood?
**Second bowl**

What is the final destination of Death and Hades after the thousand years?
**Lake of fire**

Which rider on a white horse in Revelation 19 is called Faithful and True?
**Jesus**

What title is written on that rider's robe and thigh?
**King of kings and Lord of lords**

How many gates does the New Jerusalem have?
**Twelve**

What precious material are the gates of the New Jerusalem made of?
**Single pearls**

What material are the streets of the New Jerusalem said to be?
**Pure gold**

Which river flows from the throne of God in the new creation?
**River of life**

What tree stands on each side of the river of life?
**Tree of life**

What covers the floor before God's throne like crystal?
**Sea of glass**

Which creatures around the throne say "Holy, holy, holy, Lord God Almighty"?
**Four living creatures**

Who casts their crowns before God's throne in worship?
**Twenty-four elders**

Which church is warned that it has the reputation of being alive but is dead?
**Sardis**

Which church is commended for enduring patiently and not denying Jesus even unto death?
**Smyrna**

Which church is rebuked for being lukewarm, neither hot nor cold?
**Laodicea**

How long do the two witnesses prophesy in Revelation 11?
**1260 days**

What happens to the two witnesses after they finish their testimony?
**They are killed**

After three and a half days, who raises the two witnesses to life?
**Breath of life from God**

What is the name of the angel of the bottomless pit described in Revelation 9?
**Apollyon**

What is the name of the great prostitute who sits on many waters?
**Babylon the Great**

What image does Babylon sit on, symbolizing her influence?
**Many waters**

Who sings a new song before the throne in Revelation 14?
**144,000 on Mount Zion**

What is written on the gates of the New Jerusalem?
**Names of the twelve tribes of Israel**

What is written on the foundations of the city wall?
**Names of the twelve apostles**

What will not be found in the New Jerusalem?
**Night**

Who will be no more in the new creation?
**Death**

What invitation ends the book of Revelation?
**"Come, Lord Jesus"**

Which island was John exiled to when he received the Revelation?
**Patmos**

What term describes the lampstands in John's vision?
**Golden**

Who holds the seven stars and walks among the lampstands?
**Son of Man**

Which creature around the throne has six wings and is full of eyes?
**Living creatures**

What do the four living creatures continuously say?
**Holy, holy, holy**

How many elders sit on their thrones around God's throne?
**Twenty-four**

What do the elders cast before the throne?
**Their crowns**

What is the color of the third horse in the Four Horsemen vision?
**Black**

What object does the rider on the black horse hold?
**Scales**

How much does wheat cost during the famine in Revelation 6?
**A denarius**

Which trumpet judgment releases a star called Wormwood?
**Third trumpet**

What is the name of the bottomless pit from which locusts emerge?
**Abyss**

What mark do the 144,000 have on their foreheads?
**Seal of the living God**

Which chapter introduces the beast rising from the sea?
**13**

How many horns does the first beast have?
**Ten**

Which beast has two horns like a lamb but speaks like a dragon?
**Second beast**

Who worships the dragon because he gives authority to the beast?
**The earth's inhabitants**

Which number is associated with the name of the beast?
**Six hundred sixty-six**

What geographical river is dried to prepare the way for the kings of the east?
**Euphrates**

What message does the eagle proclaim in Revelation 14?
**Three woes**

Which chapter depicts the measuring of the temple and worshipers?
**11**

How many days do the two witnesses prophesy?
**1260**

Which plague is poured out in the second bowl?
**Sea turns to blood**

What does the fifth bowl, poured on the throne of the beast, cause the kingdom to become?
**Dark**

Who sits on the great white throne during the final judgment?
**God**

What is thrown into the lake of fire at the Great White Throne judgment?
**Death and Hades**

Which vision shows a new heaven and new earth?
**Revelation 21**

What bright street material makes up the New Jerusalem's main street?
**Pure gold**

How many gates does the New Jerusalem have?
**Twelve**

Which river flows from the throne in Revelation 22?
**River of life**

What tree stands on either side of the river of life?
**Tree of life**

What covers the floor before God's throne like crystal?
**Sea of glass**

Which church is told it has the reputation of being alive but is dead?
**Sardis**

Which church is commended for holding fast his name and not denying faith?
**Smyrna**

Which church is warned for being lukewarm?
**Laodicea**

Which church hears "whoever conquers, I will give the hidden manna"?
**Ephesus**

Which church is criticized for having abandoned their first love?
**Ephesus**

Which church is rebuked for tolerating the teaching of "Jezebel"?
**Thyatira**

Which church is praised for not denying Christ's name, even in death?
**Smyrna**

Which church is promised a pillar in the temple of God?
**Pergamum**

Which church is promised white garments if they overcome?
**Sardis**

Which church is encouraged to keep Jesus' works until he comes?
**Philadelphia**

Which church is told they will sit with Jesus on his throne if they overcome?
**Thyatira**

Which church is urged to be zealous and repent?
**Laodicea**

Which church is promised that Jesus will come in and dine with them if they open the door?
**Laodicea**

Which church is warned about coming judgment if they do not repent of immorality?
**Thyatira**

Which church is told to be watchful, for Christ comes like a thief?
**Philadelphia**

What color is John's hair described as in Revelation 1?
**White like wool**

What do the seven stars in Jesus' right hand represent?
**Angels of the churches**

Which part of Jesus is described as like a flame of fire?
**His eyes**

What symbol stands for the seven churches in Revelation 1?
**Lampstands**

How does John describe Jesus' voice in Revelation 1?
**Like the roar of many waters**

What do the twenty-four elders cast before God's throne?
**Their crowns**

Which of the four living creatures is described as like a flying eagle?
**One of the four living creatures**

How long is there silence in heaven after the seventh seal is opened?
**About half an hour**

Which trumpet brings hail and fire mixed with blood that burns a third of earth and trees?
**The first trumpet**

Which star falls from heaven and makes a third of the waters bitter?
**Wormwood**

Which church is told that the one who conquers will not be hurt by the second death?
**Philadelphia**

How many angels are released from the Euphrates to kill a third of mankind?
**Four angels**

What number is written on the beast's forehead in Revelation 13?
**666**

Which river is dried up to prepare the way for the kings of the east?
**Euphrates**

Who sits on the white horse in Revelation 19 wearing a robe sprinkled with blood?
**The Word of God (Jesus)**

What name is written on the rider's robe and thigh in Revelation 19?
**King of kings and Lord of lords**

How many bowls of God's wrath are poured out in Revelation 16?
**Seven**

Which bowl turns the rivers and springs into blood?
**The third bowl**

What covers the cup that pours out God's wrath in Revelation 21?
**Nothing—Heaven and earth flee** (no hiding place)

Which sea is called the "sea of glass" before God's throne?
**Sea of glass**

Which city does the angel measure with a reed in Revelation 11?
**The temple of God**

For how many days do the two witnesses prophesy?
**1,260 days**

What happens to the two witnesses after they finish their testimony?
**They are killed by the beast**

How long do they lie dead before being resurrected?
**Three and a half days**

Which chapter introduces the woman clothed with the sun?
**Revelation 12**

Who wages war in heaven against the dragon?
**Michael**

What color is the dragon in Revelation 12?
**Red**

How many horns does the beast from the sea have?
**Seven**

Which beast performs great signs to deceive those on earth?
**The second beast (false prophet)**

Who worships the beast in Revelation 13?
**All whose names are not written in the Lamb's book of life**

What mark is required to buy or sell in Revelation 13?
**The mark of the beast**

Which angel says, "Fear God and give him glory"?
**First angel**

What sweetly tasting book does John eat?
**Little scroll**

Which gate of the New Jerusalem is made of a single pearl?
**Each of the twelve gates**

How many foundations of the city wall are decorated with jewels?
**Twelve**

What precious material are the city's streets made of?
**Pure gold**

Which river flows from the throne of God?
**River of the water of life**

What tree yields twelve kinds of fruit and bears fruit every month?
**Tree of life**

Which church is commended for enduring persecution and remaining faithful even to death?
**Smyrna**

Which church is rebuked for having abandoned its first love?
**Ephesus**

Which church is warned to repent of being lukewarm?
**Laodicea**

Which church is praised for keeping Jesus' word and not denying his name?
**Philadelphia**

Which church is told its works are incomplete and to hold fast what it has?
**Sardis**

Which church is condemned for tolerating a false prophetess named Jezebel?
**Thyatira**

What is the name given to the great prostitute in Revelation 17?
**Babylon the Great**

On how many waters does Babylon sit?
**Many waters**

Which chapter describes the New Jerusalem descending out of heaven?
**Revelation 21**

What will no longer exist in the new creation?
**Death**

What invitation does the Spirit give at the end of Revelation?
**"Come"**

Which creature in John's vision has seven horns and seven eyes?
**The Lamb**

Who tells John "Do not weep" when he sees no one worthy to open the scroll?
**One of the elders**

Which song do the victorious ones sing before the throne in Revelation 15?
**Song of Moses**

Which sea creature is mentioned as not being able to enter the New Jerusalem?
**Sea (the sea itself)**

Which chapter describes the sealing of the 144,000?
**Revelation 7**

What are the 144,000 sealed servants wearing?
**White robes**

Which of the seven trumpet judgments brings locust-like creatures from the abyss?
**Fifth trumpet**

What command does the second angel give in Revelation 14?
**"Babylon the great is fallen"**

What warning does the third angel proclaim in Revelation 14?
**Not to worship the beast**

Which city is called "the great prostitute" in Revelation 17?
**Babylon**

What color is the dragon described in Revelation 12?
**Red**

Which archangel is named as fighting the dragon in Revelation 12?
**Michael**

Which mountain is called the place where the beast and false prophet are thrown alive?
**The lake of fire**

Who measures the temple and altar but excludes the outer court in Revelation 11?
**An angel**

Which feature of the New Jerusalem is twelve times twelve stadia?
**Its length**

What precious stone is the first foundation of the New Jerusalem?
**Jasper**

Which tree in the new earth yields its fruit every month?
**Tree of life**

What flows from under the throne of God and of the Lamb?
**River of the water of life**

Which gate of the New Jerusalem never shuts by day because there is no night?
**Twelve gates**

Whose names are written on the twelve foundations of the city wall?
**The twelve apostles**

Which trumpet judgment darkens a third of the sun, moon, and stars?
**Fourth trumpet**

Which bowl turns the rivers and springs into blood?
**Third bowl**

Which horsemen are called by name (fourth only by name "Death")?
**Death** (fourth)

What is the color of the fifth horse?
**Black**

Which church is told to "hold fast what you have" so no one will seize your crown?
**Philadelphia**

Which church is told, "You have a reputation of being alive, but you are dead"?
**Sardis**

Which church is warned not to tolerate the teaching of "Jezebel"?
**Thyatira**

Which church is urged to be zealous and repent?
**Laodicea**

Which church is promised to eat from the tree of life if they conquer?
**Ephesus**

What do the twenty-four elders wear when they worship?
**White garments**

Which bowls of wrath are poured out directly on the throne of the beast?
**Fifth bowl**

Which trumpet calls for repentance from kingdom claims?
**Second trumpet**

Which angel shouts "It is done," signaling the seventh bowl?
**Seventh angel**

Which entity is said to be the light of the city of God?
**The Lamb**

Which offering is said never to cease before God's throne?
**Worship** *(constant)*

What does the measuring reed measure in Revelation 21?
**The city, its gates, and walls**

Which feast's imagery is used to describe the final marriage supper of the Lamb?
**Feast of Tabernacles**

Which sea outside the New Jerusalem's gates is mentioned?
**None; there is no sea**

Which river's water heals the nations in Revelation 22:2?
**River of life**

What command closes the book after the invitation "Come"?
**"Take the water of life freely"**

Which voice from heaven says "Behold, I am coming soon"?
**Jesus**

What does "Alpha and Omega" signify in Revelation?
**Beginning and end**

Which title does Jesus give Himself as having the seven spirits of God?
**The First and the Last**

Which promise is given to "the one who conquers and keeps my works until the end"?
**Authority over the nations**

Which feature of New Jerusalem's wall is measured at 144 cubits?
**Thickness**

Which star-starved plague is unleashed in the sixth trumpet?
**Four angels released**

Which "great mountain" is cast into the sea, making a third of the sea blood?
**Not named** (a great mountain)

What precious stone is the first foundation of the New Jerusalem?
**Jasper**

Which Greek term does John use for the churches addressed in Revelation 2–3?
**Ekklesia**

What does the mighty angel hold in Revelation 9:1 when he unlocks the abyss?
**Key**

What phrase describes the "sea" before God's throne in Revelation 4:6?
**Glass like crystal**

Which voice commands the four living creatures to "Worship him who lives forever and ever"?
**Elders' voice**

What is the numerical measurement of the New Jerusalem's wall height?
**144 cubits**

Which heavenly precursor announces the seven bowl judgments?
**Seven angels**

What is the first of the four living creatures described as being like?
**A lion**

Which church is praised for "holding fast my name, and you did not deny my faith"?
**Philadelphia**

Which heavenly document is sealed with seven seals?
**Scroll**

Which judgment follows the seventh trumpet in Revelation 11?
**The kingdom proclamation**

What is the form of God's throne seen by John in Revelation 4?
**Sapphire**

Who gives John a golden reed to measure the city and temple?
**Angel**

Which chapter describes the "great multitude that no one could number, from every nation"?
**Revelation 7**

Which living creature has the face of a man?
**One of the four living creatures**

Which beast from the earth is also called the false prophet?
**Second beast**

Which seal unleashes riders that conquer with a bow?
**First seal**

What mark identifies the 144,000 servants on their foreheads?
**Seal of God**

Which bowl turns the rivers and springs into blood?
**Third bowl**

What does the woman clothed with the sun cast at the dragon's feet?
**Her child**

Which star is named in Revelation 8:11 as making waters bitter?
**Wormwood**

Which eagle calls out three woes in Revelation 8?
**Flying eagle**

What area is made desolate after the second trumpet judgment?
**A third of the earth**

Which number describes the authority of the beast in Revelation 13:5?
**Forty-two months**

Which chapter introduces the vision of the seven golden lampstands?
**Revelation 1**

Who holds the seven trumpets in Revelation 8?
**Seven angels**

Which trumpet brings a great star falling on a third of the rivers?
**Third trumpet**

What title is given to the one on the white horse in Revelation 19?
**Faithful and True**

Which dragon is thrown down from heaven in Revelation 12?
**Ancient serpent**

Which venue is measured in Revelation 11?
**Temple**

Which second resurrection occurs after the thousand years?
**Final resurrection**

What becomes of Death and Hades after the final judgment?
**Thrown into lake of fire**

Which prophetic song is sung by those who conquer the beast?
**Song of Moses**

What feature of the New Jerusalem is described as "twelve thousand stadia"?
**Length, width, and height**

Which resource flows from the throne of God through the city?
**River of life**

Which earthly king is symbolized by the fourth beast in Daniel, referenced in Revelation 13?
**Antichrist (composite)**

What color is the fourth horse of the apocalypse?
**Pale**

Which chapter ends with the words "Even so, come, Lord Jesus"?
**Revelation 22**

What invitation follows "Let the one who thirsts come" in Revelation 22?
**Take the water of life freely**

What precious material are the gates of the New Jerusalem made from?
**Pearl**

Which Old Testament book is quoted in Revelation 4 with "Holy, holy, holy"?
**Isaiah**

What sound accompanies the opening of the seventh seal?
**Silence in heaven**

Which tree along the river yields fruit each month and whose leaves heal the nations?
**Tree of life**

Who stands by the sea of glass holding harps given by God?
**Those who conquer the beast**

What does the phrase "keen as a two-edged sword" refer to in Revelation 1?
**Voice**

Which period is described as the time of the Gentiles trampling the holy city?
**Forty-two months**

Which age-long period comes before the final judgment, per Revelation 20?
**Thousand years**

Which vow does the Lamb make to the one who overcomes in Sardis?
**White garments**

Which closing vision shows no temple because God and the Lamb are its temple?
**New Jerusalem**

What does the woman in Revelation 19 ride?
**A white horse**

Which vision includes lightning, thunder, and voices coming from the throne?
**Seven seals**

Which voice in Revelation 4 calls the twenty-four elders to worship?
**The voice of the living creatures**

What do the twenty-four elders cast before God's throne?
**Their crowns**

Which seal unleashes cosmic disturbances—sun darkened, moon turned to blood?
**Sixth seal**

What element of creation is said to mourn when the sixth seal is opened?
**Sun and moon**

Which song do the victors over the beast sing in Revelation 15?
**Song of Moses and the Lamb**

Who stands beside the sea of glass with harps of God?
**Those who had conquered the beast**

Which symbol in Revelation 14 announces "Babylon is fallen"?
**Flying angel**

How many times is the word "Amen" used to affirm the seven bowls of wrath?
**Seven**

What precious material are the foundations of the New Jerusalem's wall made of?
**Jewels**

Which two words describe the gates of the New Jerusalem?
**Each gate is a single pearl**

What covers the floor before God's throne like crystal?
**A sea of glass**

Which creature around the throne is said to have a voice like thunder?
**Living creatures**

What word describes the voice of Jesus in Revelation 1?
**Like many waters**

Which figure does the Lamb call "the faithful witness"?
**Christ**

What role does the second beast play in Revelation 13?
**Enforces worship of the first beast**

Which number is associated with the beast's name in Revelation 13:18?
**Six hundred sixty-six**

What does the rider on the pale horse bring?
**Death**

Which trumpet releases a plague of locusts that do not harm foliage?
**Fifth trumpet**

Which bowl turns the Euphrates River dry for the kings of the east?
**Sixth bowl**

Which judgment causes the earth to split and islands to flee away?
**Seventh bowl**

What invitation follows "Surely I am coming soon" in Revelation 22?
**"Amen. Come, Lord Jesus!"**

www.ingramcontent.com/pod-product-compliance
Lightning Source LLC
Chambersburg PA
CBHW050847160426
43194CB00011B/2060